The Complete
FAMILY CHRISTMAS

The Complete FAMILY CHRISTMAS

INDEX

Published in 1997 by Merehurst Limited
Ferry House, 51–57 Lacy Road, Putney,
London SW15 1PR

This edition published 1997 for INDEX
Unit 1, Garrard Way, Kettering NN16 8TD

ISBN 1-897730-51-9

A catalogue record for this book is available from the British Library.

Editor: Alison Leach
Design: Anita Ruddell

Photography:
Christmas in Cross Stitch by Marie-Louise Avery
Decorative Christmas Dough by James Duncan
Christmas Flower Projects by Jacqui Hurst
Creative Christmas Cakes by James Duncan
Favourite Christmas Recipes by Alan Marsh

Colour separation by Bright Arts, (HK) Limited
Printed in Hong Kong by Midas Printing Limited

CONTENTS

Christmas in Cross Stitch

Julie Hasler

INTRODUCTION

Christmas is one of the happiest times of the year, for adults and, even more, for children. Churches are lit with candles for the service which we call the Christ Mass; carol singers go from house to house, and people kiss under the mistletoe as traditional signs of friendship. We decorate our houses with holly and ivy, and festoon the Christmas tree with glittering ornaments and lights. We have a traditional Christmas dinner with all the family and friends gathered round the table, pull crackers, dress up in paper hats and, afterwards, play traditional games.

The most exciting part of all, for the children, is the giving and receiving of presents, just as the shepherds and kings gave presents to the newborn baby Jesus in Bethlehem nearly two thousand years ago. In celebration of the festive season, I have designed a whole range of Christmas projects, both for the home and to give as presents.

Each cross stitch design is carefully charted and has an accompanying colour key and full instructions for making up the project. Also included is a Basic Skills section, which covers everything from how to prepare your fabric and stretch it in an embroidery hoop or frame, to mounting your cross stitch embroidery over card ready for display. Some of the designs are very simple and are aimed at beginners; others are more challenging, with many colours and shaded effects for the more experienced stitcher, or one who is eager to expand existing skills.

Whatever your level of skill or interest in the craft, you will enjoy being able to create items from the wide range of projects offered, suitable for children and adults of all ages.

BASIC SKILLS

Preparing the fabric

Even with an average amount of handling, many evenweave fabrics tend to fray at the edges, so it is a good idea to overcast the raw edges, using ordinary sewing thread, before you begin.

The instructions

Each project begins with a full list of the materials that you will require; Aida and Lugana are both fabrics produced by Zweigart. Note that the measurements given for the embroidery fabric include a minimum of 3cm (1¼ in) all around to allow for stretching it in a frame and preparing the edges to prevent them from fraying.

Colour keys for stranded embroidery cottons – DMC, Anchor or Madeira – are given with each chart. It is assumed that you will need to buy one skein of each colour mentioned, even though you may use less, but where two or more skeins are needed, this information is included in the main list of requirements.

To work from the charts, particularly those where several symbols are used in close proximity, some readers may find it helpful to have the chart enlarged so that the squares and symbols can be seen more easily. Many photocopying services will do this for a minimum charge.

Before you begin to embroider, always mark the centre of the design with two lines of basting stitches, one vertical and one horizontal, running from edge to edge of the fabric, as indicated by the arrows on the charts.

As you stitch, use the centre lines given on the chart and the basting threads on your fabric as reference points for counting the squares and threads so as to position your design accurately.

Working in a hoop

A hoop is the most popular frame for use with small areas of embroidery. It consists of two rings, one fitted inside the other; the outer ring usually has an adjustable screw attachment so that it can be tightened to hold the stretched fabric in place. Hoops are available in several sizes, ranging from 10cm (4in) in diameter to quilting hoops with a diameter of 38cm (15in). Hoops with table stands or floor stands attached are also available.

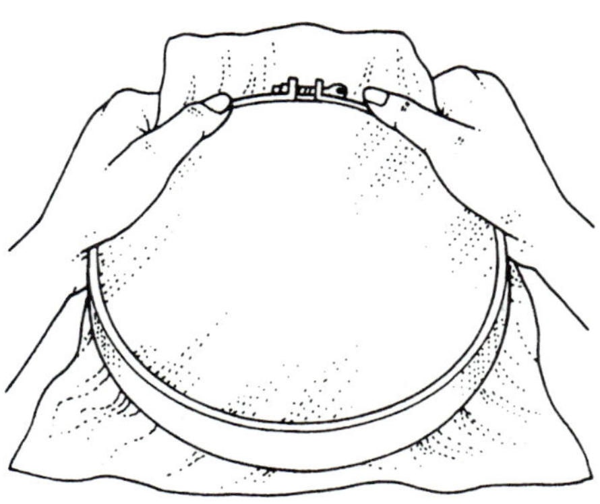

1 To stretch your fabric in a hoop, place the area to be embroidered over the inner ring and press the outer ring over it with the tension screw released. Tissue paper can be placed between the outer ring and the embroidery, so that the hoop does not mark the fabric. Lay the tissue paper over the fabric when you set it in the hoop, then tear away the central embroidery area.

2 Smooth the fabric and, if necessary, straighten the grain before tight-

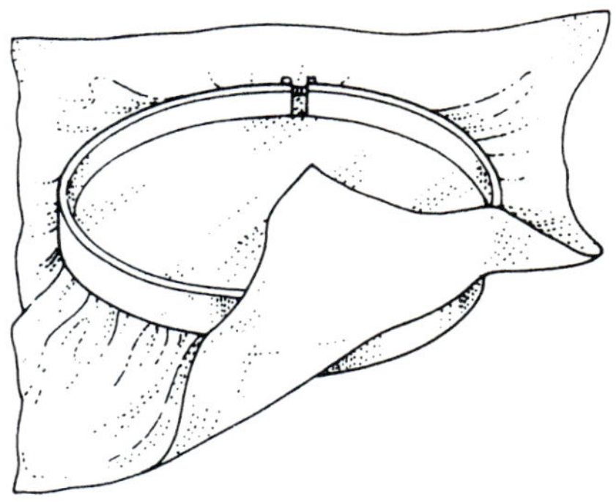

ening the screw. The fabric should be evenly stretched.

Extending embroidery fabric

It is easy to extend a piece of embroidery fabric, such as a bookmark, to stretch it in a hoop.

Fabric oddments of a similar weight can be used. Simply cut four pieces to size (in other words, to the measurement that will fit both the embroidery fabric and your hoop) and baste them to each side of the embroidery fabric before stretching in the hoop in the usual way.

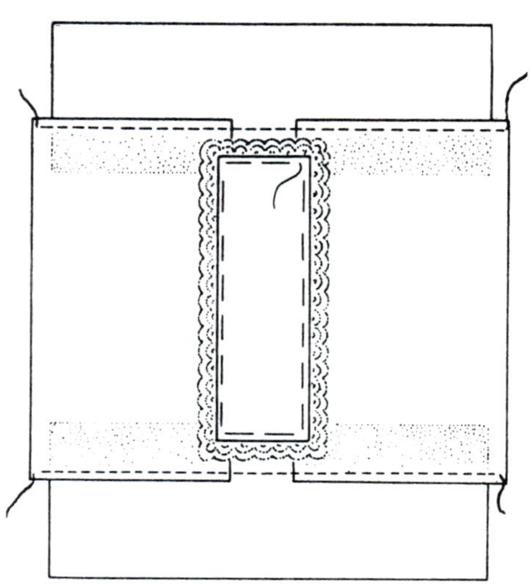

Working in a rectangular frame

Rectangular frames are more suitable for larger pieces of embroidery. They consist of two rollers, with tapes attached, and two flat side pieces, which slot into the rollers and are held in place by pegs or screw attachments. Available in different sizes, either alone or with adjustable table or floor stands, frames are measured by the length of the roller tape, and range in size from 30cm (12in) to 68cm (27in).

As alternatives to a slate frame, canvas stretchers and the backs of old picture frames can be used. Provided there is sufficient extra fabric around the finished size of the embroidery, the edges can be turned under and simply attached with drawing pins (thumb tacks) or staples.

1 To stretch your fabric in a rectangular frame, cut out the fabric, allowing at least an extra 5cm (2in) all around the finished size of the embroidery. Baste a single 12mm (1/2 in) turning on the top and bottom edges and oversew strong tape, 2.5cm (1in) wide, to the other two sides. Mark the centre line both ways with basting stitches. Working from the centre outwards and using strong thread, oversew the top and bottom edges to the roller tapes. Fit the side pieces into the slots, and roll any extra fabric on one roller until the fabric is taut.

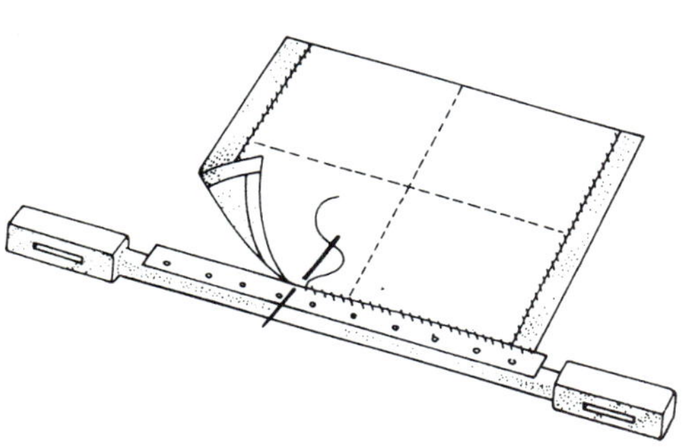

2 Insert the pegs or adjust the screw attachments to secure the frame. Thread a large-eyed needle (chenille

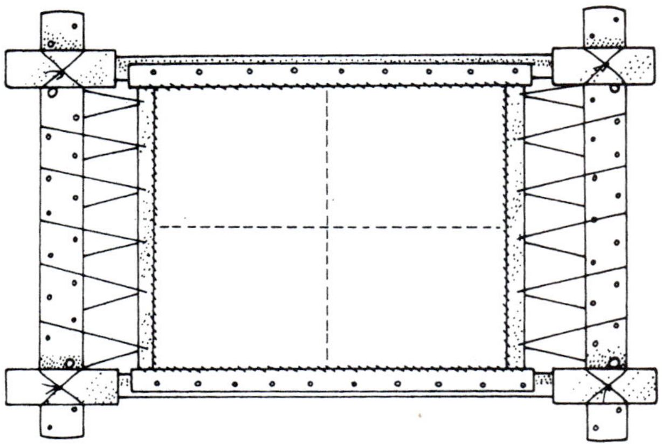

needle) with strong thread or fine string and lace both edges, securing the ends around the intersections of the frame. Lace the webbing at 2.5cm (1in) intervals, stretching the fabric evenly.

Enlarging a graph pattern

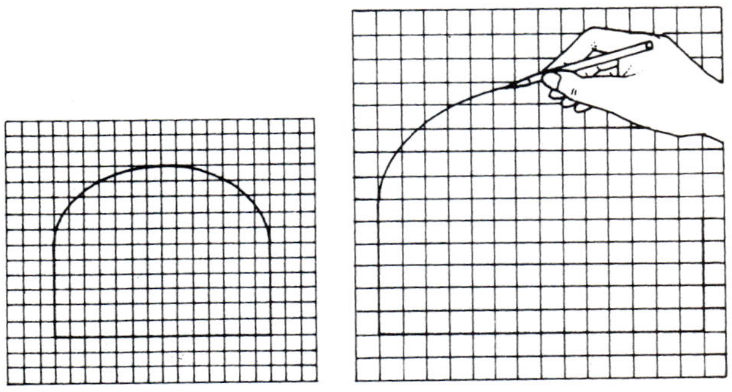

To enlarge a graph pattern, you will need a sheet of graph paper ruled in 1cm (3/8 in) squares, a ruler and a pencil. If, for example, the scale is one square to 5cm (2in) you should first mark the appropriate lines to give a grid of the correct size. Copy the graph freehand from the small grid to the larger one, completing one square at a time. Use a ruler to draw the straight lines at first and then copy the freehand curves.

To bind an edge

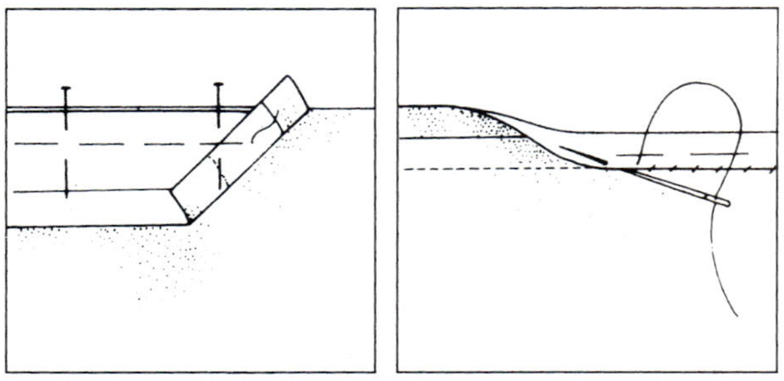

1 Open out the turning on one edge of the bias binding and pin in position on the right side of the fabric, matching the fold to the seamline. Fold over the cut end of the binding. Finish by overlapping the starting point by about 12mm (1/2 in). Baste and then machine stitch along the seamline.

2 Fold the binding over the raw edge to the wrong side, baste and, using matching sewing thread, neatly hem to finish.

Piped seams

Contrasting piping adds a special decorative finish to a seam and looks particularly attractive on items such as cushions and cosies.

You can cover piping cord with either bias-cut fabric of your choice or a bias binding; alternatively, ready-covered piping cord is available in several widths and many colours.

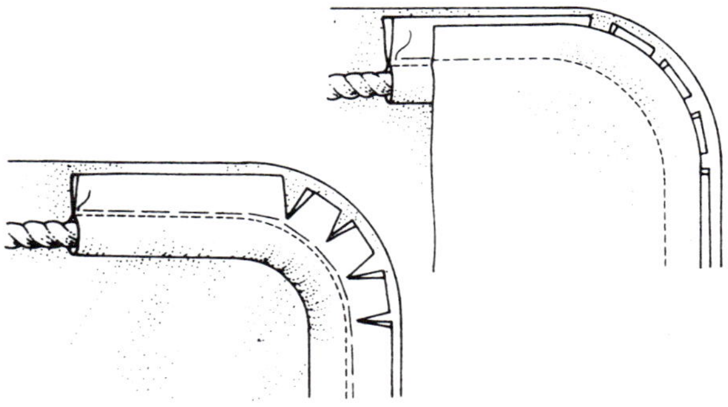

1 To apply piping, pin and baste it to the right side of the fabric, with seam lines matching. Clip into the seam allowance where necessary.

2 With right sides together, place the second piece of fabric on top, enclosing the piping. Baste and then either hand stitch in place or machine stitch, using a zipper foot. Stitch as close to the piping as possible, covering the first line of stitching.

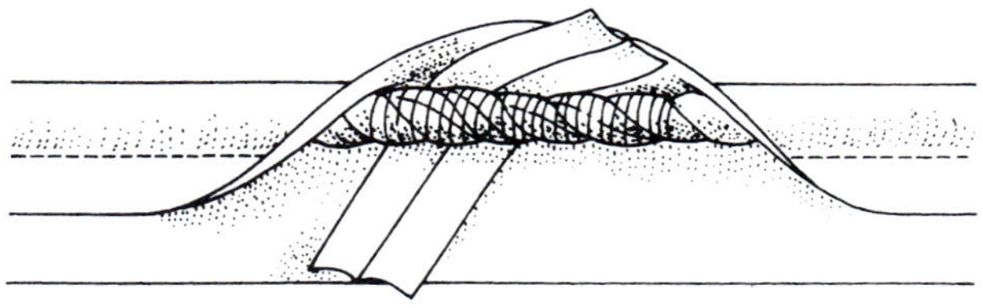

3 To join ends of piping cord together, first overlap the two ends by about 2.5cm (1in). Unpick the two cut ends of bias to reveal the cord. Join the bias strip as shown. Trim and press the seam open. Unravel and splice the two ends of the cord. Fold the bias strip over it and finish basting around the edge.

Mounting embroidery

The cardboard should be cut to the size of the finished embroidery, with an extra 6mm (¼ in) added all around to allow for the recess in the frame.

Lightweight fabrics

1 Place the embroidery face down, with the cardboard centred on top, and basting and pencil lines matching. Begin by folding over the fabric at each corner and securing it with masking tape.

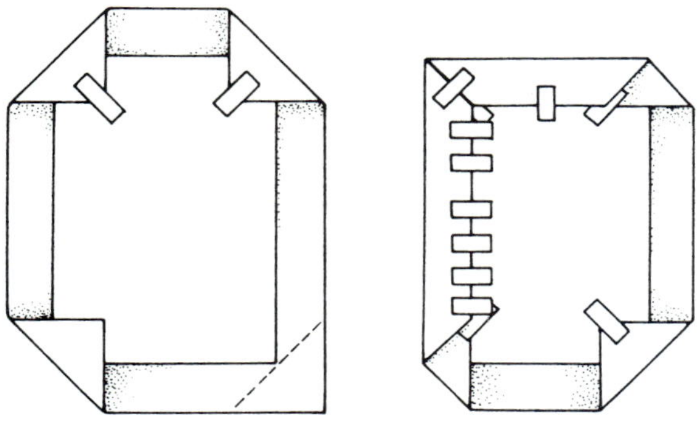

2 Working first on one side and then the other, fold over the fabric on all sides and secure it firmly with pieces of masking tape, placed about 2.5cm (1in) apart. Also neaten the mitred corners with masking tape, pulling the fabric tightly to give a firm, smooth finish.

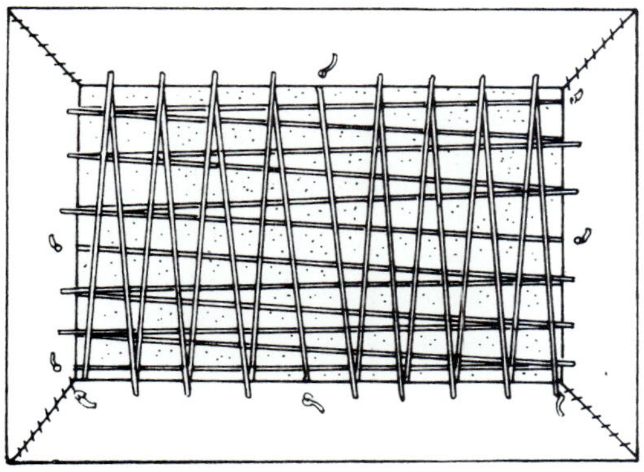

Heavier fabrics

Lay the embroidery face down, with the cardboard centred on top; fold over the edges of the fabric on opposite sides, making mitred folds at the corners, and lace across, using strong thread. Repeat on the other two sides. Finally, pull up the stitches fairly tightly to stretch the fabric firmly over the cardboard. Overstitch the mitred corners.

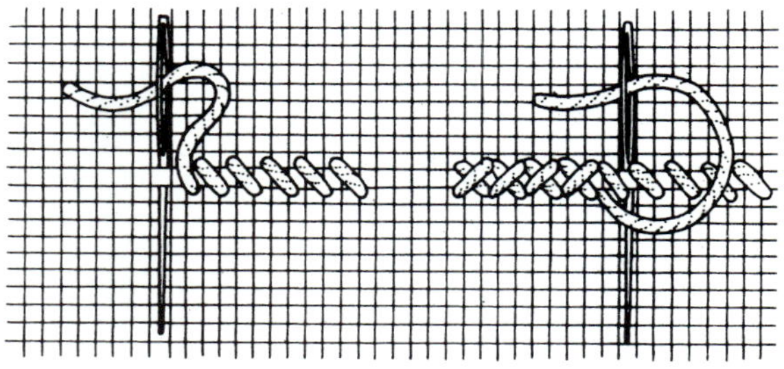

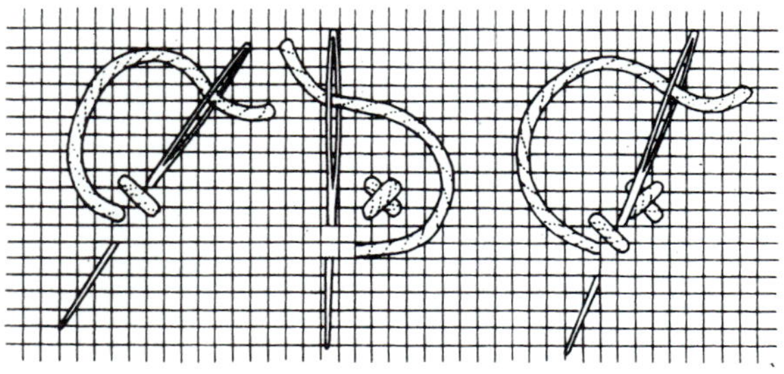

Cross stitch

For all cross stitch embroidery, the following two methods of working are used. In each case, neat rows of vertical stitches are produced on the back of the fabric.

When stitching large areas, work in horizontal rows. Working from right to left, complete the first row of evenly spaced diagonal stitches over the number of threads specified in the project instructions. Then, working from left to right, repeat the process. Continue in this way, making sure each stitch crosses in the same direction.

When stitching diagonal lines, work downwards, completing each stitch before moving to the next.

Backstitch

Backstitch is used in the projects to give emphasis to a particular foldline, an outline or a shadow. The stitches are worked over the same number of threads as the cross stitch, forming continuous straight or diagonal lines.

Make the first stitch from left to right; pass the needle behind the fabric and bring it out one stitch length ahead to the left. Repeat and continue in this way along the line.

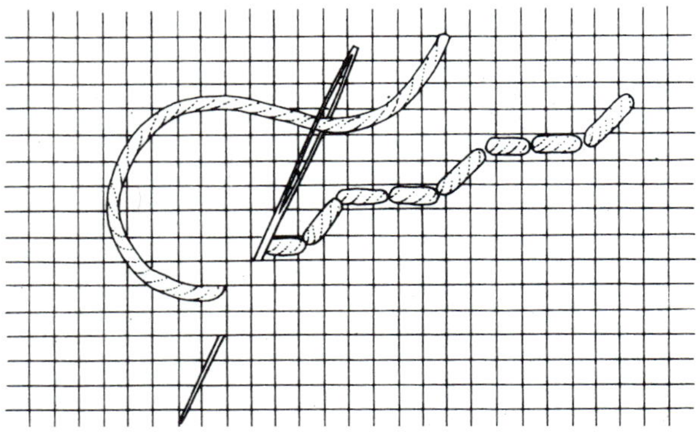

Festive Table Linen

A set of hand-embroidered Christmas table linen, complete in every detail – even individual placecards – will delight your family and guests, and set the scene for one of the happiest days of the year.

Festive Table Linen

For the set of six plastic napkin holders, placecards and placemats, and the single table runner (sizes given below), you will need:

six napkin holders
15x7.5cm (6x3in) white, 22-count Hardanger fabric (sufficient for six napkin holders)
15x7.5cm (6x3in) ultra-soft, medium-weight, iron-on interfacing, to back the napkin holders
six red placecards, with 2.3cm (⅞ in) circular cut-outs
15x10cm (6x4in) white, 18-count Aida fabric (sufficient for six placecards)
15x10cm (6x4in) of ultra-soft, medium-weight, iron-on interfacing, to back the placecards
six 40cm (16in) square dinner napkins
six 33x48cm (13x19in) placemats
33x97cm (13x38in) table runner
stranded embroidery cotton in the colours given in the panel
No26 tapestry needle
NOTE The napkin holders, placecards, napkins, placemats and runner are all obtainable from specialist suppliers, see page 224.

★

Napkin holders

1 Using rows of basting stitches, divide the Hardanger fabric into six equal sections. Take the holly design from the Christmas bows border, and embroider one holly motif at the centre of each section, using two strands of embroidery cotton in the needle throughout.

2 Press the finished embroidery. Iron the interfacing to the back of the fabric, then cut along the basted lines to separate the six holders. For each holder, trim the fabric to measure 4.3x3.8cm (1⅝ x 1½ in), and place the embroidery inside the clear plastic holder.

Placecards

1 Using rows of basting stitches, divide the Aida fabric into six equal sections. Take the holly design from the Christmas bows border, and embroider one motif at the centre of each section, using two strands of embroidery cotton in the needle throughout.

2 Press the finished embroidery. Iron the interfacing to the back of the fabric, then cut along the basted lines to separate the six holders. For each placecard, trim the fabric to measure 3.8cm (1½ in) square.

3 Position your design behind the round aperture. When you are happy that it is correctly centred, use a small piece of clear tape to hold it while you seal the card. Remove the backing strip from the panel on the left of the placecard; fold it over, and press firmly to seal the two halves of the placecard together. You can then add the names or wording you require, perhaps using a gold or silver pen.

Table linen

All of the designs are stitched over two threads of the 26-count fabric used for these ready-prepared table linens, and two strands of embroidery cotton are used in the needle throughout.

1 The dinner napkins feature the Christmas Bows border, which runs along the side edges, 2.5cm (1in) in from the fringe.

2 For the placemats, embroider the holly border, again placing it along the side edges, 2.5cm (1in) in from the fringe.

3 For the table runner, start by marking the centre with two lines of basting stitches (see page 8). Stitch the holly wreath at the centre of the runner, then measure out for 25cm (10in) on each side of the central vertical line. Stitch the holly border at this point on each side of the runner.

4 When you have completed the holly borders, embroider a Christmas bows border down each side, 2.5cm (1in) out from the holly border, and the same distance in from the fringed edge.

Napkin

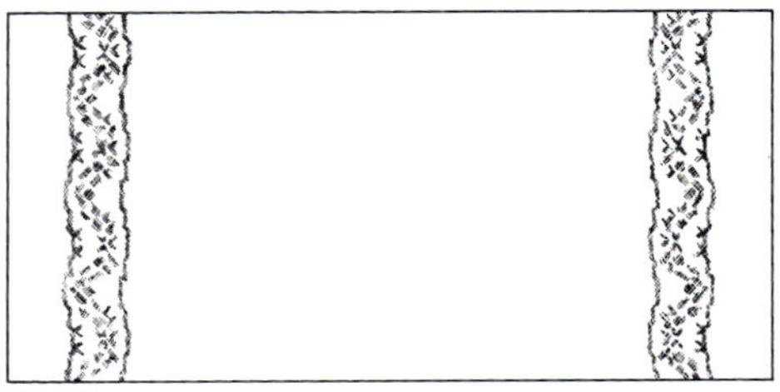

Placemat

Table runner

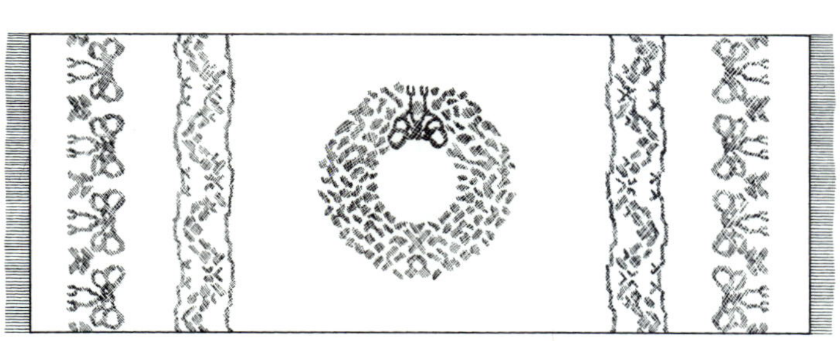

	TABLE LINEN	DMC	ANCHOR	MADEIRA
●	Bright orange red	606	335	0209
•̇	Bright Christmas green	704	256	1308
/	Kelly green	702	226	1306
II	Christmas green	699	923	1303
V	Bright canary yellow	973	297	0105
O	Medium tangerine orange	941	304	0203
X	Light loden green	3364	843	1603
■	Khaki	370	888	2112

NOEL

Tree Decorations and Gift Tags

Brighten up your Christmas tree with these unusual tree decorations and gift tags. You can hang small gifts on the tree with the gift tags attached, or place larger gifts around the base of the tree.

Tree Decorations and Gift Tags

For three tree decorations, each measuring about 9x8cm (3½ x3¼in), you will need:

38x12.5cm (15x5in) white, 16-count Aida fabric
38x12.5cm (15x5in) medium-weight, iron-on fabric interfacing
60cm (24in) red ribbon, 6mm (¼ in) wide
stranded embroidery cotton in the colours given in the appropriate panel (starred colours used for backstitching only)
gold metallic thread
No26 tapestry needle
Framecraft 'Christmas shapes' - tree, Santa and bell (for suppliers, see page 224)

For four gift tags, each measuring 5cm (2in) square, with an aperture measuring 3cm (1¼in), you will need:

12.5cm (5in) square white Hardanger fabric, with 22 threads to 2.5cm (1in)
12.5cm (5in) square medium-weight, iron-on fabric interfacing
stranded embroidery cotton in the colours given in the appropriate panels
gold metallic thread
No26 tapestry needle

★

Tree decorations

1 Divide the Aida strip into three square sections, using lines of basting stitches. With two strands of embroidery cotton in the needle, complete the cross stitch embroidery, making sure that each design is centred within its section. Iron the interfacing to the wrong side of the fabric, to prevent it from fraying, and then cut along the basted lines to separate the three designs.

2 Place each Christmas shape over the relevant embroidered design, ensuring that the embroidered design is centred within the shape, and draw around the edge of the shape with a soft pencil.

3 For each shape, take the paper template provided; centre this within your pencil lines and draw around this with a soft pencil. This is your cutting line. Cut your fabric to size carefully and place it, right side down, in the shape. Place the paper template on the reverse side of your embroidery. Next, peel the backing off the felt and carefully place it over the back of the 'Christmas shape'. Thread the ribbon through the hole, ready for hanging the shape on the tree.

TREE DECORATIONS	DMC	ANCHOR	MADEIRA
● Gold thread	-	-	-
II Bright Christmas green	700	229	1304
X Bright Christmas red	666	46	0210
• Silver thread	-	-	-
V Dark violet	552	100	0713

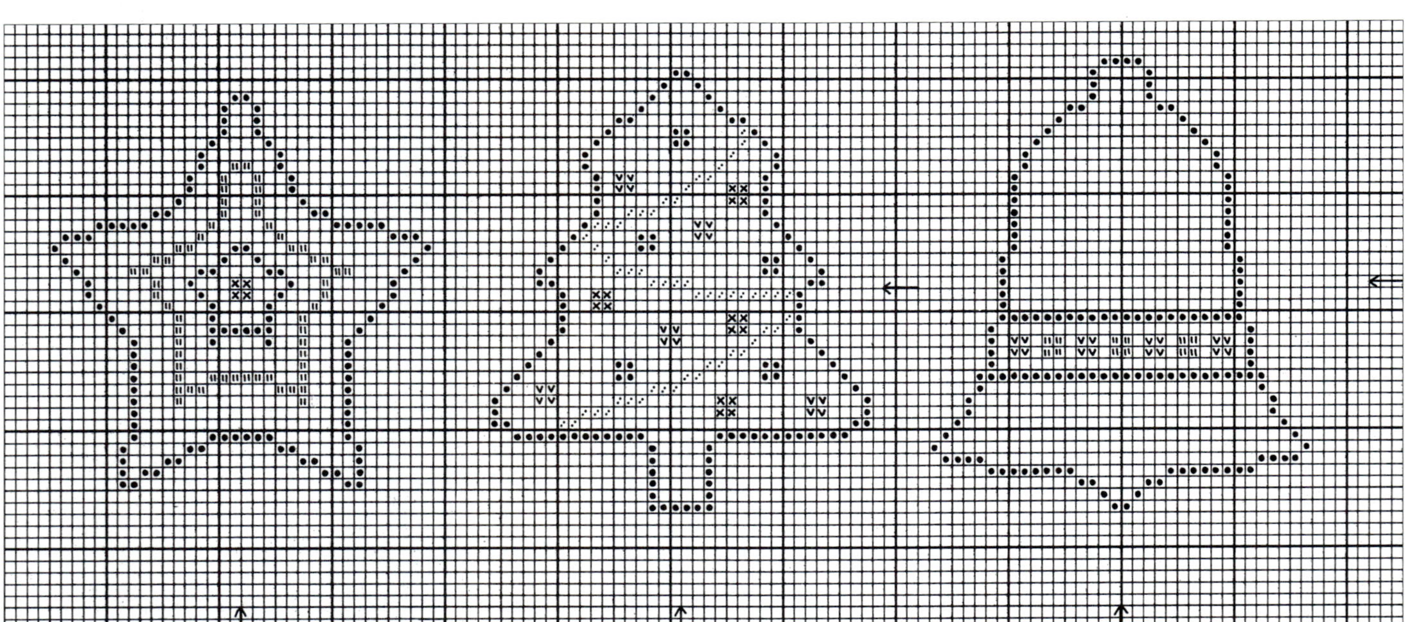

NOEL	DMC	ANCHOR	MADEIRA
/ Dark Kelly green	701	227	1305
V Bright Christmas red	666	46	0210

Note: backstitch lettering in bright Christmas red.

SNOWMAN	DMC	ANCHOR	MADEIRA
● Black	310	403	Black
V Pumpkin orange	971	316	0203
/ Bright Christmas red	666	46	0210
II Dark Kelly green	701	227	1305
• White	White	2	White
Light steel grey*	318	399	1802

Note: backstitch with light steel grey.*

Gift tags

1 Divide the Hardanger fabric into four equal sections, using horizonal and vertical lines of basting stitches. Complete the cross stitch embroidery, with one strand of embroidery cotton in the needle throughout, ensuring that each design is centred within a section. Press the finished embroidery and then iron the interfacing to the wrong side of your fabric, to prevent it from fraying. Cut along the basted lines to separate the designs.

2 For each design, place the embroidery so that it shows through the aperture in the gift tag. Use a soft pencil to mark cutting lines on the wrong side of the fabric, slightly larger than the aperture, and then trim to size. Place the design in position again. It helps if you use a small piece of clear adhesive tape to hold part of the design in position before you seal the two halves together. Remove the backing strip from the panel on the left; fold it over and press firmly to seal the two halves of the gift tag together. You can add a piece of embroidery silk or narrow ribbon to complete the tag.

PUDDING	DMC	ANCHOR	MADEIRA
II Dark Kelly green	701	227	1305
C Bright Christmas red	666	46	0210
• White	White	2	White
Light steel grey*	318	399	1802
/ Medium brown	433	371	2008
● Dark forest brown	938	381	2005

Note: backstitch with light steel grey.*

REINDEER	DMC	ANCHOR	MADEIRA
• White	White	2	White
Light steel grey*	318	399	1802
● Black	310	403	Black
V Bright Christmas red	666	46	0210
/ Beige brown	840	379	1912
II Spice brown	3064	914	2312

Note: backstitch with light steel grey.*

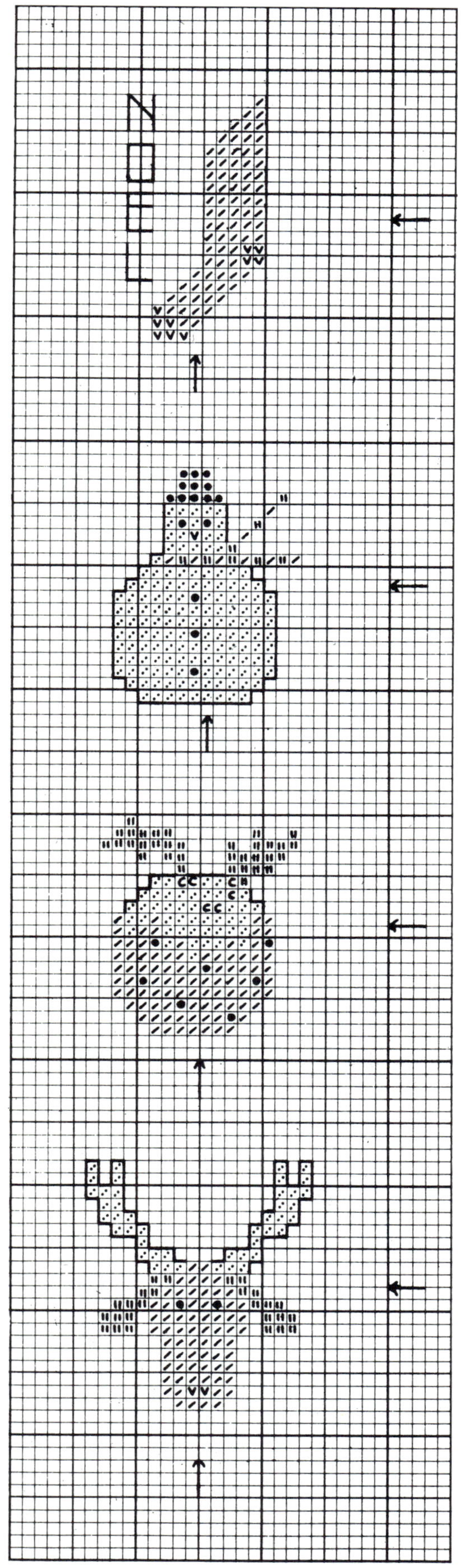

Glass Jars and Decorative Mats

These beautiful cut-glass lead crystal jars, accompanied by pretty mats, make gifts which are both useful and decorative. They can adorn a dressing table, an occasional table, or even a mantelpiece. Why not fill them with brightly coloured sweets for Christmas?

Glass Jars and Decorative Mats

For each cut-glass jar, with a lid measuring 6.5cm (2½in) in diameter, you will need:

10cm (4in) square ecru, 25-count Lugana fabric
stranded embroidery cotton in the colours given in the appropriate panel
No26 tapestry needle

For each mat, measuring 16cm (6¼in) square, you will need:

16cm (6¼in) square Christmas red, 14-count Aida fabric
stranded embroidery cotton in the colour given in the appropriate panel
No24 tapestry needle

★

Glass jars

1 For each design, prepare the fabric, marking the centre with basting stitches, and stretch it in a hoop (see page 9). Using one strand of embroidery cotton in the needle throughout, complete your chosen design. Press the finished embroidery, leaving the basting stitches in place.

2 Gently remove all parts from the glass jar lid. Centre the design within the lid, and draw around the outer edge, marking the fabric. Remove the lid and cut the fabric to size.

3 To assemble the lid, replace the clear acetate and place your design in the lid, with the right side against the acetate. Place the sponge behind your design. Push the metal locking disc very firmly into place, using thumb pressure, with the raised side of the disc facing the sponge. When the locking disc is tightly in position, use a little glue to secure the flock lid lining card.

Decorative mats

1 For each mat, complete the cross stitch embroidery, working from the centre outwards and using two strands of embroidery cotton.

2 Press if required and then fray the edges by removing threads, one at a time, to a depth of 6mm (¼in). You can either leave the frayed edge as it is, or secure it with hemstitching, using a matching thread.

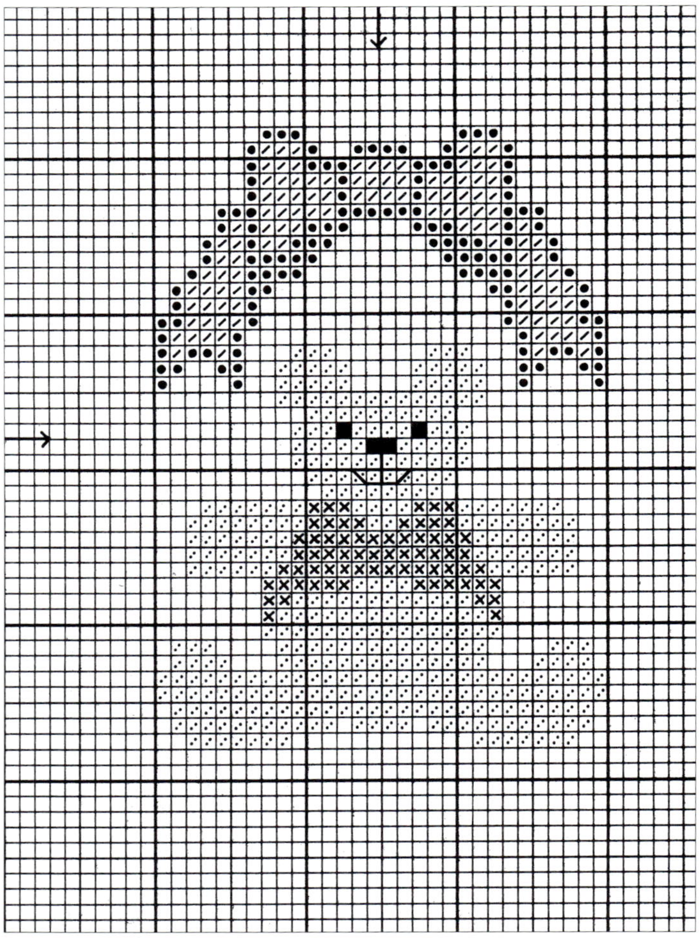

GLASS JAR	DMC	ANCHOR	MADEIRA
■ Black	310	403	Black
● Bright Christmas green	700	229	1304
/ Chartreuse	703	238	1307
⁘ Christmas gold	783	307	2211
X Bright Christmas red	666	46	0210
II Steel grey	414	400	1801
C Pale grey	415	398	1803

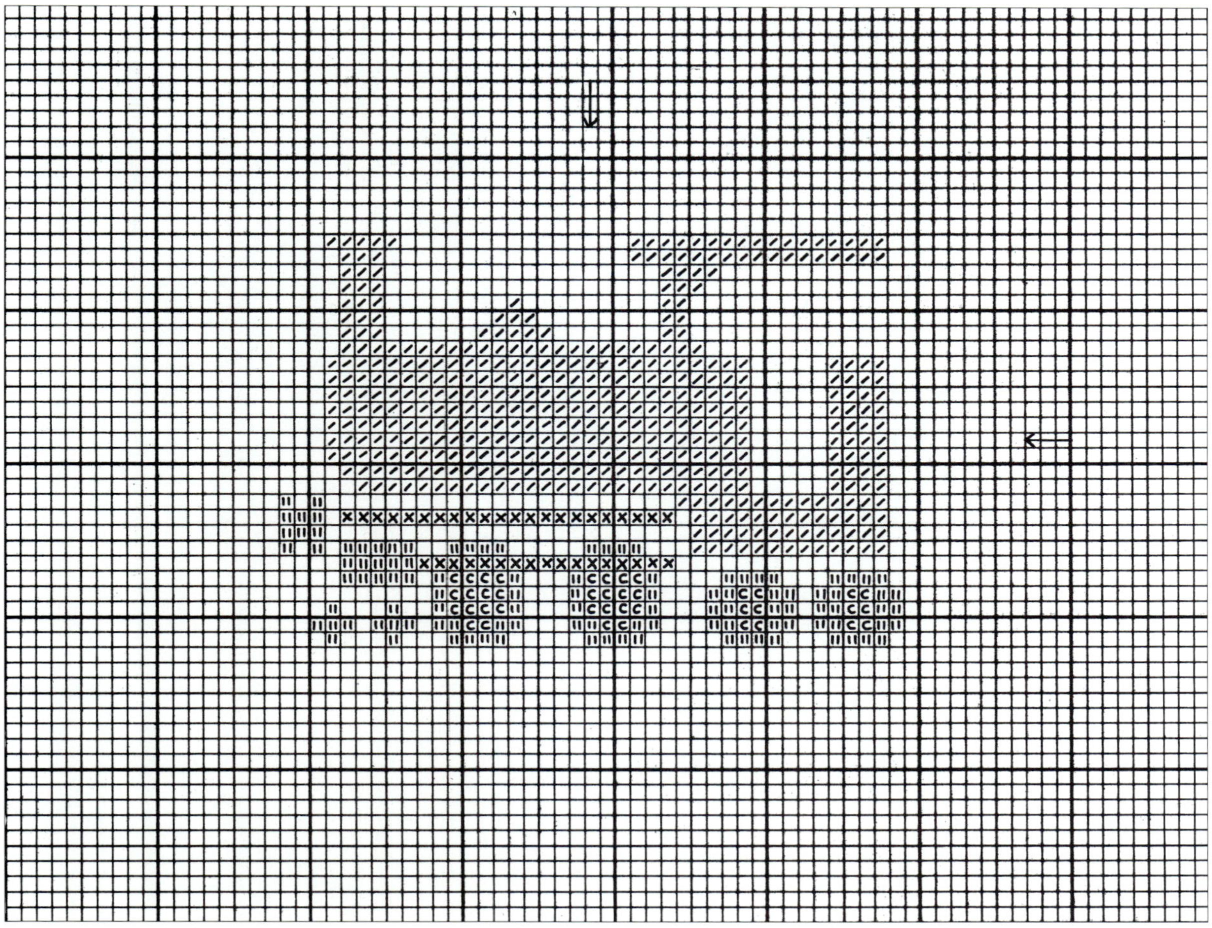

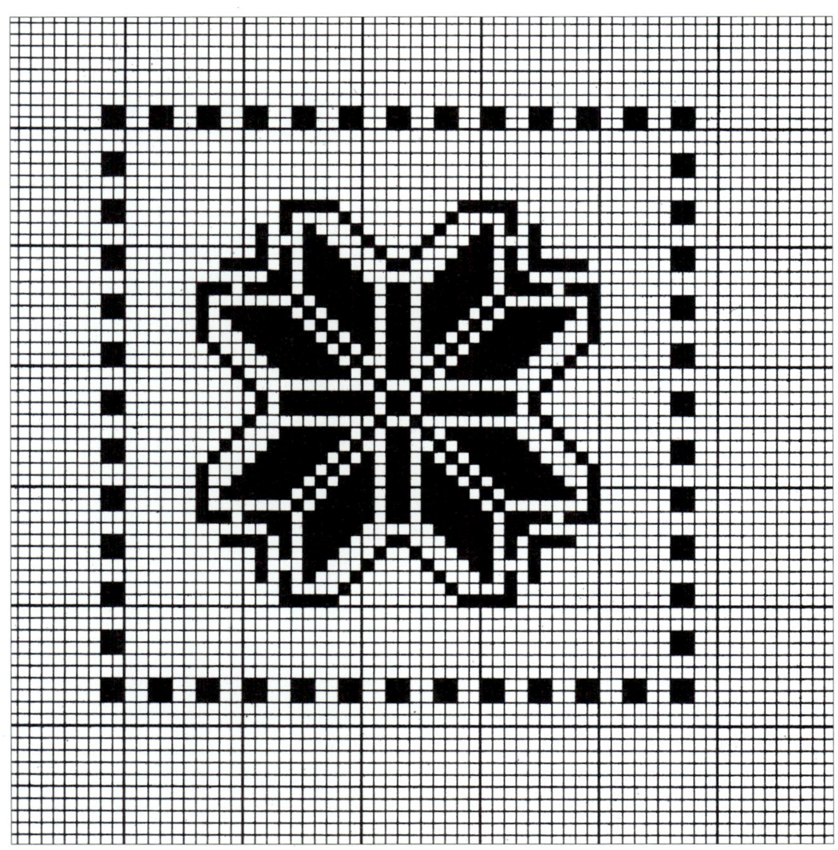

MAT	DMC	ANCHOR	MADEIRA
■ White	White	2	White

CHRISTMAS CRACKERS

These pretty Christmas crackers offer a novel way of wrapping gifts. Each cracker can be filled with sweets, jewellery or other small gifts such as a packet of seeds or a selection of different coloured ballpoint pens.

Christmas Crackers

For each cracker, measuring 23cm (9in) long and 3.8cm (1 ½ in) in diameter, you will need:

28x19cm (11x7½ in) white, holly green or Christmas red, 14-count Aida fabric
1.12m (1⅛ yd) red or green ribbon, 6mm (¼in) wide
stranded embroidery cotton in the colours given in the appropriate panel
gold metallic thread
No24 tapestry needle
cardboard tube from the centre of a toilet roll
double-sided adhesive tape

The embroidery

Prepare the fabric, marking the centre with basting stitches, and stretch it in a hoop (see page 8). Using two strands of embroidery cotton in the needle throughout, complete your chosen design. Remove basting stitches and press the finished embroidery, pressing a 12mm (½ in) seam allowance to the wrong side down each long edge.

Making the cracker

1 Fray the two short edges for 2.5cm (1in), removing the cross threads of Aida one at a time.

2 Place the embroidery face down on a firm, flat surface. Put a strip of double-sided adhesive tape along the complete length of one of the pressed seam allowances (on the wrong side of the embroidery).

3 Put another strip of double-sided tape along the length of the cardboard tube. Lay the taped tube against the seam allowance. Make sure that the tube is centred, so that an equal amount of fabric extends beyond the tube at each end.

4 Carefully roll the fabric around the tube, pressing the taped seam allowance firmly where the fabric meets.

5 Cut the ribbon into two equal lengths; tie one length in a bow around one end of the cracker. Place your gift inside the cardboard tube, and tie the remaining length of ribbon into a bow around the other end of the cracker, which is now ready to be hung on the tree.

ROBIN	DMC	ANCHOR	MADEIRA
II Very light topaz yellow	727	293	0110
/ Light emerald green	912	209	1212
● Light red	350	11	0213
■ Black	310	403	Black
⁘ Medium cocoa brown	407	882	2310
C Chocolate	632	936	2311
◢ Dark beige brown	839	905	1913

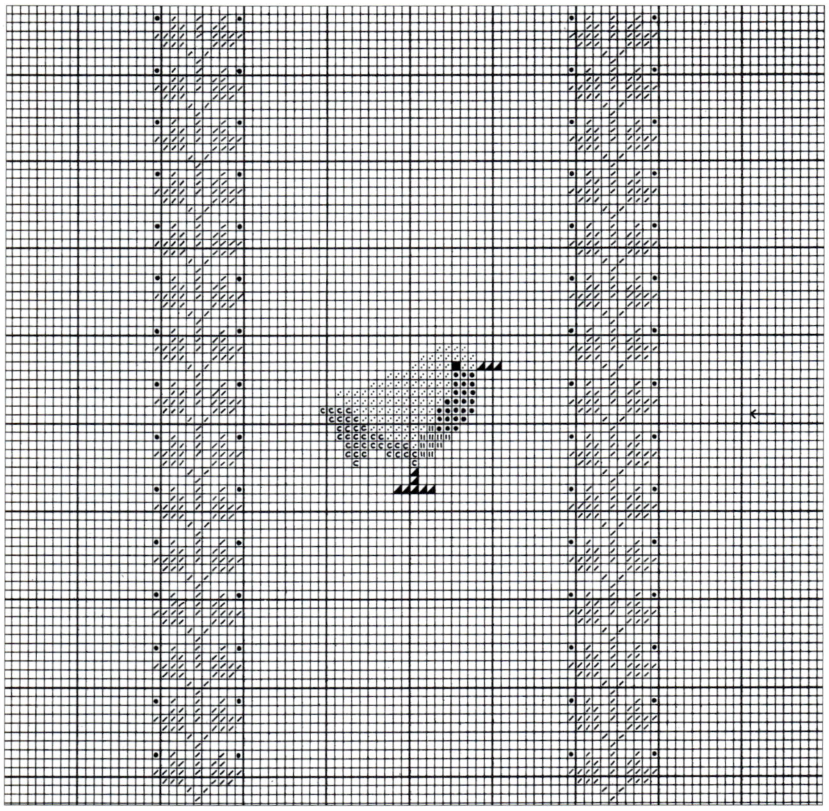

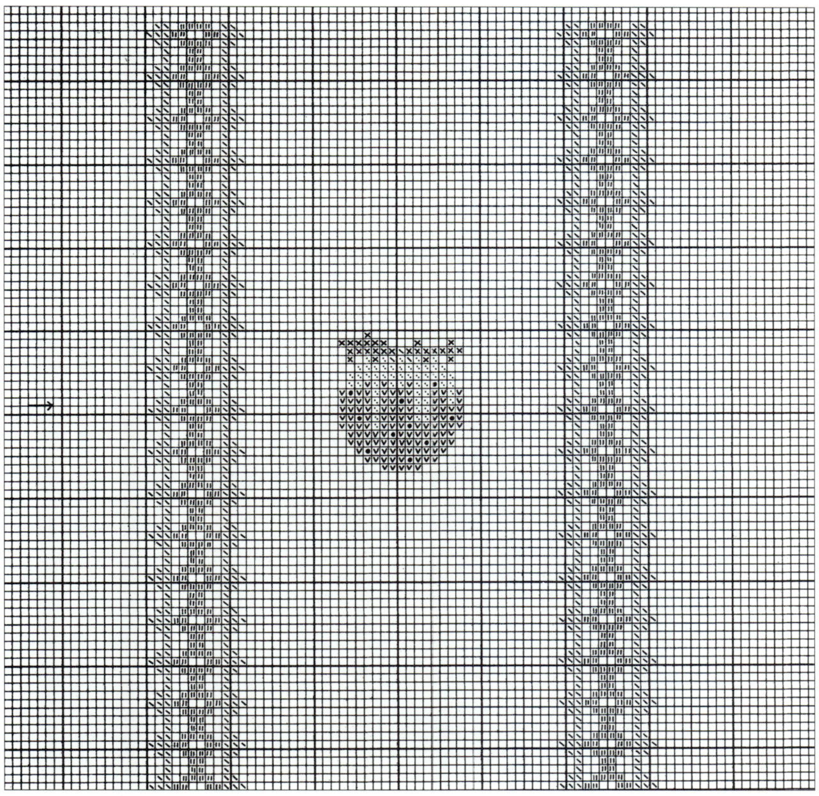

PUDDING		DMC	ANCHOR	MADEIRA
⁄	Red	349	13	0212
‖	Gold thread	-	-	-
☒	Light chartreuse green	704	256	1308
⁚	White	White	2	White
V	Tan brown	436	363	2011
●	Dark coffee brown	801	357	2007

WREATH		DMC	ANCHOR	MADEIRA
⧅	Chartreuse	703	238	1307
☒	Red	349	13	0212
⁚	White	White	2	White

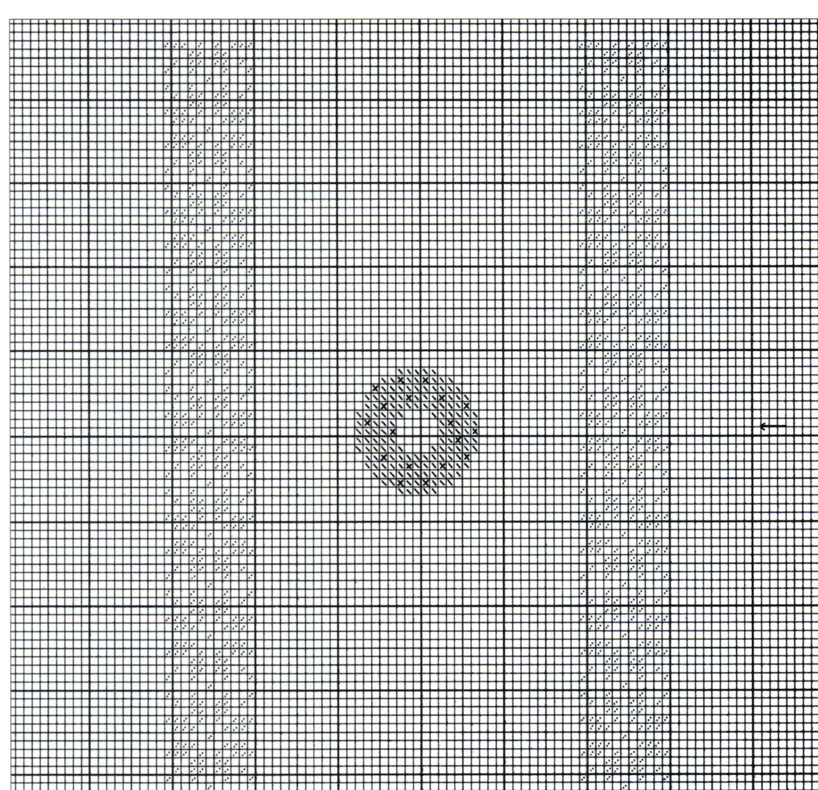

QUILTED WALL HANGING

In days gone by, Christmas used to go on for twelve days and nights until January 6th. The song 'The First Day of Christmas' highlights this traditional time, the new line of each verse telling of an amazing gift that the lady was sent on each day.

1
2
3
4
5
6
7
8
9
10
12

QUILTED WALL HANGING

For the wall hanging, measuring 60x82cm (24x32in), you will need:

23cm (9in) squares 18-count Aida fabric – five of navy, four of Christmas red, and three of holly green
70x84cm (28x33in) green cotton fabric, for the backing and hanging loops
63x84cm (25x33in) thin batting (wadding)
stranded embroidery cotton in the colours given in the appropriate panel (starred colours used for backstitching only)
gold and silver metallic threads
No26 tapestry needle
white quilting thread
two 60cm (24in) lengths of dowelling

★

The embroidery

One by one, prepare each Aida square, marking the centre with horizontal and vertical lines of basting stitches, and set it in a hoop or frame (see page 9). Embroider one of the designs on the square, using two strands of embroidery cotton in the needle for cross stitching, and finishing with the backstitching, made with one strand only in the needle. When you have embroidered all the squares, press each finished embroidery gently on the wrong side, using a steam iron.

Making the hanging

1 Position the designs as shown in the photograph. Join the squares in horizontal rows, taking 12mm (½in) seam allowances and pressing all seams to one side, then join the horizontal rows. For hanging loops, cut six strips of the green fabric, each 7.5x11.5cm (3x4½in). Also from the green fabric, cut a piece measuring 63x84cm (25x33in) for the backing. Fold each green strip in half lengthwise, right sides facing, and stitch down the long side. Turn right side out and press.

2 Lay the backing right side down on a flat surface. Smooth it out; place the batting (wadding) on top, and then the embroidery, right side up. Pin the three layers together and baste diagonally across from corner to corner, and straight across from edge to edge, and then in rectangles, starting close to the centre and spaced about 10cm (4in) apart. Using the quilting thread, quilt by hand or machine along the lines joining the squares, stopping 2.5cm (1in) away from the outer edge of the quilt.

3 Bring the edge of the backing over the batting. Fold the hanging strips so that the short edges meet and position three at the top and three at the bottom of the hanging, concealing the raw edges between the batting/backing and the top fabric. Stitch the loops firmly to the batting/backing layers. Fold in the raw edge of the top fabric all around and slipstitch in place, making sure that the stitches do not show on the right side.

4 Place the lengths of dowelling through the loops to complete your wall hanging.

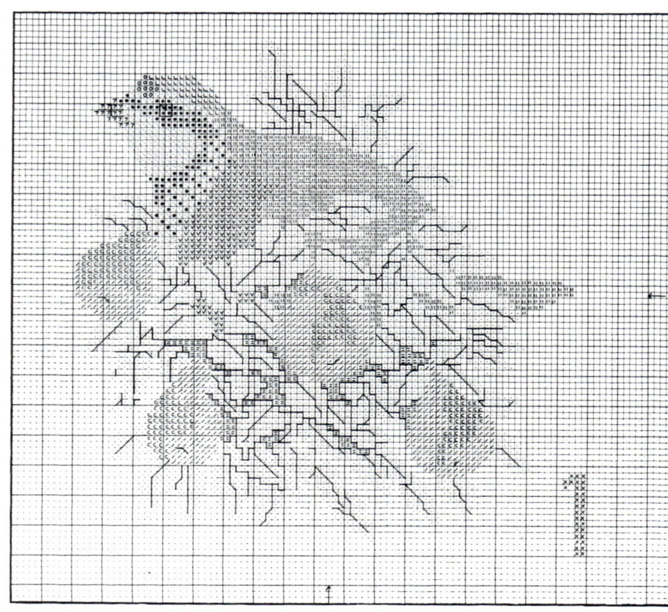

FIRST DAY OF CHRISTMAS

		DMC	ANCHOR	MADEIRA
II	Avocado leaf brown	830	277	2114
☒	Gold thread	-	-	-
●	Black	310	403	Black
L	Light copper	922	324	0310
/	Golden brown	977	307	2301
	Dark golden brown*	975	352	2303
C	Topaz yellow	725	306	0108
•	Light forest green	989	256	1401
	Dark green*	319	246	1313
V	Light old gold	676	891	2208
☰	Dark forest green	987	245	1403
⁛	White	White	2	White
O	Pale grey	415	398	1803
7	Medium copper	920	339	0312
	Very dark beaver grey*	844	401	1810

Note: backstitch golden brown in dark golden brown; light forest green in dark green*, and medium copper grey in very dark beaver grey*.*

SECOND DAY OF CHRISTMAS

		DMC	ANCHOR	MADEIRA
⁄	Very light pearl grey	762	397	1804
•	White	White	2	White
X	Gold thread	-	-	-
■	Black	310	403	Black
C	Pale blue	794	120	0907
V	Baby pink	818	48	0502
I	Light baby pink	819	892	0501
●	Very dark steel grey	413	401	1713
Z	Medium blue	826	161	1012
\	Topaz yellow	725	306	0108
II	Pale grey	415	398	1803
L	Light steel grey	318	399	1802
	Steel grey*	414	400	1801
☰	Dark forest brown	938	381	2005
⁚	Light old gold	676	891	2208
O	Dark old gold	680	901	2210
N	Avocado leaf brown	830	277	2114
Λ	Light salmon red	761	8	0404

Note: backstitch around eyes in black; other backstitching is in steel grey.*

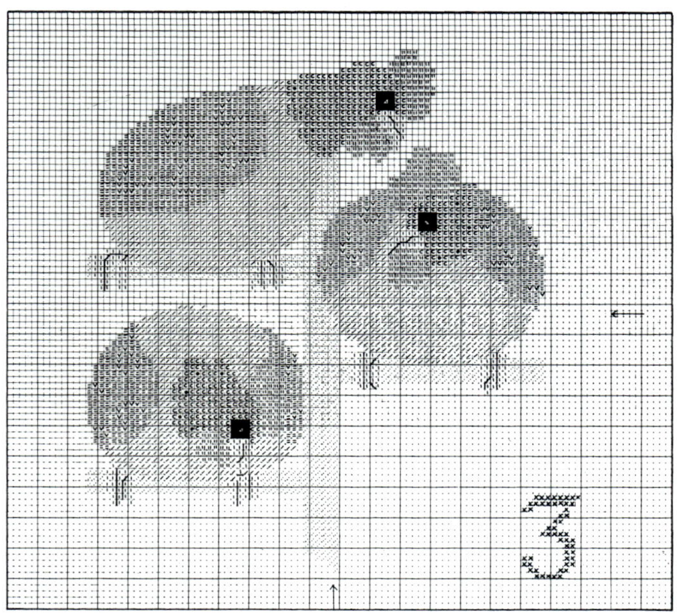

THIRD DAY OF CHRISTMAS

		DMC	ANCHOR	MADEIRA
X	Gold thread	-	-	-
■	Black	310	403	Black
⁄	Topaz yellow	725	306	0108
•	White	White	2	White
●	Dark electric blue	995	410	1102
II	Bright orange red	606	335	0209
⁚	Dark hazelnut brown	420	375	2104
I	Light old gold	676	891	2208
	Medium topaz brown*	782	307	2212
V	Very dark copper	918	341	0314
C	Tangerine orange	740	316	0202
☰	Copper	921	338	0311

Note: backstitch in medium topaz brown.*

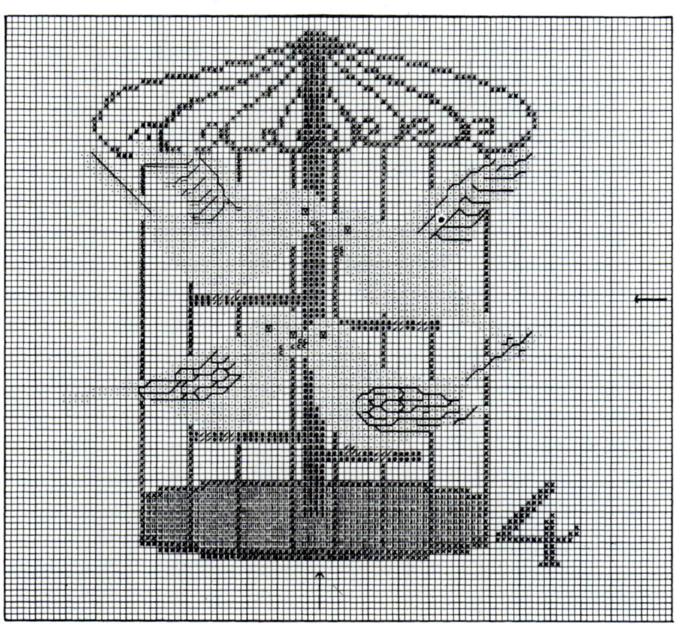

FOURTH DAY OF CHRISTMAS

		DMC	ANCHOR	MADEIRA
X	Gold thread	-	-	-
●	Very dark coffee brown	898	360	2006
II	Dark old gold	680	906	2210
C	Light old gold	676	891	2208
V	Very dark mahogany brown	300	352	2304
⁄	Pale grey	415	398	1803
	Steel grey*	414	400	1801
•	Black	310	403	Black

Note: backstitch with steel grey.*

The first day of Christmas, my true love sent to me
A partridge in a pear tree

The second day of Christmas, my true love sent to me
Two turtle doves and a partridge in a pear tree

The third day of Christmas, my true love sent to me
Three French hens, two turtle doves and a partridge in a pear tree

The fourth day of Christmas, my true love sent to me
Four colly birds,
three French hens, etc.

The fifth day of Christmas, my true love sent to me
Five gold rings,
four colly birds, etc.

The sixth day of Christmas, my true love sent to me
Six geese a-laying,
five gold rings, etc.

FIFTH DAY OF CHRISTMAS

		DMC	ANCHOR	MADEIRA
☒	Gold thread	-	-	-
ǁ	Medium garnet red	815	43	0513
	Dark garnet red*	814	44	0514
C	Bright Christmas red	666	46	0210
/	Christmas green	699	923	1303
•	Kelly green	702	226	1306
	Very dark evergreen*	890	218	1314
	Green metallic Kreinik Balger Cord* 008C			

Note: backstitch leaf green in very dark evergreen; around medium garnet red with dark garnet red*, and around all leaves with two strands of Kreinik green metallic*.*

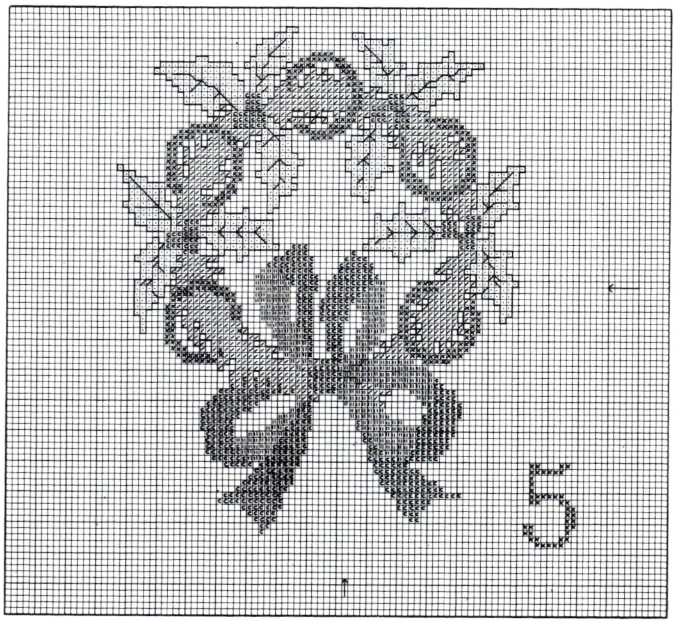

The seventh day of Christmas, my true love sent to me
Seven swans a-swimming, six geese a-laying, etc.

The eighth day of Christmas, my true love sent to me
Eight maids a-milking, seven swans a-swimming, etc.

The ninth day of Christmas, my true love sent to me
Nine drummers drumming, eight maids a-milking, etc.

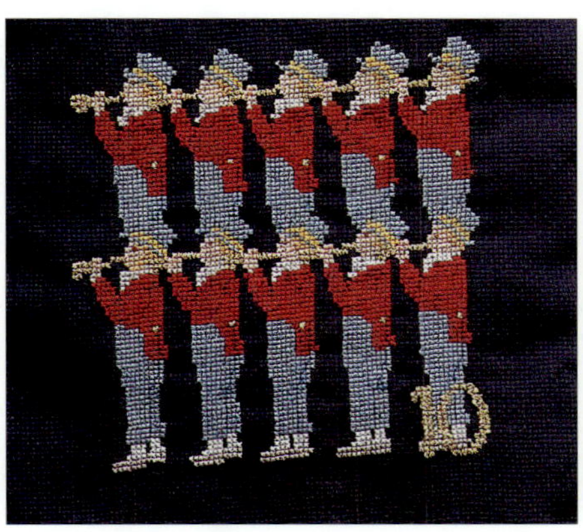

The tenth day of Christmas, my true love sent to me
Ten pipers piping, nine drummers drumming, etc.

The eleventh day of Christmas, my true love sent to me
Eleven ladies dancing, ten pipers piping, etc.

The twelfth day of Christmas, my true love sent to me
Twelve lords a-leaping, eleven ladies dancing, ten pipers piping, nine drummers drumming, eight maids a-milking, seven swans a-swimming, six geese a-laying, five gold rings, four colly birds, three French hens, two turtle doves, and a partridge in a pear tree.

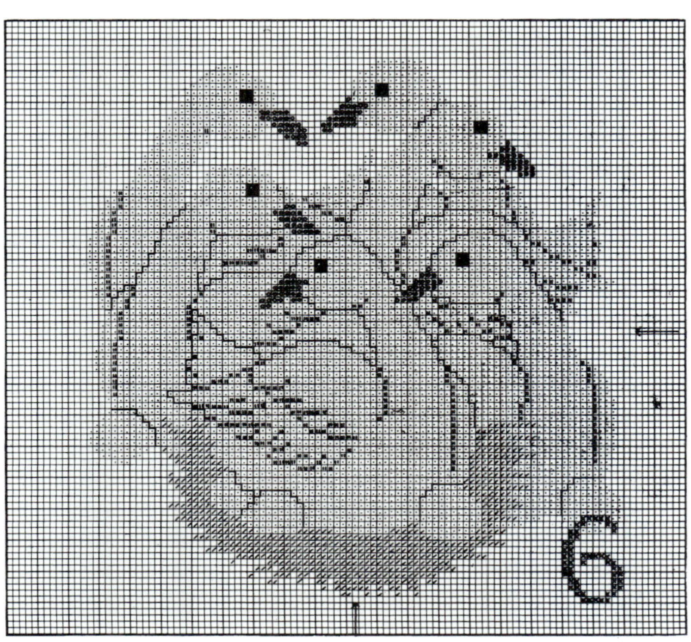

SIXTH DAY OF CHRISTMAS

		DMC	ANCHOR	MADEIRA
■	Black	310	403	Black
☒	Gold thread	-	-	-
⊡	White	White	2	White
	Medium steel grey*	317	400	1714
O	Pumpkin orange	971	316	0203
II	Pale grey	415	398	1803
/	Christmas gold	783	307	2211

Note: backstitch around white with steel grey.*

SEVENTH DAY OF CHRISTMAS		DMC	ANCHOR	MADEIRA
X	Gold thread	-	-	-
/	Aqua	959	186	1113
V	Medium tangerine orange	741	304	0201
■	Black	310	403	Black
•	White	White	2	White
	Medium steel grey*	317	400	1714
II	Pale grey	415	398	1803

Note: backstitch around white in medium steel grey.*

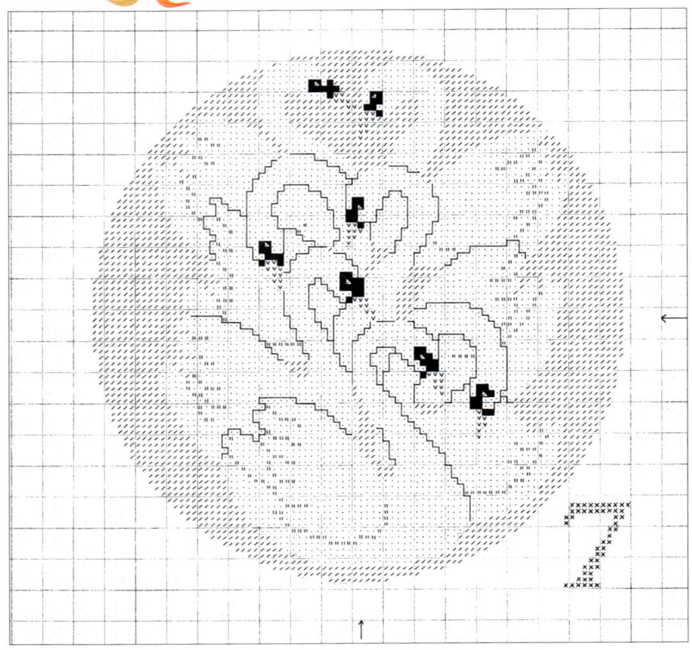

EIGHTH DAY OF CHRISTMAS		DMC	ANCHOR	MADEIRA
X	Gold thread	-	-	-
/	Medium golden brown	976	309	2302
	Very dark copper*	918	341	0314
•	White	White	2	White
	Light steel grey*	318	399	1802
⁚	Light peach	754	6	0305
	Medium peach*	352	9	0303
●	Black	310	403	Black
V	Dark golden brown	975	352	2303
\	Delft blue	809	130	0909
	Dark Delft blue*	798	146	0911
=	Christmas gold	783	307	2211
H	Light topaz yellow	726	295	0109
II	Pale grey	415	398	1803
O L	Medium brown	433	371	2008
C	Medium pink	899	27	0505
	Very dark rose red*	326	59	0508
I	Golden wheat	3046	887	2206
	Dark golden wheat*	3045	888	2103
Y	Tan brown	436	363	2011
◢	Very dark coffee brown	898	360	2006
Z	Steel grey	414	400	1801

Note: backstitch around medium golden brown with very dark copper; white and black with light steel grey*; light peach with medium peach*; Delft blue with very dark Delft blue*; medium pink with very dark rose red*; golden wheat with dark golden wheat*, and tan brown with medium brown.*

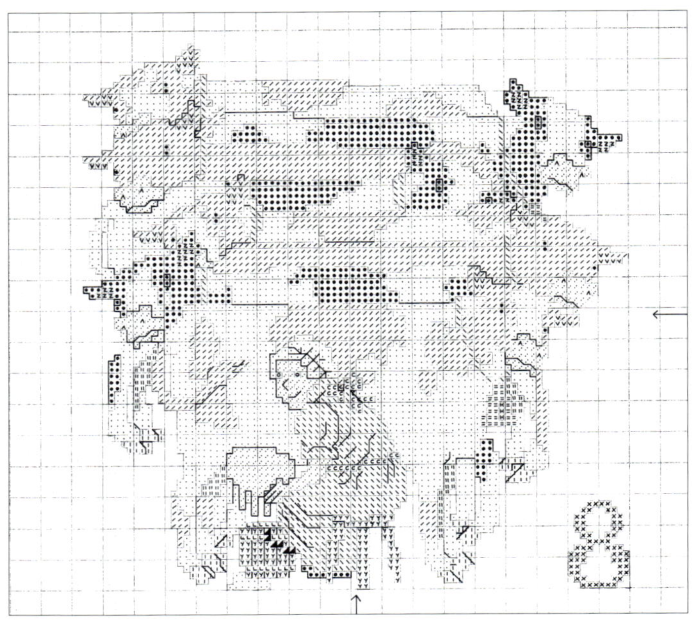

NINTH DAY OF CHRISTMAS		DMC	ANCHOR	MADEIRA
X	Gold thread	-	-	-
O	Medium topaz brown	782	307	2212
	Dark golden brown*	975	352	2303
●	Black	310	403	Black
	Steel grey*	414	400	1801
/	Off white	746	368	0101
	Golden wheat*	3046	887	2206
⁚	Bright orange red	606	335	0209
	Garnet red*	816	20	0512
=	Topaz yellow	725	306	0108
V	White	White	2	White
•	Light peach	754	6	0305
	Medium peach*	352	9	0303
■	Medium brown	433	371	2008
II	Pale grey	415	398	1803
Z	Tan brown	436	363	2011
I	Medium mahogany brown	301	349	2306

Note: outline medium topaz brown with dark golden brown; black with steel grey*; off white with golden wheat*; bright orange red with garnet red*, and light peach with medium peach*, and make the eyes with french knots in medium brown.*

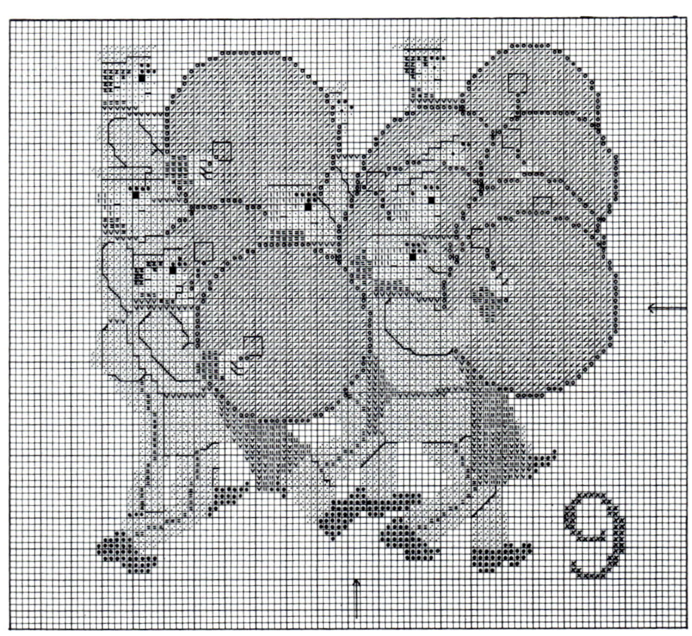

TENTH DAY OF CHRISTMAS		DMC	ANCHOR	MADEIRA
☒	Gold thread	-	-	-
•	Light peach	754	6	0305
	Medium peach*	352	9	0303
●	Medium beige grey	644	830	1907
	Very dark beige grey*	640	903	1905
I	White	White	2	White
	Light steel grey*	318	399	1802
/	Light blue	813	160	1013
	Dark blue*	825	162	1011
⁚	Bright Christmas red	666	46	0210
	Dark garnet red*	814	44	0514
C	Topaz yellow	725	306	0108
II	Tan brown	436	363	2011
✛	Medium brown	433	371	2008

Note: outline light peach with medium peach; medium beige grey with very dark beige grey*; white with light steel grey*; light blue with dark blue*, and bright Christmas red with dark garnet red*, and make french knots with medium brown.*

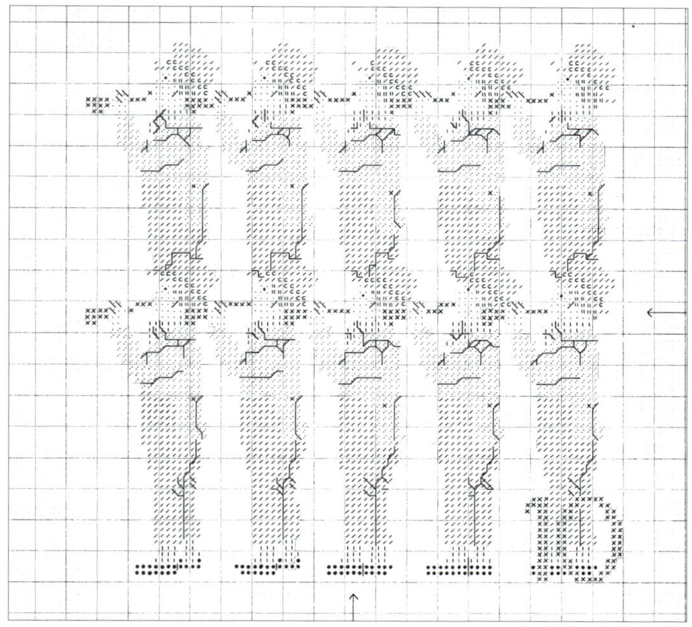

ELEVENTH DAY OF CHRISTMAS		DMC	ANCHOR	MADEIRA
☒	Gold thread	-	-	-
•	Light peach	754	6	0305
	Medium peach*	352	9	0303
C	Melon orange	3340	329	0214
	Medium salmon red*	3328	11	0408
⁚	Light violet	554	96	0711
	Dark violet*	552	100	0713
–	Light old gold	676	891	2208
	Dark old gold*	680	901	2210
V	Silver thread	-	-	-
/	Aqua	959	186	1113
	Medium aqua*	943	188	1203
I	White	White	2	White
	Light steel grey*	318	399	1802
Z	Hazelnut brown	869	944	2105

Note: outline light peach with medium peach; melon orange with medium salmon red*; light violet with dark violet*; light old gold with dark old gold*; aqua with medium aqua*, and white with light steel grey*, and use the eyes with french knots in hazelnut brown.*

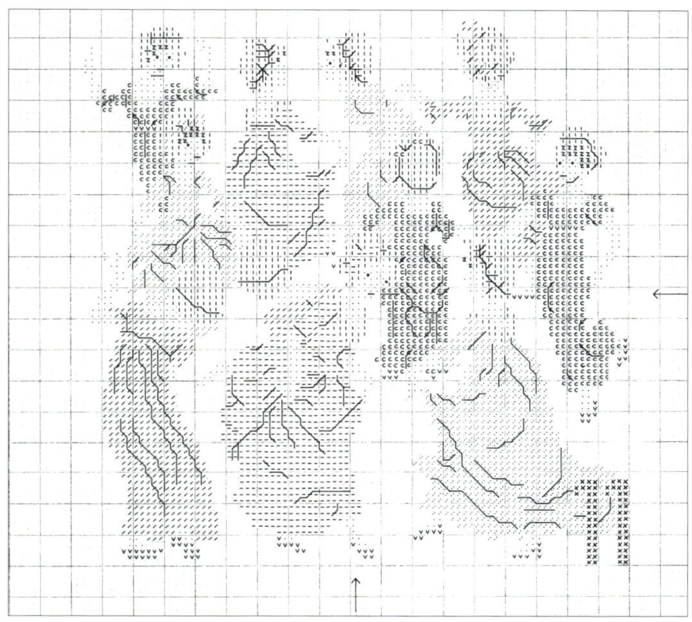

TWELFTH DAY OF CHRISTMAS		DMC	ANCHOR	MADEIRA
☒	Gold thread	-	-	-
•	Light peach	754	6	0305
	Medium peach*	352	9	0303
Z	Light brown	434	309	2009
O	Medium topaz brown	782	307	2212
I	White	White	2	White
	Light steel grey*	318	399	1802
/	Bright orange	608	333	0206
	Medium Christmas red*	304	47	0509
⁚	Kelly green	702	226	1306
	Christmas green*	699	923	1303

Note: outline light peach with medium peach; white with light steel grey*; bright orange with medium Christmas red*, and Kelly green with Christmas green*.*

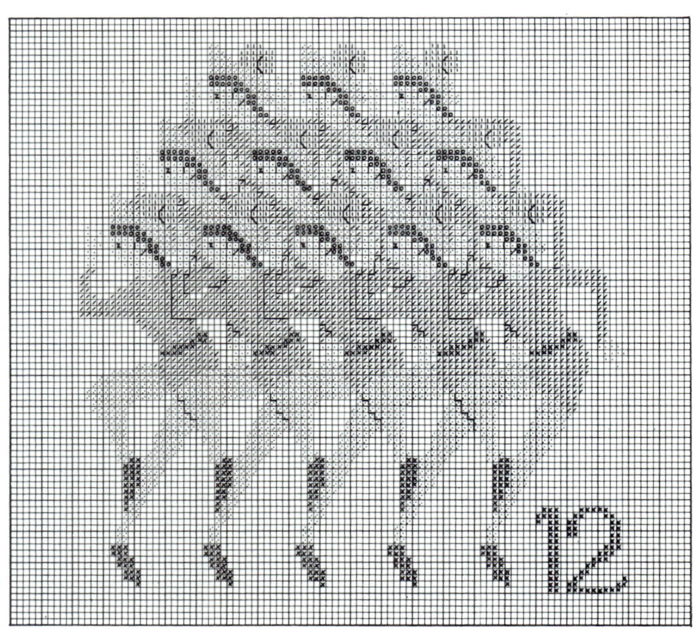

Christmas Cards

Personalized greetings cards containing a small embroidery are a pleasure to make or receive. Christmas cards first became popular in the late Victorian era. Early cards were decorated with flowers, then came the more traditional Christmas themes, such as holly, robins and snow scenes, followed by nativities and angels.

XMAS

Christmas Cards

For each card, the large cards measuring 16x11cm (6¼x4¼in), and the small cards 9x12cm (3½x4¾in), you will need:

stranded embroidery cotton in the colours given in the appropriate panel (starred colours used for backstitching only)
No26 tapestry needle
double-sided adhesive tape
appropriate card, as listed below (for suppliers, see page 224)

For the Noël card:
16x11cm (6¼x4¼in) white, 18-count Aida fabric
large holly green card with a rectangular cut-out

For the Xmas card:
16x11cm (6¼x4¼in) silver fleck, 20-count Bellana fabric
large holly green card with a circular cut-out

For the Shepherd card:
16x11cm (6¼x4¼in) white, 20-count Bellana fabric
large holly green card with an oval cut-out

For the Bethlehem card:
9x12cm (3½x4¾in) sky blue, 22-count Hardanger
small Christmas red card with a rectangular cut-out

For the Santa card:
9x12cm (3½x4¾in) silver fleck, 20-count Bellana fabric
small Christmas red card with a rectangular cut-out

For the Robins card:
16x11cm (6¼x4¼in) of silver fleck, 20-count Bellana fabric
large Christmas red card with an oval cut-out

★

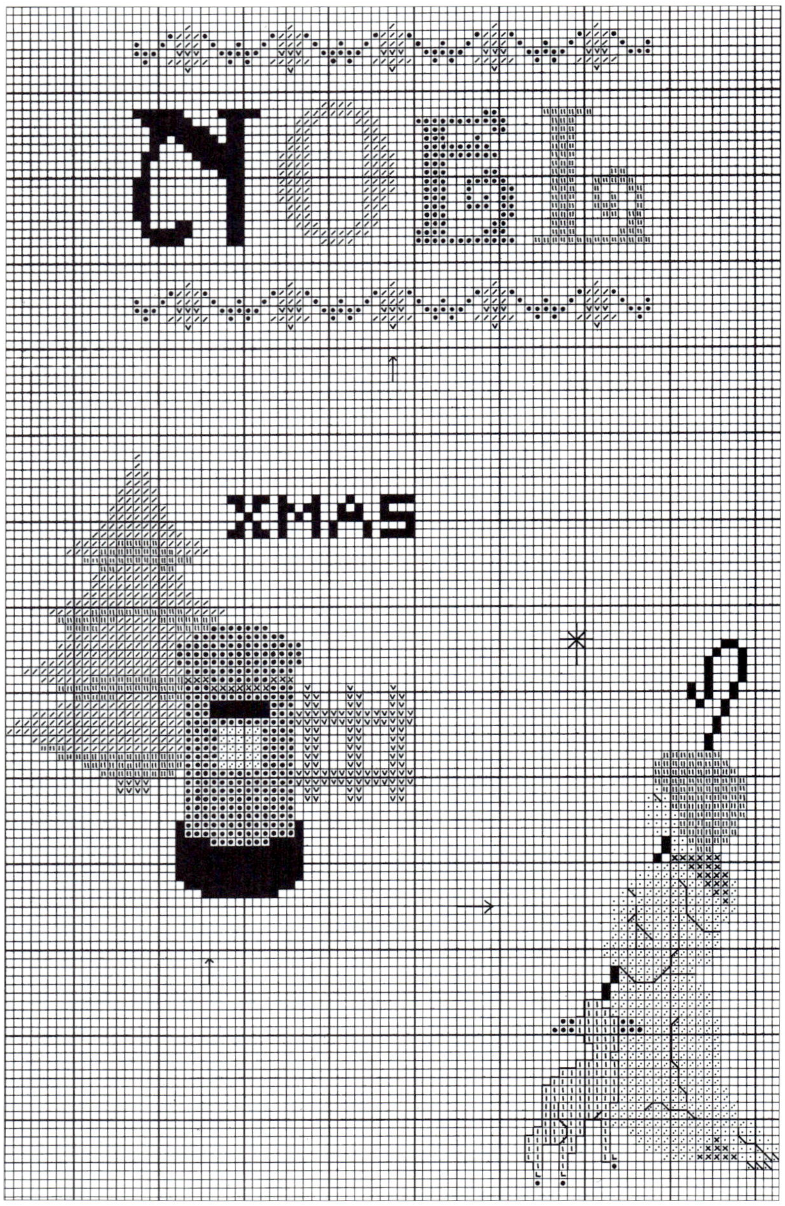

NOEL	DMC	ANCHOR	MADEIRA
● Dark Kelly green	701	227	1305
/ Topaz yellow	725	306	0108
V Medium topaz yellow	782	307	2212
■ Bright Christmas red	666	46	0210
II Dark violet	552	100	0713

The embroidery

Each card is made in the same way. To economize on fabric, you could make the Santa, Robins and Xmas cards on a single piece of fabric, providing you leave sufficient space around each design.

Prepare the fabric, marking the centre (of each design, if you are stitching several on a single piece) with horizontal and vertical lines of basting stitches (see page 8). Set the fabric in a hoop, and complete the cross stitch embroidery, using one strand of embroidery cotton in the needle throughout. When you have completed the embroidery, gently press the finished piece from the wrong side, leaving the basting stitches in position at this stage.

Making up the cards

1 Trim the embroidery to measure slightly larger all around than the card window, then centre it behind the window, using the basting stitches as guidelines. Make

XMAS	DMC	ANCHOR	MADEIRA
Black	310	403	Black
Kelly green	702	226	0306
Christmas green	699	923	1303
Medium brown	433	371	2008
Dark Christmas red	498	47	0511
Light red	350	11	0213
White	White	2	White

SHEPHERD	DMC	ANCHOR	MADEIRA
Medium brown	433	371	2008
Very light brown	435	365	2010
Light peach	754	6	0305
Medium peach*	352	9	0303
Dark antique mauve	315	896	0810
Antique mauve	316	894	0809
White	White	2	White
Black	310	403	Black
Light steel grey	318	399	1802
Silver thread*	-	-	-

Note: backstitch around light peach with medium peach; white with light steel grey, and star with silver thread*.*

BETHLEHEM	DMC	ANCHOR	MADEIRA
Silver thread	-	-	-
Black	310	403	Black
White	White	2	White
Light peach	754	6	0305
Dark aqua	958	187	1114
Light steel grey	318	399	1802
Light loden green	3364	843	1512
Dark loden green	3362	846	1514

ROBINS	DMC	ANCHOR	MADEIRA
Pale grey	415	398	1803
Black	310	403	Black
Dark forest brown	938	381	2005
Medium brown	433	371	2008
Medium yellow	744	301	0112
Very light mahogany brown	402	347	2307
Light red	350	11	0213

SANTA	DMC	ANCHOR	MADEIRA
Bright Christmas red	666	46	0210
Light peach	754	6	0305
White	White	2	White
Light steel grey*	318	399	1802
Kelly green	702	226	0306
Black	310	403	Black
Medium peach	352	9	0303

Note: backstitch string in black; around white with light steel grey.*

light pencil marks on the back of the embroidery and the back of the window, to act as registration marks.

2 Remove the basting stitches, then replace the card in the window. Use double-sided adhesive tape to secure the card in position, then press the backing down firmly.

Christmas Stocking

This lovely embroidered stocking is just the right size to hold sweets and small toys, even a little teddy. It is a present which will delight any child at Christmas.

For the Christmas stocking (photograph, pages 6-7), measuring about 31x28cm (12 1/4 x11in), you will need:

two 38x30cm (15x12in) pieces holly green, 14-count Aida fabric
1.5m (1 2/3 yd) red bias binding, 12mm (1/2 in) wide
stranded embroidery cotton in the colours given in the panel
No24 tapestry needle
red sewing thread

The embroidery

Take one of the two pieces of Aida fabric; prepare it for embroidery and set it in a hoop or frame (see page 9). Embroider the design; work the cross stitch first, using two strands of embroidery cotton in the needle, and then the backstitch, using one strand. Gently press the finished embroidery on the wrong side, using a steam iron.

Making the stocking

1 Trace the stocking template on good quality tracing paper, marking the position of the arrows. Centre this over the embroidery; mark and then cut out the shape. Reversing the tracing paper pattern, cut a mirror-image shape from the remaining piece of Aida.

2 Place the two pieces with wrong sides together and baste around the edge. Machine stitch, taking a 12mm (1/2 in) seam allowance and leaving the top open. Trim the edge to within 6mm (1/4 in) of the stitching line and remove basting stitches.

3 Pin and baste the red bias binding all around the stitched edge and around the open top edge of the stocking. Stitching through all layers, stitch the binding in position. If you intend to hang the stocking, make a small hanging loop from a short length of the binding and stitch this to the top of the stocking, at the back seam.

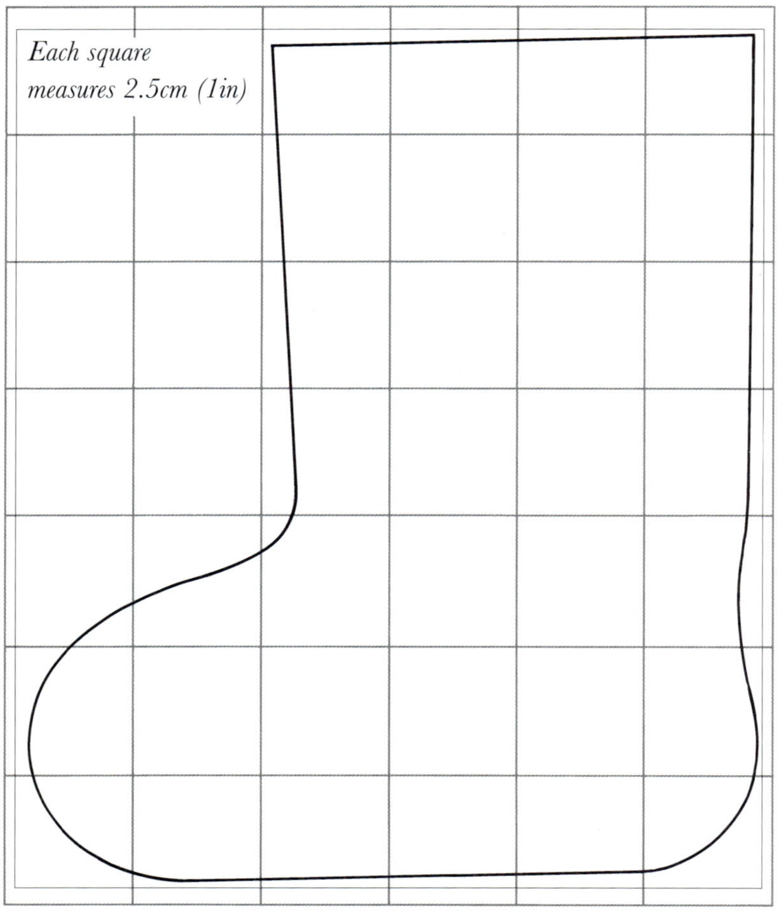

STOCKING		DMC	ANCHOR	MADEIRA
/	Bright Christmas red	666	46	0210
C	Medium garnet red	815	43	0513
⁚	White	White	2	White
X	Topaz yellow	725	306	0108
●	Black	310	403	Black
II	Medium steel grey	317	400	1714
•	Light peach	754	6	0305
Λ	Medium peach	352	9	0303
H	Medium Delft blue	799	130	0910
V	Royal blue	797	132	0912
I	Golden wheat	3046	887	2206
O	Dark golden wheat	3045	888	2103
=	Medium violet	553	98	0712
L	Light Chartreuse green	704	256	1308
Z	Very light golden yellow	3078	292	0102

Note: backstitch white with medium steel grey; light peach with medium peach and golden wheat with dark golden wheat.

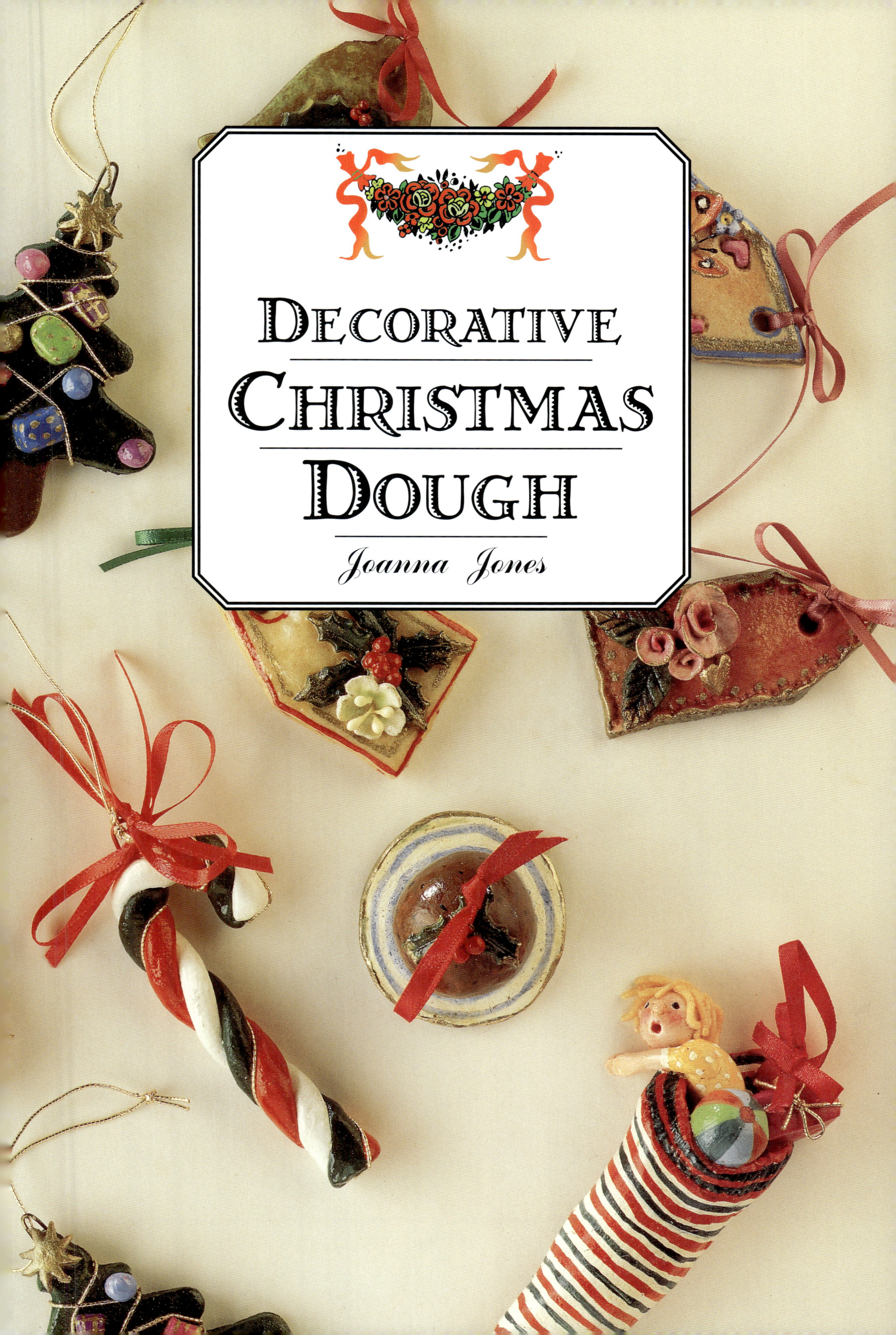

Decorative Christmas Dough

Joanna Jones

Decorative Christmas Dough

Introduction

It somehow seems fitting that we should make gifts and decorations for the ancient festival of Christmas with a material as old and as basic as dough. In fact, some things, such as the nativity scene, have been traditionally made in dough of one kind or another for centuries.

Now that dough modelling is so popular, it seems extraordinary that so little information was available not very long ago when I first became fascinated by the craft. Thanks to a casual encounter with an American lady in the book department of a large store, I finally acquired the precious salt dough recipe for which I had been searching in vain. The recipe I scribbled down was extremely basic and consisted of flour, salt and water. I have since modified it slightly, adding a little oil in an attempt to alleviate the dough modeller's curse ... cracking!

I cannot stress enough how important it is to knead the dough thoroughly, but I am also well aware that, despite zealous kneading, the demon cracks can still appear. Hours after the piece has been baked you may actually hear the dough cracking.

Basic Recipes, Equipment & Modelling Techniques

Basic dough

250g (8oz/2 cups) plain (all-purpose) flour
125g (4oz/½ cup) salt
2 teaspoons cooking oil

1 Thoroughly mix the flour and salt in a bowl and then add the oil and 125ml (4fl oz/½ cup) water. Stir the water and oil into the flour mixture and start to bind the ingredients into a dough. Discard the spoon at this point and mix the dough with your hand, adding more water gradually by sprinkling it into the mix with your fingertips. By adding the water drip by drip, you will know the instant the dough is ready. It should be firm enough not to stick to your hands but not so dry that it is crumbly.

2 Turn the dough out onto a smooth work surface and then knead it very thoroughly for at least 10 minutes, until the dough is very smooth, pliable and very slightly warm.

Notes: the basic dough is a salt dough. Where a quantity of basic dough is listed, be sure to use the above recipe, not the bread dough (below). You may use the cheapest available flour; because brands differ, the amount of water needed to bind the dough varies.

Bread dough

The ingredients for bread dough are totally different from those in salt dough and the result is a dough of such a fine texture that it is possible to make flowers with petals as delicate as porcelain. As it is so delicate, this dough is only really suitable for making small objects. Larger pieces look more attractive and are easier to make using salt dough.

Both types of dough require kneading; unfortunately the bread dough has to be kneaded for 15–20 minutes, during which time your hands are in such a mess that you really need to plan ahead before you start. Before kneading bread dough, rub a lavish quantity of hand cream into your hands.

125g (4oz/4 slices) day-old white bread without crusts
3 tablespoons P.V.A. glue
1 tablespoon white acrylic paint
1 teaspoon glycerine (glycerol)

1 Break the bread into small pieces about the size of sugar cubes and place them in a bowl. Add the remaining ingredients, wiping the sticky glue and paint off the spoon each time with a piece of the bread.

2 Bind the mixture together by stirring it with a spoon until it forms a ball. Scoop up the dough with your hands and knead it between your palms for 15–20 minutes. Your hands will be completely coated with white paint and glue at first, but persevere and very soon you will notice that the ball of dough will be growing smoother and your hands will be cleaner.

3 If after 30 minutes the dough is either far too wet or too dry, add more breadcrumbs to wet dough or a little more glycerine to dry dough and continue to knead.

4 Wrap the ball of dough in cling film (plastic wrap) and put it into an airtight container in the refrigerator until you need to use it. It will keep for months if stored in this way.

Note: when you have taken the dough from the bowl, make sure that you fill the bowl with water and place the spoon in it, otherwise the mixture will have dried hard by the time you are free to do the washing up.

After many years of teaching dough modelling, I know that at some time during the kneading exercise you are more than likely to doubt me, but have faith ... you *will* end up with a beautiful ball of smooth white dough, which will be slightly softer than plasticine.

Kneading bread dough

Knead the dough by pressing it first into one palm and then into the other. Be firm about this action and do not spread the dough by stroking the fingers of one hand against the palm of the other. If you are kneading bread dough properly you should actually feel the effect on your pectoral muscles.

As you work, the glue and paint on your hands will gradually be taken up by the ball of dough, which will become very smooth and supple. When kneaded sufficiently there should be absolutely no sign of any bread.

Quantities

Some projects call for smaller quantities of bread dough, but it is not worth making less than the amount given above; just store the leftover dough in the refrigerator ready for making another model.

Drying

Bread dough takes about 6 hours to dry at room temperature; the exact length of time depends on the size of individual pieces.

Colouring bread dough

Flatten a small chunk of bread dough out slightly. Squeeze a little gouache or water-colour paint onto the dough and then fold the dough over it and knead it. Continue kneading until the paint is well distributed and the colour is even, adding more paint or dough until the colour is right.

This is an undeniably messy business and you may well be tempted to leave the dough white and paint it when dry. This is not always a good idea because, although you invariably paint over the coloured dough, there are nooks and crannies that you cannot reach without smudging something else, so it helps if it is almost the same colour and you can leave it unpainted.

Colouring the dough also seems to refine it, making it less coarse.

Egg glaze

Egg glaze gives salt dough a lovely golden colour if you paint it on before baking. To make a glaze, beat an egg with 1 tablespoon water. Do not glaze dough that you intend to paint later as it will prevent the paint from flowing on easily. If you require a really deep colour, you may repeat the application of glaze every 20 minutes or so throughout the cooking time.

Salt Dough Modelling Techniques

Kneading salt dough

As soon as all the ingredients are thoroughly bound together, tip the ball of dough out onto a lightly floured smooth surface. Take hold of the dough with both hands, then press down and push it away from you with the base of your palms.

Alternate this action with a sideways folding movement to keep the ball of dough roughly the same size and shape as it is kneaded. Continue kneading for at least 10 minutes, by which time the dough should be smooth and very slightly warm.

It is essential to knead the dough firmly and for the recommended time to avoid problems when modelling.

Rolling ropes

Roll a piece of well-kneaded salt dough into a rough sausage shape on a lightly floured board. Place the fingers of both hands together in the middle of the sausage and work them out towards the ends, rolling the dough backwards and forwards. Repeat until the rope is the required length and thickness. By using your fingers rather than the palms of your hands, you both exert less pressure and have more control, and your rope is more likely to be of even thickness.

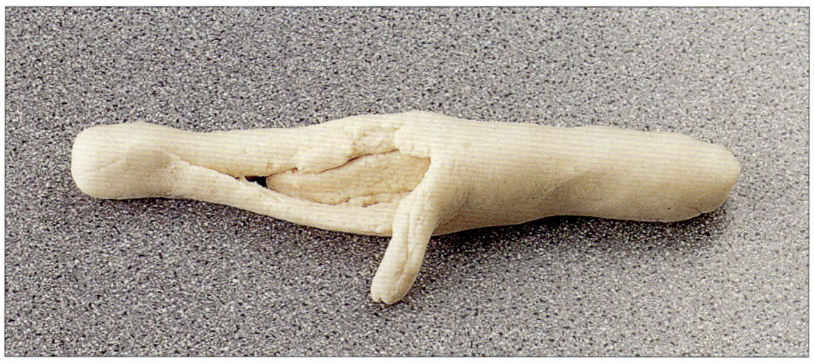

Dough which has not been thoroughly kneaded splits when it is rolled into a rope.

Making a twist

Lay two ropes of the same length and thickness side by side. Starting in the centre, twist them around each other, then work outwards, first to one end and then to the other. Fix the ropes together at both ends. By working from the middle, you are less likely to stretch the dough and end up with a twist which has one thin end and one thick end.

Making a twist.

Making hair

Dough is extruded through a garlic press, clay gun or a fine sieve, such as a nylon tea strainer to make hair. Whichever method you use, try to give your figures a recognizable style, rather than leaving the dough in a tangled mess, and avoid wispy arrangements or stray locks as these tend to break off.

Garlic press Fill the press with a smooth ball of dough, then push it through the holes. If the resultant strands are long enough, cut them off using a sharp knife. If you want longer hair, re-charge the press with dough, before cutting the first batch off and push some more through.

Wet the head and then, transferring single strands of hair on some well-floured plastic tweezers, gradually build up the hair style.

Clay gun There are two or three different types of clay gun available from specialist sugarcraft shops. They all work along similar lines and may be used for a variety of different effects. To make hair, fit one of the sieve-like discs into the end of the gun and load the tube with slightly dampened dough.

Pull the trigger to push strands of dough out onto a lightly floured board. Then use floured plastic tweezers to pick up little clumps of hair and transfer these to the dampened head.

Clay-gun hair is usually much finer than garlic-press hair and with care it can be extruded in waves, straight onto the head of the figure. It can also be coaxed into curls after it has been arranged on the head by using a cocktail stick (toothpick) or modelling tool.

Fine sieve I use this for short, male styles, for little dolls and for a permed effect. Soften the dough slightly with a little water and, using the back of a wooden spoon, push it through the sieve. The more you press, the longer the hair on the other side of the sieve will be, but as this method gives a very compact effect, it is best to reserve it for short styles.

Remove the hair from the back of the sieve with a sharp knife and transfer it directly to the head.

Pushing dough through a fine sieve to make hair.

Curls For creatures such as cherubs, who simply must have big fat curls, the only solution is to roll them by hand.

Make several very small tapering ropes about 12mm (½in) in length and, starting at one end, roll each rope into a coil. Dot these all over the head at different angles; I usually reserve one, which is coming slightly uncurled, for the forehead.

Making arms and hands

Lay two suitable ropes of dough side by side on a floured board. Flatten the ends closest to you with a finger, then use a sharp knife to cut a small triangle of dough from the inside edge of each of the flattened pieces to represent the space between the thumb and the first finger.

Make three small cuts along the bottom edge of each piece to represent the fingers and trim these to the appropriate lengths. Using the sharp knife or a damp paint brush, carefully round the ends of the fingers and thumbs.

While the arms are still lying side by side, trim the tops of them diagonally so that the two diagonals form a 'V'; these slanting ends will eventually fit on either side of the body at the shoulder.

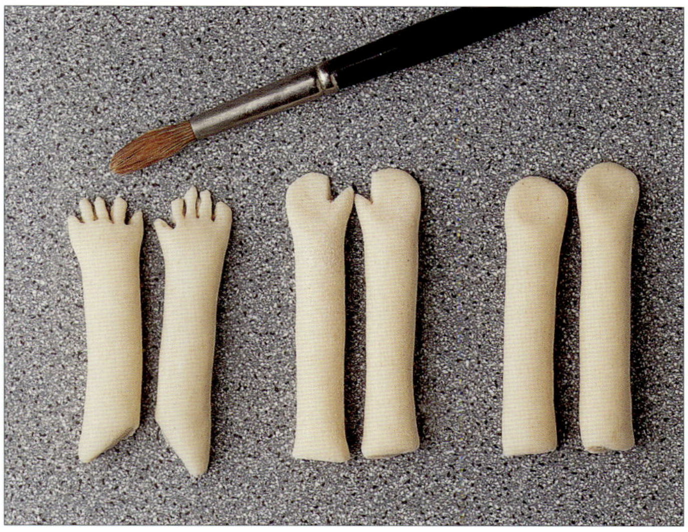

Modelling hands.

Making legs and feet

To make legs and feet that are wearing boots or shoes, lay two suitable ropes of dough together on a floured board. Leave the bottom ends of these ropes untrimmed so that they retain their rounded appearance.

Lay a finger across one of the ropes, about 12mm (½ in) from the rounded end, and roll the rope very gently to make a slight indentation. Dab a spot of water on the indentation and then bend the rounded end up at right angles to form a foot. Make the other foot in the same way.

If you wish to give the appearance of boots, fix a very thin rope of dough around each leg, just above the ankle or halfway up the calf.

To make legs with bare feet, lay the ropes side by side as before, but trim both bottom ends diagonally so that together they form a 'V'. Make four small cuts along the diagonal edges to represent toes and round each toe off, either with a sharp knife or a damp brush. As bare feet are generally used on flying angels or cherubs I do not usually bend them at the ankle, but if you want that effect treat them as above.

While the legs are still together, trim the top ends diagonally so that together they form a 'V'; these diagonals fit on either side of the body.

Making a frill

Use a fluted round cutter of a suitable size to cut out a circle of thinly rolled dough. Use a smaller round cutter to remove the centre of the fluted circle.

Using a cocktail stick (toothpick) like a very small rolling pin, roll out each of the flutes around the circle, with a gentle rocking motion. Flour the cocktail stick repeatedly while you work. When you have frilled the complete ring, cut it into the required lengths.

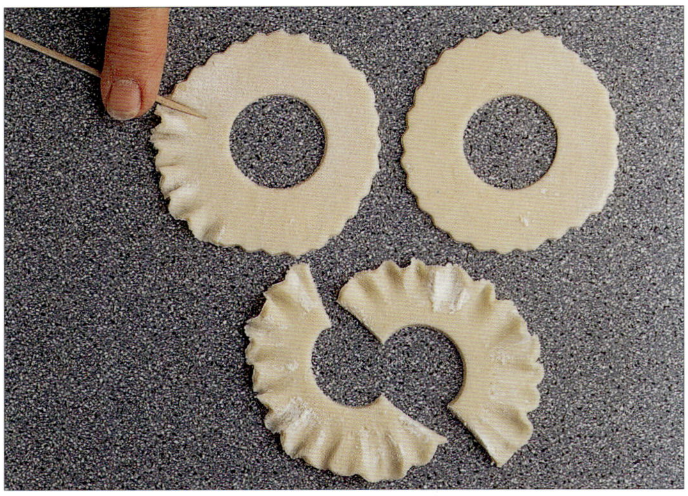

Making a frill.

Modelling a robin

Take a small ball of well-kneaded dough and pull out one side slightly. Model this into a rounded head with a pinched-in neck and a small beak.

Pull the other end of the dough out to a point to suggest long tail feathers.

Use a small leaf cutter to make two wings and feather these with the back of a knife. Finish using a cocktail stick (toothpick) to indent two eyes in the dough.

Veining leaves

There are cutters available for making a wide variety of leaves, but the most useful is the rose leaf which can usually double up for other types.

To vein the rose leaf, use the back of a knife to mark a central vein and then add four or five pairs of smaller veins coming from it.

Leaves like ivy and holly have such distinctive shapes that you really have to buy the proper cutter. Use the back of a knife to give both of them a central vein only. The ivy cutter will also double for a grape vine leaf.

Making flowers with a primrose cutter

The primrose cutter is another very versatile piece of equipment which can also be used to make a variety of other flowers.

PRIMROSE OR PRIMULA Cut the shape out of thinly rolled dough and fix the flower in position, then make a hole in the middle with the pointed end of a modelling tool.

CHRISTMAS ROSE Cut out a flower and lay it in the palm of your hand, then gently press each petal with the rounded end of a modelling tool to thin and slightly cup the petals. Fix the flower in position and fill the centres with five shortened stamens.

DOG ROSE Make the flowers as for a Christmas rose, but use slightly longer stamens. The main difference is in the painting of the dog rose.

Making hanging hooks

The most successful hanging hooks are made from traditional hairpins. Trim them to length, as necessary for your project, using wire cutters. The trimmings from the straight-sided pins may be bent into hooks as well.

PAINTING AND VARNISHING

Painting brings dough models to life and makes them look interesting. Unfortunately, most of the models you see for sale have been painted with unsuitable paints and the results are crude.

You could use two or three old saucers instead of a palette, but a 'Chrysanthemum' palette is the most useful and china will not stain in the same way as plastic. Paints of different types, brushes, palettes and spirit-based acrylic varnish are all available in art shops, but you will probably need to go to a do-it-yourself store to purchase oil-based polyurethane varnish.

Absorbent kitchen paper is handy for wiping brushes and to lay your model on while you are painting. I also have a sharp craft knife and some cotton buds so that I can erase the inevitable mistake, wiping it off with the bud or scraping it off with the knife.

For models made with bread dough you will also need a chunk of polystyrene (styrofoam) of the kind used for packaging or flower arranging and hand cream which should be as non-sticky as possible.

Paints

Water-colours These come in small cakes or tubes and they give a transparent finish. They are perfectly all right for dough modelling and I use them if I want to preserve the look of natural salt dough with just a gentle wash of colour. I use water-colours mostly on bread dough where they can be blended to get the most delicate and realistic effects, especially on flowers.

Acrylic paints In my opinion, these are not suitable for dough modelling. Their natural tendency to dry quickly is accentuated by the porous quality of both salt dough and bread dough. This gives rise to patchiness and makes blending impossible.

Craft paints These are the little pots of ready-mixed paint for craft workers. Provided that they are water-based and non-acrylic, these are fine for dough and are especially good if you do not have sufficient confidence to mix colours.

Poster paints It is possible to use these on dough, but the results tend to be rather garish and powdery.

Gouache paints or Designer colours These are the paints that I use most; so, of course, you would not expect me to say anything but good about them! They come in a range of traditional colours and are perfect for dough modellers. They can be used in an opaque way or watered down and they allow plenty of time for blending.

Brushes

The rough surface of salt dough is very hard on brushes; therefore I would advise you generally to use artists' synthetic brushes. They lose their points very quickly though, so it is useful to buy one or two of the more expensive sable brushes for occasions when a fine point is essential. Sables are also the best brushes to use on bread dough which does not wear them out as quickly as salt dough.

I have used a rigger brush on many occasions in these projects and it is absolutely invaluable if you like to be decorative in your painting by adding a few stripes, checks and tartans. This is a completely straight and narrow brush with hairs about 2.5cm (1in) long. You may buy a synthetic rigger without any qualms as it does not necessarily have a point to go blunt. Charge a rigger well with paint and use its complete length to draw straight lines.

Varnishes

Salt dough is extremely susceptible to damp and has to be varnished with quite strong varnish to seal it. A good-quality clear, gloss, oil-based polyurethane varnish is best. The sparkle varnishing gives to your work more than compensates for the slight yellowing it may cause.

Do not use a water-based acrylic varnish, even if it does say 'polyurethane' on the tin. Although this does not cause yellowing, being water-based it will smudge your painting and ruin it. It is often advisable to use a stronger sealant, such as yacht varnish, on bowls or other pieces that are going to be used or handled a lot. Since this varnish gives an even more yellow finish, use darker colours when painting.

Keep a small soft brush solely for applying varnish and clean it in turpentine or white spirit (mineral spirits), before rinsing it in warm, soapy water.

Bread dough may be varnished with artists' quality spirit-based, acrylic varnish which is clear and quick-drying. This varnish is not as strong as polyurethane, but it has the advantage of not yellowing.

Paint terms and techniques

Pure This means the colour as it comes from the tube with just enough water added to make it flow.

Watery or thin Mix the paint with more water than usual, but stop short of making it transparent.

Transparent Mix the paint with so much water that you are adding just a suggestion of colour to the dough.

Wash A wash is a transparent layer of paint. This sometimes refers to a thin application of paint over a thicker one.

Painting faces

Start the doll's face by painting on some flesh colour and then, while this is still damp, mix a little more cadmium red into part of the mixture to get a pink. Work this into the cheeks so that it blends gently into the background colour. If you find this difficult, blend with a clean damp brush. Reserve some of the pink mixture, in case you need to return to it for making corrections.

For a standard dough dolly, whose eyes and mouth have been made with a cocktail stick (toothpick), run a little pale blue around the inside of the eye holes and some mid-pink around the inside of the mouth to complete the face. It can look good to blend a touch of pink onto the fingertips and toes, especially with angels and children.

In cases where you have only modelled the nose and have left the eyes and mouth blank, start off in the same way by painting the flesh colour and blending the cheeks, and then continue by painting two very pale blue almonds for the eyes. When dry, encircle the almond shapes with thin black lines and paint in any eyelashes and eyebrows.

Paint a coloured iris in each eye and choose the position and size of them to give expression. Small irises surrounded by white look amazed, whereas large ones painted towards the corners can look quite sultry. When the irises are dry, surround them with a thin black line and paint a small black dot in the middle.

Use a medium pink for the mouth, making it a little browner for a man. Paint the central line between lips with the most care as you can make someone look very jolly or utterly miserable, depending on whether the corners turn up or down. Finally, add moustaches, beauty spots or eye shadow.

Using a rigger brush to paint stripes.

Painting patterns

SPOTS AND DOTS Use the tip of the brush to paint evenly spaced dots of a similar size all over the dry base colour. If you are feeling adventurous, you might try larger spots with golden circles painted around them on, say, a clown's outfit or a ballet dancer's skirt.

TARTANS Use a rigger brush and the main colour for a background. When dry, paint horizontal lines in broad strokes, leaving enough room between the strokes to add another line later. Paint similar vertical lines in the same colour. Then, holding the rigger up on end to produce a thinner stroke, paint a different colour between all the previous lines. For a more complicated tartan effect, you may also paint a very thin line down the middle of all the broad lines; this works particularly well in black.

FLOWERS To produce a very simple daisy petal, hold an artists' brush on its point and move it back slowly while allowing more and more of it to touch the surface. Complete the stroke by lifting the brush back onto its point and away from the work. Practise this stroke on paper first and then, when you have perfected it, make several widely spaced dots over the area that you want to cover and encircle each with a ring of daisy petals. For variation, put single polka dots among the flowers.

The cracking problem

★ Cracking is the bane of a dough modeller's life and even though there does not seem to be a clear-cut solution, there are some tips which might help. Do not model with dough that is too soft, because it has a tendency to dent and cracks form along the dents as it dries. Soft dough can be caused by too much water or by too little salt.

★ Make sure that you knead your dough thoroughly so that no air remains; trapped air expands in the oven and it then cracks the dough.

★ If the dough is too dry, it will actually be covered in minute cracks before baking, and these will inevitably expand in the heat.

★ I have added a little oil to the basic dough mixture to help alleviate the problem of cracking, but do not be tempted to add more oil as the dough will then take hours longer to bake and end up stuck to the baking sheet. You will then probably still crack it, trying to prise it off!

★ Cook dough at as low a temperature, and for as long as possible; in fact, you should think of the process as 'drying' rather than 'cooking'. I have given good average times and settings for drying dough, but if you are willing to experiment with your oven, you may find that leaving the dough in for a much longer time at a lower setting will avoid the problem of cracking.

Decorative Christmas Dough

Paints used for projects

Paint	Christmas Wreath	Nativity Scene	Carol Singers	Festive Table Centrepiece	Napkin Rings	Christmas Place Names	Christmas Napkin Rings	Rocking Horse	Christmas Stockings	Father Christmas	Christmas Tree Angel	Christmas Labels	Candelabra	Winged Head Cherub	Garlanded Cherub
Lemon Yellow	★			★								★			
Cadmium Yellow	★	★	★						★	★	★				
Yellow Ochre		★	★	★					★						
Ultramarine	★	★	★						★		★			★	★
Olive Green			★	★	★	★	★			★		★	★		★
Fir Green	★		★					★	★						
Viridian													★		
Saffron Green									★						
Linden Green				★	★										
Rose Madder														★	★
Cadmium Red	★	★	★	★			★			★	★	★			
Rose Pink									★	★					
Alizarin Crimson											★				
Red Ochre		★													
Spectrum Red	★					★	★					★			★
Flame Red								★	★	★					
Magenta			★												
Spectrum Violet			★												
Burnt Sienna		★	★												
Raw Umber	★											★			
Jet Black		★	★	★	★			★	★	★					
Permanent White	★	★	★		★			★	★	★	★	★	★	★	
Gold	★	★	★					★		★	★	★		★	★

★ Leave the dough in the oven to cool down slowly after it has cooked and you have turned off the heat.

★ To repair a crack quickly, fill it with a hard-drying glue and use reasonably thick paint to cover the glue. Alternatively, fill it with soft dough, then smooth it over and bake it again. Rub it down with fine sandpaper before painting. You may also use fine surface filler, following the instructions on the packet.

Christmas Wreath

Traditionally, holly wreaths are meant to be hung on the front door as a sign of welcome but unless you live in particularly sunny climes, I would hang this dough wreath inside the house or it is likely to soften.

1¼ quantities basic dough, see page 44
25cm (10in) plate
large holly leaf cutter
primrose cutter
stamens
large and small leaf cutters
cocktail stick (toothpick)
large plastic drinking straw
hanging hook, see page 48
1m (1⅛yd) wide red ribbon

1 Lay the plate on a baking sheet and draw around it with a pencil. If the sheet is very dark you may need to use a coloured pencil. Make a thick rope from half the dough, long enough to encircle the plate – about 70cm (28in). Lay the rope on the mark and join the ends by trimming each at an opposite slant and fixing them with water. Press the ring flat with your fingers until it is about 4cm (1½in) wide.

2 Make the arms and legs for the cherub (see page 47). Lay them at the top of the ring so that the finished cherub will cover the join, but do not secure the left hand. Model a generous pear shape for the body and lay this on the arms and legs. Separate the buttocks by making a line with the back of your knife.

3 Make a head with a smiling mouth, and fix this facing forwards and resting on the left arm. Roll out some dough to 3mm (⅛in) thick and cut out two large leaves. Lay these together on the board and notch the outside edges of both to make a pair of wings. Fix the wings onto the cherub's back with the notched edge uppermost.

4 Make five pencil-thin ropes about 15cm (6in) kong and drape these over and around the wreath so that they appear to be one continuous rope wound around it. Start the first one on the inside, just under the cherub's legs, and lay it diagonally across the wreath so that it finishes on the outside. Trim the ends of all the ropes at a slant so that they fit neatly against the sides of the wreath. Start the second rope on the inside and not quite opposite the first one and lay this across the wreath in the same way. Continue around the wreath in this fashion until the last rope ends close to the cherub's right hand.

5 Cut out 30–35 holly leaves and arrange these in groups of four or five on each of the ropes. Arrange similar groups between these, directly on the wreath, leaving a space of about 7.5cm (3in) at the bottom of the wreath. Make several holly berries from balls of dough and put three or four in the centre of each group of leaves. Place one berry in the left hand of the cherub, as if he were picking them.

6 Make a robin (see page 48), and sit him on the wreath close to, and facing, the cherub. Cut out about ten primroses and flatten their petals slightly (see page 48). Keeping the space at the bottom, place flowers symmetrically around the wreath. Push three shortened stamens into the centre of each.

7 Finally, use the drinking straw to make two holes, 5cm (2in) apart, in the space and push a hanging hook into the top behind the cherub. Bake in a preheated oven at 145°C (290°F/Gas 1½) for 2½ hours.

Flesh colour

To make flesh colour you need permanent white, cadmium yellow and cadmium red. Take the white first and add a little water, then add a small amount of yellow and mix it in well. Follow this with a very small amount of the red and mix it in well. If the mixture looks too orange, add more white. The result should be a pale peach colour and definitely not pink or orange.

Painting and finishing

Mix up some flesh colour and paint all the cherub apart from his wings and hair. While still wet, mix a spot of

cadmium red with watery white and blend this into his cheeks, fingers and toes, running a little into the line of his mouth. Paint his wings white and then add a touch of ultramarine to make a pale blue. Blend this colour into the ends of his wings and also use it to paint his eyes. When his wings are quite dry, tip their very ends with gold and use the same colour to paint his hair.

Add a little fir green to watery burnt umber to paint the holly branch and leave to dry. Paint each bunch of leaves separately using pure fir green, with lemon yellow blended along the edges. Use pure spectrum red to paint the berries.

Paint the flowers white and work on only two or three at a time to blend a mixture of lemon yellow and a touch of fir green into their centres and onto their stamens before the white dries. Mix a little raw umber into some white to paint the robin's head, back and wings. When this is dry, paint his chest and under his chin with spectrum red. Take some fairly fluid raw umber onto a fine brush and paint a stylized feather pattern on his back, tail and wings; add a dot of the same colour to his eyes. Decorate his feathers with little dots of gold. Varnish the wreath. When dry thread the ribbon through the holes in the bottom and tie a bow.

NATIVITY SCENE

It is worth taking trouble with this project which could well become a family heirloom. Although it will spend most of its time packed away in a box along with other Christmas decorations, once a year its moment will come – and who knows how many generations will admire your artistry or even try to emulate it when the paint begins to fade?

1¼ quantities basic dough, see page 44
plastic ruler
clay gun or garlic press
retracted ballpoint pen
5cm (2in) round fluted cutter
modelling tool
kitchen foil
fine sieve
medium daisy cutter
2 hanging hooks, see page 48
egg glaze, see page 45
rigger brush

1 Take a handful of dough and make a 20cm (8in) long, finger-thick rope (see page 46). Lay this on a baking sheet. Make two more ropes about twice as thick and 15cm (6in) long. Score these lengthways with the side of a ruler to represent columns, then stand one at each end of the first rope and secure with a little water. Make a rope similar to the first and lay it across the top of the columns. To shape the roof, roll one more finger-thick rope, about 25cm (10in) long, and fix its ends to the ends of the rope across the top of the columns. Curve the rope upwards so that it forms a domed roof.

2 Pass dough through a clay gun or garlic press to make short lengths of thatching for the roof. Gradually build up a thatch to cover the domed roof and fill the roof space, also to cover the rope across the bottom of the roof.

3 To make the back of Mary's chair, if you are using a clay gun, fit the disc that resembles a clover leaf and twist the dough as it comes through. Cut two 5cm (2in) lengths of the twist and lay them about 2.5cm (1in) apart in the middle of the stable. Place a tiny ball of dough on each. If you are not using a clay gun, make two small ropes with a ball on each.

4 Model a small figure with a long skirt but no petticoat, see Carol Singers (page 57). Make the head but do not mark the eyes and mouth, just model a small nose. Make a very thin rope of dough for the neckline of the dress and indent it with a retracted ballpoint pen. Use the same method to decorate the hem of the dress.

5 When the figure is dressed, bend the legs into a sitting position and secure her so that she looks as though she is on the chair. Make a small oval of dough for the baby's body and attach a little ball of dough at one end for the head. Add a tiny nose and wrap the baby in a shawl made by cutting out a circle of rolled-out dough with the fluted cutter. Mark a faint pattern on the shawl with the pointed end of a modelling tool. Arrange the baby in Mary's arms and attach some hair made by extruding dough through a clay gun.

6 Cut a long strip of thinly rolled dough measuring 18 x 6.5cm (7x2½ in). Mark the middle and use this point as a guide for cutting a curve along one side. The strip should still be 6.5cm (2½in) wide at the ends, but the curve should taper its width to only 4cm (1½in) in the middle. Drape this strip over Mary's head, making folds in the ends.

7 Make legs, arms and a body for Joseph (see page 47). Set the arms aside. Cut a triangle from thinly rolled dough, measuring 9cm (3½in) across the base and 12.5cm (5in) along the sides. Cut 12mm (½in) off the apex of the triangle to shape the neck of the robe. Fit the dough around Joseph with the cut-off top around his neck. Secure Joseph beside Mary, draping any spare dough in his robe.

8 Fix two thin ropes around Joseph's wrists to make cuffs. Fix the arms onto the body, so that one is around Mary and the other rests across Joseph's body. Flatten a thin rope of dough around the neck of Joseph's robe and indent it with a retracted ballpoint pen. Make a round ball of dough for Joseph's head and add a wedge-shaped nose. Use the clay gun to make a beard and hair for Joseph. Shape a slightly droopy moustache on his face.

9 To make the sheep, roll four thin, 4cm (1½in) long ropes and make a little cut in the middle of one end of each. Arrange these in pairs on the stable base, next to Mary. Cover the tops of the legs with a flattened oval of dough for the body, supporting it on a small pad of foil to prevent it falling back on the baking sheet. Model a small ball of dough into a slightly pointed sheep's face and rest it on Mary's cloak, looking at the baby. Flatten two very small balls of dough into cupped ears with the rounded end of a modelling tool. Fix these on the sheep.

10 Make dozens of tiny ropes and roll them up into curls. Secure them to cover the top of the sheep's head and all the body. Secure a few more curls together to make a tail.

11 Roll two pencil-thin ropes and make feet at one end (see page 47). Lay these on the thatched roof. Cut out a triangle of rolled-out dough with a 10cm (4in) base and sides. Still keeping the triangle in shape, tuck the sides under and lay it over the legs with the feet protruding to make the angel's robe.

12 Make a round ball of dough for the head and attach it to the pointed end of the robe. Make a trumpet by rolling out a thin 4cm (1½ in) rope which is slightly thicker at one end. Widen the thick end into a trumpet shape with the rounded end of a modelling tool. Secure the thin end of the trumpet against the angel's face and lay the rest along the left-hand column of the stable.

13 Make hands and arms, and attach cuffs made from very small ropes; secure the arms to the robe. Place the hands on the trumpet. Make a nose from a tiny ball of dough and attach it above the trumpet. Make hair from dough pressed through a fine sieve (see page 46).

14 To make wings, cut out two triangles from thinly rolled dough, measuring 4cm (1½ in) across each base and 5cm (2in) along the sides. Lay these beside each other, base down, then trim off the outside corner of each. Use a sharp knife to cut pointed shapes into the outer edges. Decorate the points with the retracted ballpoint pen. Place the wings on the angel with the straight sides innermost and the tops of the triangles close to the head.

15 Roll out some dough to 6mm (¼ in) and use the daisy cutter to make a star. Secure this firmly to the straw thatch overhanging the left-hand side of the roof. Secure a hanging hook into each side of the roof and brush the roof, columns and base with egg glaze. Bake in a preheated oven at 145°C (290°F/Gas 1½) for about 3 hours.

Stripes and checks

Use a rigger brush (see page 49) to make these designs. If you have never used a rigger before, I would practise first on a piece of paper. Make the paint quite runny, but still opaque, and completely cover the long hairs in your brush with it. Wipe the brush on the side of your palette to make sure that all the hairs are lying straight and then draw your lines, using as much of the length of the brush as you can.

Painting and finishing

Mix up flesh colour and paint the faces and hands of all the figures, also Joseph's feet (see page 52). Paint Mary with her eyes closed, looking down at the baby. Add a little red ochre to white to make the deep pink of Mary's dress. Add some white to ultramarine to mix the colour of her cloak.

Paint Joseph's robe in pure burnt sienna and leave to dry. Use a rigger brush to paint on wide stripes with diluted yellow ochre. Mix cadmium yellow and ultramarine to make a dull green and paint more stripes.

Make up a watery permanent white and paint the baby's shawl and angel's robe and wings. While the wings are wet, blend first a little watery ultramarine, then some thin cadmium red into their edges. Paint the sheep's wool with the same watery white, but do not worry too much about getting paint into all the nooks and crannies, as leaving some dough bare will give the coat depth.

Use pure jet black to paint shoes on Joseph's feet and the face and legs of the sheep. When the sheep is quite dry, add pale blue eyes and tint the inside of the ears with watery cadmium red. Finally, use gold to paint the star and angel's trumpet, then paint a design along the hem of the robe and the decoration on the wings. Add a few golden highlights on the hair. Trim the edge of Mary's cloak with gold and paint a circle and dot pattern over the outside.

CAROL SINGERS

This Dickensian-looking group is a good example of the important role painting takes when trying to produce attractive dough models.

1¼ quantities basic dough, see page 44
fine sieve
cocktail stick (toothpick)
5cm (2in) and 2.5cm (1in) fluted round cutters
small blossom plunger cutter
garlic press or clay gun
retracted ballpoint pen
3 hanging hooks, see page 48

1 Roll a handful of dough into a fat rope, about 18cm (7in) long. Lay this on a baking sheet. Make two 6.5cm (2½in) long ropes for legs and shape quite large shoes at their ends (see page 47); put these to one side.

2 Roll out half of the remaining dough to 3mm (⅛in) thick. To make the trousers, cut two 6.5x5cm (2½ x2in) rectangles and wrap them around the legs, securing them with a little water at the back.

3 Make a fairly portly oval of dough for the man's body and fix on top of the legs. The join will not show. Cut out a 6.5cm (2½in) square of dough and cut into two triangles. Wrap one around the right-hand side (*his* right side) of the man's chest so that the cut edge runs across him. Overlapping the first triangle slightly, cover his left side in the same way. Before securing this piece, trim off the point of the triangle where it crosses over to shape the coat front.

4 Cut a pear-shaped piece of dough, about 4.5cm (1¾in) across the fattest part and 6.5cm (2½in) high. Cut a deep notch in the broad end so that it looks a little like a heart shape and fix this upside down on the figure's back to make coat-tails. Eventually, his right-hand coat-tail will not show because of the female figure but make sure that the left-hand tail is pulled slightly to the side so that it will show from the front.

5 Attach the man to the base rope about 2.5cm (1in) from the right side. Cut two small, tapering strips of dough for lapels and secure them in place. Make buttons for the coat from four tiny balls of flattened dough.

6 Make a pair of arms and hands (see page 47), and wrap two thin ropes of dough around these to make cuffs. Attach the arms to the body at the shoulders but leave the hands free. Make a small carol sheet out of a thin piece of dough, about 4x2.5cm (1½x1in). Roll up one end to make a scroll, then arrange it in the hand so that it looks as if the man is holding it.

7 Make a ball of dough for his head. Mark the eyes and an open, singing, mouth with a cocktail stick (toothpick). Make a nose from a small ball of dough. Use the 2.5cm (1in) round cutter to cut out the brim of the hat. Squeeze its edges between your thumb and forefinger to make them thin and to slightly enlarge the brim.

8 Make a short cylinder of dough for the crown of the hat and score it with the back of a knife to make it look slightly battered. Fit the crown on the brim, then put the hat on his head at a slight angle. Push a small amount of dough through the sieve and arrange it in little patches, sticking out from under the hat and on the cheeks to make hair and sideburns.

9 Cut two thin strips of dough 7cmx12mm (2¾ x½ in). Press the strips gently against the finest strip cutter so that they are indented along their length to look like ribbed knitting. Cross these strips across the man's chest and around his neck to make a scarf. Push some dough through a garlic press to make a fringe for the scarf (see page 46).

10 Make the lady a slightly thinner set of legs and feet, measuring 6.5cm (2½in) long and lay them on the work surface. Make a far slimmer oval of dough for her body and fix it to her legs. Cut a fluted circle of thinly rolled dough and frill the edges with a cocktail stick (see page 48). Remove the centre of the circle with the 2.5cm (1in) round cutter, then cut the frilled ring to make a strip. Fit this just above the lady's ankles, to represent the edge of her petticoat.

11 Cut a 16.5x5cm (6½ x 2in) rectangle of thinly rolled out dough and lay it vertically on the surface. Dampen a point in the middle of the top edge of the dough. Fold about 2.5cm (1in) of dough inwards on each side of the damp spot, making an inverted pleat. Dust some flour over the top of this pleat to take up any spare moisture and then roll the top 6mm (¼in) of it with a rolling pin to secure it in place. Trim the top edge straight again and trim the side edges of the rectangle at a slant, so that the top is slightly narrower.

12 Fit the pleated skirt around the lady's waist and fold the edges underneath her body. The bottom of the skirt should cover the top edge of the frill to conceal the fact that there is no petticoat. Arrange the hemline of the skirt so that the frill shows a little. The top edge of the skirt will not show.

13 Make two arms and a scroll of carols and fit these in a similar way to the man's arms. Make a little round head for the lady and mark the features as before but give her a smaller nose; do not add the hair and hat yet.

14 Cut a triangle of thinly rolled dough, 10cm (4in) across the base and with 11.5cm (4½in) sides. Drape this around the lady's shoulders like a shawl. Cross over the front corners of the shawl. Flatten a small oval of dough and attach it where she might have a brooch to hold the shawl in place. Make some thick fringing for the shawl with short lengths of dough from the garlic press.

15 Cut out a 5cm (2in) circle of rolled-out dough and cut it in half. Fit one half over the back of her head to represent the back of her bonnet, then fit the other half so that it overlaps the first slightly and comes forward to form a peak. Shape the second half by pressing the dough lightly between your thumb and forefinger. Decorate the join with a row of small flowers made using a blossom plunger cutter.

16 Attach a few short strands of dough extruding through the garlic press on either side of her face to represent ringlets. Cut four very thin strips of dough with a fine strip cutter to make ribbons for her bonnet. Run one strip under her chin, then notch the ends of two more strips. Attach these to the first strip at one side of her face and let the notched ends hang down over her shawl. Make a bow with the fourth strip and fix this under her cheeks, over the ribbons.

17 To make the lamp-post make a 15cm (6in) long rope, quite thick at one end and tapering to pencil-thin at the other. Wrap three thin ropes of dough around it at even intervals for decoration. Fix the fatter end to the base to the left of the lady.

18 Lay another thin 2.5cm (1in) long rope across the top of the lamp-post. Stand two more equally thin, 12mm (½in) long ropes on either end of the first to produce a 'U' shape and top this off with the small, hand-modelled triangle of dough, about 4.5cm (1¾in) across the bottom and 2cm (¾in) on each side. Decorate the top of the triangle with two small balls of dough, the top being the smallest. Model a tiny flame and attach it to the middle of the lamp. Then use the retracted ballpoint pen to indent the bottoms of the triangle and the lamp, and the three decorative ropes.

19 Cover the base with several flattened balls of dough, packed tightly together to represent cobble stones.

20 Make two dog's legs by rolling two very thin ropes about 2.5cm (1in) long. Then model a haunch with a leg attached by rolling a 2.5cm (1in) long rope the same thickness as the first pair of legs at one end but growing thicker towards the other end. Flatten the thick end slightly. Make three short cuts in the bottom of each leg to represent paws.

21 Model an oval of dough for the dog's body and lean this at a slight angle against the male figure's left leg. Fit the two front legs to the front of the body and the haunch and leg to the back, so that the dog appears to be sitting down. Model a smaller oval of dough for the head and fix this onto the dog, tipped up in the direction of the man's face. Mark two eyes and an open mouth with a cocktail stick so that the dog appears to be joining in the singing. Cut two triangular ears and fit these well back on the dog's head to accentuate the angle of the head. Make a 2.5cm (1in) long tapering rope and fit this on the dog for a tail. Finally, add a small triangular knob of dough just above the mouth for his nose and score the whole dog with a cocktail stick to simulate fur.

22 Push a hanging hook into each end of the base and one into the female figure's hat. Bake in a preheated oven as 145° (290°F/Gas 1½) for about 3 hours.

Painting and finishing

Paint the faces of the figures with flesh colour (see page 52). Use yellow ochre to paint the man's trousers and while this is drying, paint his jacket fir green. When both jacket and trousers are dry, paint his scarf and gloves in pure cadmium red. Then use a fine brush or preferably a rigger and the same colour to paint the checks on his trousers. When dry use some fir green to paint a finer check between the red lines (see page 56). Use jet black to paint his lapels, buttons, hat, boots and cuffs.

Paint the lady's shawl in a mixture of white and ultramarine. While this is drying, paint her skirt pure magenta and use this colour to paint a fine check on her shawl. Leave to dry thoroughly. Using ultramarine and white again, mix a slightly darker blue to paint another check between the first lines on the shawl.

Paint the bonnet, ribbons and gloves in pure spectrum violet and the flowers on the bonnet with a mixture of pale violets and magentas.

When the dress is completely dry, paint a triangular pattern all over it in white, using three small dots. Make the white a little more watery and paint both the scrolls and her petticoat and cuffs. When the scrolls are dry, make a few uneven black lines on them to represent writing and paint her boots and the markings on his gloves black. Paint a miniature portrait on her brooch.

Paint the dog mainly burnt sienna, just dabbing a little white on his chest, tail and paws when the base is dry. Paint his nose and eyes black, putting a little crescent of white at the bottom of his eye when the black is dry. Mix some pink from cadmium red and white, and paint the inside of the dog's mouth.

Paint the lamp-post watery olive green; leave to dry. Paint the balls and the indentations in gold. Mix bright orange using cadmium red and yellow for the flame, and add a dab of pure cadmium yellow while the paint is still wet.

Mix some white and black together in rather a watery consistency and paint this onto the cobbles. While the paint is still wet, add some watery dabs of blues, violets and pinks to give it some life – but don't overdo it.

Festive Table Centrepiece and Napkin Rings

Festive Table Centrepiece

By the time the food has been set on the festive dinner table, there is not very much room for a centrepiece and many of my more extravagant efforts have ended up on the sideboard or – worse still – under it.

hand cream
½ quantity bread dough, see page 44
cadmium red gouache or water-colour paint
waxed paper
large and medium rose leaf cutters
cling film (plastic wrap)
modelling tool
small black stamens
olive green gouache or water-colour paint
holly leaf cutter
primrose cutter
gold spray paint
piece of tree bark, about 20cm (8in) long
sauce bottle top
fast-drying glue
lemon yellow gouache or water-colour paint
jet black gouache or water-colour paint
small yellow stamens
linden green gouache or water-colour paint
spirit-based clear gloss acrylic varnish
candle
50cm (20in) wide green ribbon

1 Rub hand cream into your hands, then take a piece of bread dough about the size of a large walnut, and colour it with cadmium red paint (see page 45). Flatten the dough into a round and place it between two pieces of waxed paper, then gently roll it out thinly.

2 Use the larger of the two rose leaf cutters to cut out 14 poinsettia bracts or petals. Knead the scraps of dough together and roll them out again; cut out ten more bracts with the smaller rose leaf cutter. Gather up the scraps again and wrap them in cling film (plastic wrap).

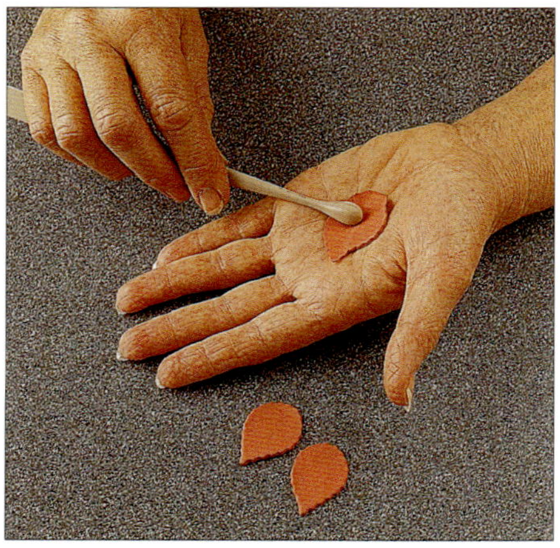

3 Rub more hand cream into your hands and on the rounded end of a modelling tool. Lay one of the bracts in the palm of your hand and carefully roll the rounded end of the modelling tool along each side of it to stretch the dough slightly and give the bract slightly undulating edges. Repeat with the remaining bracts and set them aside on a piece of waxed paper to dry.

4 Roll the remaining red dough into eight small balls to represent holly berries. Trim most of the stalk from one of the black stamens and fix it into one berry; repeat with the other berries, then set them aside to dry with the leaves.

5 Take a slightly larger piece of white dough than before and colour it with olive green paint (see page 45). Roll this out between waxed paper, then cut out eight leaves with the large rose cutter and seven holly leaves. Roll the edges of the rose leaves as before and set these and the holly leaves aside to dry.

6 Roll out a small piece of the white dough as before and use the primrose cutter to cut out five Christmas roses. Rub more hand cream into your hands and on the rounded end of the modelling tool. Lay a flower in the palm of your hand and gently press and roll each of the petals with the modelling tool before finally pressing it in the middle so that it cups slightly. Repeat with the remaining flowers, then set them aside on waxed paper to dry. Finally, make about 20 very small white balls and leave these to dry.

Painting and finishing

Make sure that the piece of bark is clean and dry, and then spray it sparsely with gold paint, so that it receives just a dusting of gold, allowing the wood to show through. Wash and dry the sauce bottle top and give that a solid coat of gold. Leave both until completely dry.

Use fast-drying glue to fix the sauce bottle top upside down on the bark to act as a candle holder.

Paint the poinsettia petals with cadmium red and the leaves with a mixture of olive green and lemon yel-

low. Allow these to dry before painting some veins on the leaves with pure olive green. Paint the holly leaves with pure olive green and the holly berries with cadmium red. Add a touch of jet black to the stamens when the berries are dry.

Paint the Christmas roses white and allow these to dry, then glue four or five yellow stamen heads into the middle of each flower. When the glue has dried, paint some watery linden green on and around the stamens, and blend this into the white with a clean damp brush. Finish the stamens by brushing some pure linden green over their tops.

Glue seven of the larger poinsettia bracts overlapping each other slightly, forming a circle on the bark and with part of the circle leaning up against

the candle holder.

Fix five small bracts inside the larger ones so that they overlap in a similar way to form the centre of the flower. Glue ten small balls into the middle of the flower and fix three or four leaves behind the outer bracts.

Make a second arrangement with the remainder of the poinsettia bracts and leaves, and position this so that it obscures the sides of the candle holder. Fill the centre with the remaining little balls.

Arrange five holly leaves together so that some lean against the candle holder and some lie on the bark. Then position five holly berries in the centre of the group. Lay the remaining holly leaves and berries close to the second poinsettia and dot the Christmas roses around singly and in pairs to balance the arrangement.

When all the flowers are in place and the glue is dry, give all the dough pieces a coat of spirit-based acrylic varnish and allow this to dry thoroughly.

Finally, fix the candle into the holder and add a bow of green ribbon; glue this at one end of the arrangement close to the candle.

Napkin Rings

If you have decided to revitalize old napkin rings, remember that they do not have to be a matching set; as long as they are similar in size, the gold spray will disguise their appearance.

4 wooden or plastic napkin rings
gold spray
¼ quantity bread dough, see page 44
olive green gouache or water-colour paint
cadmium red gouache or water-colour paint
waxed paper
medium and very small holly leaf cutter
primrose cutter
yellow and black stamens
P.V.A. glue
spirit-based acrylic varnish
clear fast-drying glue
1.25m (1⅓ yd) narrow green ribbon

1 Spray the napkin rings gold, giving them several thin coats and leaving the recommended time between applications.

2 Colour about a third of the dough with olive green paint (see page 45). Flatten the dough into a circle and then roll it out thinly between two sheets of waxed paper. Cut out eight of each size holly leaf and mark a central vein on each of them. Brush some P.V.A. glue on the backs of two large leaves and lay these on one of the rings, so that they meet end to end and follow the curve of the ring. Glue two small leaves in front of the first two at a slight angle. Fix holly leaves on the other rings.

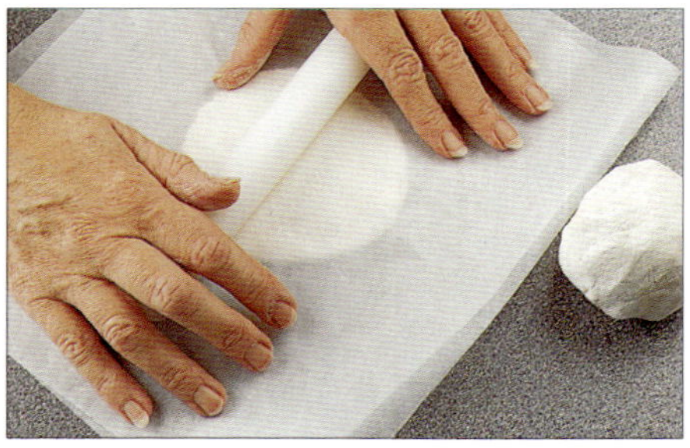

3 Roll out half the remaining dough between waxed paper as before. Use the primrose cutter to cut out eight Christmas roses and shape them with a modelling tool.

4 Take one of the napkin rings and glue two Christmas roses side by side where the larger holly leaves meet. Trim most of the stalks from 12 yellow stamens and push six of them carefully into the centre of the flowers. Decorate the other rings similarly.

5 Colour the remaining dough red (see page 45), and roll this into 12 small balls to represent holly berries. Trim most of the stalk from 12 of the black stamens and push one of these into each of the berries. Glue the berries in threes between the flowers and holly leaves. Leave for about 6 hours, until the dough has set and the glue has dried.

Painting and finishing

Paint the holly with pure olive green and the berries with cadmium red. Then paint the Christmas roses white and, before this is quite dry, dab the centres with a little watery linden green. When the Christmas roses are completely dry brush some pure linden green across the tops of the stamens. Paint the stamens in the berries jet black.

Varnish with spirit-based acrylic varnish and allow this to dry thoroughly. Use fast-drying glue to attach a bow of green ribbon, tucking it in behind the Christmas roses.

Place Names and Napkin Rings

Christmas Place Names

These salt-dough place names do not take much longer to make than a batch of mince pies, but if you pack them away carefully after Christmas, they will last far longer!

¾ quantity basic dough, see page 44
5cm (2in) fluted round cutter
cocktail stick (toothpick)
thin plastic drinking straw
egg glaze, see page 45
very small holly leaf cutter
1.5m (1⅔ yd) narrow red ribbon
fast-drying glue

1 Roll out about a third of the dough to 6mm (¼ in) thick and cut out six 6.5cm x 12mm (2 ½ x ½ in) strips; set these aside.

2 Roll out some more dough to 3mm (⅛ in) thick and cut out six fluted circles. Frill the edges of the circles with a cocktail stick (toothpick) (see page 48), leaving their centres complete. Cut a third from each frilled circle and set these pieces aside. Use a thin plastic drinking straw to make ribbon eyelet holes at regular intervals about 12mm (½ in) in from the frilled edge of the remaining pieces.

3 Lay the large pieces on a baking sheet and fix one of the strips, side on, along the unfrilled edge of each of them. Coat these with egg glaze and bake them in a preheated oven at 145°C (280°F/Gas 1½) for about 30 minutes or until firm.

4 Make similar eyelet holes in the remaining sections and set them aside with the rest of the dough; cover with a lightly dampened cloth.

5 Stand the baked pieces up so that the frilled part stands up like a shell at the back. Roll six very thin ropes and use these to stick the smaller frilled pieces on top of the front of the strips. Brush the front and the back of the larger frilled pieces with egg glaze.

6 Roll out some dough thinly and cut out 12 very small holly leaves. Arrange these in pairs on the fronts of all the holders and add a few very small balls of dough for berries.

7 Return the holders to the oven, standing them upright, and bake for about 1 hour at the same temperature. If the base of a holder has risen or becomes slightly puffy during the first baking, lay a metal knife handle across it during the second cooking.

Painting and finishing

Paint the holly leaves with pure olive green and allow to dry. Then paint the edges of the frills, the holly berries and some lining on the base in spectrum red. Varnish in the usual way and allow to dry.

Start threading a piece of ribbon from each end of the back frill on one of the holders. Leave the tails of the ribbon at the back of the holder and thread the pieces of ribbon through the eyelets until they meet in the middle. Tie the ends into a small bow at the front and trim off any excess ribbon. Trim the ribbon tails, leaving just enough to secure them in place with a dab of fast-drying glue. Finish all the holders in the same way.

Christmas Napkin Rings

These Christmas napkin rings make a charming, rustic addition to the table, particularly if you make matching place names.

4 cardboard cylinders from kitchen paper or toilet rolls
cooking foil
¾ quantity basic dough, see page 44
plastic ruler
5cm (2in) fluted round cutter
cocktail stick (toothpick)
2.5cm (1in) round cutter
small holly leaf cutter
thin plastic drinking straw
egg glaze, see page 45
rigger brush
1m (1⅛yd) narrow red ribbon
fast-drying glue

1 Cover the cardboard cylinders with foil and set aside. Roll out half the dough to 6mm (¼in) thick; using a well-floured plastic ruler and a sharp knife, cut four 2.5cm (1in) wide strips long enough to fit around the cylinders. Wrap the strips around the cylinders and fix the ends together with a little water. Flour the joins lightly in case they are damp and then stand the cylinders and rings, joins downwards, on a baking sheet.

2 Roll out some more dough to 3mm (⅛in) thick and cut out four circles with the fluted cutter. Frill the edges of the circles with a cocktail stick (toothpick) (see page 48), and then remove the middle of each with the small round cutter to make rings.

3 Cut the rings in half and then fix two halves facing each other, on either side of the top of each napkin ring. If the frills are likely to fall back, prop them up with foil.

4 Cut out 12 holly leaves and arrange in groups of three on top of each ring, adding a few small balls of dough for berries. Starting on either side of the holly, use a thin drinking straw to make two or three holes around the sides of the rings; these will be used for threading ribbon.

5 Paint the rings, excluding the holly, with egg glaze and bake in a preheated oven at 145°C (290°F/Gas 1½) for about 1½ hours.

Painting and finishing

Paint all the leaves with olive green and leave to dry. Paint the berries and the edge of the frill with spectrum red. Use a rigger brush to paint a single red line around each of the rings on either side of the ribbon holes.

Varnish in the usual way; you may like to use yacht varnish as the napkin rings could come into contact with liquid. When the varnish is dry, thread the ribbon through the holes and glue the ends neatly on the inside. Add a small bow as shown.

Rocking Horse

¼ quantity basic dough, see page 44
2.5cm (1in) round cutter
retracted ballpoint pen
modelling tool
hanging hook, see page 48
30cm (12in) narrow red ribbon

1 Model a handful of dough into a pear shape with a slightly elongated neck. Flatten this slightly and put it to one side. Make three pencil-thin, 5cm (2in) long ropes and trim one end of each at a slant. Use the back of a knife to indent a line around each rope to make a hoof.

2 Lay two of the legs on a baking sheet, with the hooves about 9cm (3¼ in) apart and the rest of the legs slanting inwards. Wet the tops of the legs and lay the pear-shaped piece on top for the body, so that it overlaps them by about 12mm (½ in). The body should be slightly tilted with the neck on your left.

3 Round the end of the third leg opposite the hoof, if necessary, by modelling it with your fingers. Shape the leg into a trotting position and fix it on top of the body so that it lies just ahead of the other front leg. Model the fourth leg in a similar way, but this time make it 6.5cm (2½ in) long and allow it to become much wider above the first 3cm (1¼ in). Make a hoof at the narrow end and mould the wide end into a haunch. Secure it to the rear of the body. The leg should lie in front of the other back leg.

4 Roll a 15cm (6in) pencil-thin rope and flatten it with your fingers before curving it under the hooves of the horse, so that three of them touch it. Fix the three legs to the rocker with a little water. Decorate it around the edge with the retracted ballpoint pen.

5 Model a small piece of dough into an oval for the head. Indent across the top of the narrower end with the back of a knife to mark the mouth. Secure the head on the body. Use the pointed end of a modelling tool to mark two nostrils and a slight indentation at either end of the mouth.

6 Flatten two very small balls of dough and secure these on the face as eyes. Indent them horizontally across the middle, with the back of a knife. Use the 2.5cm (1in) round cutter to cut a circle of thinly rolled dough and divide it into four wedges. Round the points on two wedges to make ears.

7 Roll a very thin rope of dough about 4cm (1½ in) long and fix it across the horse's face as a nose band. Make an indented pattern on the nose band with the pointed end of a modelling tool and make a tiny ring of dough to go at one end of it. Use the 2.5cm (1in) cutter to cut out a circle of rolled-out dough and cut it in half. Take one of the semi-circles and thin and enlarge it slightly between your fingers and thumb. Place this on the horse's back as a saddle and indent the edges of it with the retracted ballpoint pen. Cut a thin strip of dough about 4cm (1½ in) long; secure it from the saddle under the horse's stomach.

8 Roll some long, thin and tapering ropes for the tail and secure in place in a bunch. Make similar, but shorter, ropes for the mane and attach along the neck and between his ears. Finally, roll a very thin rope for reins and loop this through the ring on the nose band and over his back. Put a hanging hook in the top of the saddle. Bake in a preheated oven at 145°C (290°F/Gas 1½) for about 1 hour.

Painting and finishing

Make up watery grey and paint the horse. While this is still wet, mix pale pink from white and a touch of flame red, add it to the muzzle and blend it into the rest of his face. Add a little more black to the grey and paint patches across the top of his back and legs.

Use pure white to paint the lower half of his eyes and dry. Use black to make a dot in the centre of the white and to run along the eyelid edge. Use black on the hooves and reins.

Paint the nose band, saddle and girth in flame red and the rocker in fir green. When dry, paint on gold decoration. Paint a gold wavy line down the middle of the rocker. Paint the nose band ring gold also.

Varnish and dry. Loop half the ribbon through the hanging hook and knot the ends together. Let the knotted end hang down behind the horse and tie a bow around the base of the looped ribbon.

CHRISTMAS STOCKINGS

½ quantity basic dough
round-ended modelling tool
plastic drinking straw
cocktail stick (toothpick)
garlic press or clay gun
30cm (12in) narrow red ribbon
15cm (6in) narrow gold cord
fast-drying glue

1 For each stocking, make a fairly thick rope measuring about 15cm (6in) long. Mould one end into a stocking foot.

2 Insert the modelling tool into the top and push out the sides of the rope until widened to about 10cm (4in) in circumference. Pinch the back of the top gently until it is about 2.5cm (1in) higher than the front. Make a hole in the back, near the top, with the straw.

3 Put your fingers into the stocking to support it, then make small indentations with the back of a knife around the edge to simulate ribbing. Go around the stocking again, making small holes at the base of the ribbing with a cocktail stick (toothpick).

4 To fill the rag doll stocking, place it on a baking sheet and mould a rectangular dough parcel. Place this on end in the back of the stocking with a ball of dough in front. Push them both into the stocking a little.

5 Make a small oval of dough for the doll's torso and place this in the stocking so that it slightly overlaps the edge, but is down far enough not to need any skirt or legs. Make two thin 2.5cm (1in) long ropes for arms and slightly flatten the rounded ends to make hands. Secure these on the body so that they flop out of the stocking. Make a small ball of dough for the head. Secure the head at a floppy angle and mark eyes and a mouth with a cocktail stick. Make the nose from a ball of dough and the hair from dough either pressed through a garlic press or a clay gun.

6 To fill the teddy bear stocking, put a square parcel of dough into the stocking, then add a small ball of dough for an orange. Prick the orange all over with a cocktail stick.

7 Make a small oval of dough for the teddy's body and indent a line down the middle with the back of a knife. Put this into the stocking leaning out. Make a head from a small pear-shaped piece of dough. Fix a tiny ball of dough at the pointed end to represent the teddy's nose, then fix the head on the body. Mark two eyes with a cocktail stick and make two ears by pressing the modelling tool into two small balls of dough. Secure the ears on the head. Make two thin ropes of dough, about 2cm (¾ in) long, for arms. Attach these so that one is flopping over the side. Model a racket out of a small circle of dough and a thin rope. Stick this, head up, into the back of the stocking.

8 Bake the stockings at 145°C (290°F/Gas 1½) for about 1 hour.

Painting and finishing

Paint the rag doll stocking white, apart from the toe, heel and ribbing; dry. Starting with the ribbing and using flame red, paint three stripes close together around the stocking. Continue with the stripes, keeping them further apart on leg and foot. Paint heel and toe solid red; dry. Paint alternate stripes in fir green. The ribbed section is red and green; the rest is red, white and green.

Mix up flesh colour (see page 52), and paint the face and most of her arms. Paint her body and sleeves in cadmium yellow. When dry, paint white spots and cuffs on her dress.

Divide the ball into eight sections. Using saffron green, ultramarine, orange made from cadmium red and cadmium yellow, and pale blue made from ultramarine and white, paint pairs of opposite sections in the same colour. Paint a dot of flame red where all the sections meet. Paint the oblong box in pure rose pink.

Paint the teddy bear stocking flame red and dry. Paint a stripe around the ribbing, the toe and heel in pure white. Paint the square box saffron green and the orange by mixing cadmium red and yellow. Use yellow ochre to paint the teddy and the middle of the racket; dry. Paint jet black strings. Paint a black cross in the middle of the orange. Paint the nose, eyes and claws black. Paint the racket frame in fir green. Varnish and dry. Thread half the ribbon through each hole and tie ends in a bow, secured with glue. Glue gold cord and bows on the boxes.

Father Christmas

The materials will make two decorations. Divide the dough in half before starting.

¾ quantity basic dough, see page 44
cocktail stick (toothpick)
garlic press
hanging hook, see page 48
30cm (12in) very thin gold cord
fast-drying glue

1 Divide a small handful of dough in half and roll two 9cm (3½ in) long, tapering ropes, finger-thick at one end and slightly less than pencil-thin at the other. Trim the thicker ends at a slant. Secure a thin rope around the thinner end of each, about 2.5cm (1in) from the end. Secure the slanting ends together with a little water and place on a baking sheet.

2 Mould a small handful of dough into a fairly thick 5cm (2in) circle, for the body. Place over the legs so that it overlaps by about 2.5cm (1in). Secure with a little water.

3 Make a pencil-thin 10cm (4in) long rope of dough and secure it around the lower edge of the circular body so that it will eventually look like fur trimming on a jacket. Make two 7.5cm (3in) long arms with hands (see page 47), and attach a thin rope around the wrist of each of these. Trim the tops of the arms at a slant and secure them to the body with a little water. Model two parcel shapes and secure the arms and hands around these as shown.

4 Secure a round ball of dough on top of the body for the head. Mark two eyes and a mouth with a cocktail stick (toothpick). Make a slightly larger than usual nose from a small ball of dough and add two small, flattened balls of dough for cheeks (see page 68). Fix two tapering wedge shapes under the nose to represent a moustache and indent this with the back of a knife to suggest hair. Make a beard and some hair from dough passed through a garlic press.

5 Roll out a small amount of dough to 3mm (⅛ in) thick and cut out a triangle with a 7.5cm (3in) base and sides. Turn the two sides under slightly, then fit the base across the front of the head, just above the eyes, to make a hat. Bend the point over slightly and secure one ball of dough on the end of the hat and a second in the middle. Fix a thin 7.5cm (3in) rope around the edge as trimming.

6 Put two small, flattened balls of dough on his coat as shown to make buttons. Make two little holes in each of these with a cocktail stick.

7 Flick the point of the cocktail stick all over the ropes around his legs, arms, hat and coat, and the bobbles on his hat to simulate fur. Put a hanging hook in his hat and bake in a preheated oven at 145°C (290°F/ Gas 1½) for about 1 hour.

Painting and finishing

Paint his face and hands flesh colour (see page 52) and the suit and hat flame red. When dry, paint the fur trimming white and the boots jet black.

Paint one parcel olive green and the other rose pink and leave to dry. Paint white dots all over the pink parcel. When dry, encircle the dots with gold. Paint gold Christmas trees on the green parcel and gold buttons on his coat. Finish the green parcel by painting red dots between the trees.

Varnish and dry. Glue lengths of cord around the parcels. Dry before gluing bows on each parcel. Tie a bow through the hanging hook.

Christmas Tree

A Christmas tree cutter was used to stamp out the decoration in basic dough. Once the parcels, decorations and a hanging hook were fixed in place, the tree was baked for about 1 hour. When painted and varnished, gold cord was used to complete the decoration.

Walking Stick

The bright walking stick is made from red, green and white ropes of bread dough, twisted together and curved into shape. Add a hanging hook at the top. When dry, the dough is given an extra coat of paint before being varnished. Gold cord and a double bow of red ribbon decorate the walking stick which is ready to hang on the Christmas tree.

CHRISTMAS TREE ANGEL

Unlike salt dough figures, bread dough people have to be made up of separate pieces which are assembled only when dry so they take a lot longer to make and care has to be taken over the proportions of all the parts.

about ⅓ quantity bread dough, see page 44
waxed paper
cocktail sticks (toothpicks)
piece of polystyrene (styrofoam)
modelling tool
retracted ballpoint pen
P.V.A. glue
garlic press

1 Roll a small piece of the dough into two thin ropes, each about 5cm (2in) long. Flatten one end of both of them slightly and make a pair of feet (see page 47). Make some thin arms and hands, about 4cm (1½ in) long (see page 47), and put these and the legs to dry on a piece of waxed paper.

2 Roll a small ball of dough for the head. Mark the eyes and a small hole for the mouth with a cocktail stick (toothpick). Make a tiny ball of dough for the nose and glue this in place. Place the head on a cocktail stick and stand it in a piece of polystyrene (styrofoam) until it dries.

3 To make the trumpet, roll a tapering rope about 2.5cm (1in) long. Insert a modelling tool in the broad end and roll this until the dough is hollowed and widened into a trumpet shape. Leave to dry.

4 Roll out another small piece of dough thinly between two sheets of waxed paper. Cut out two triangles with equal sides of 3cm (1¼ in) each. Cut three fairly deep notches in one side of each triangle to make wings, and then indent a pattern on these feathery pieces with the retracted pen.

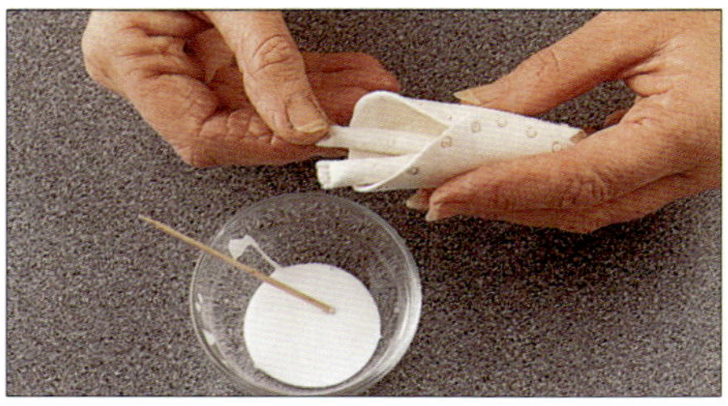

5 When the legs are dry, flatten a small ball of dough into a circle large enough to make the angel's gown. Indent the edge of the circle with the ballpoint pen and then curve and glue it into a cone. Glue the legs inside the gown so that the toes show beneath the edge of the dough. Push a short hanging hook into the back of the gown.

6 Use smaller circles of dough to make sleeves in a similar way to the gown. Lay on waxed paper to dry.

7 When the head is dry, flatten two very small balls and glue them onto the face as puffed-out cheeks. Thin the edges of the cheeks and mould them onto the face. Keeping the head fixed into the polystyrene on the end of the cocktail stick, gradually glue on strands of dough from a garlic press to build up hair.

8 Glue the thin end of the trumpet into the mouth of the angel and support the other end on crumpled paper until the glue has dried.

9 When dry, glue the head onto the point of the gown. Attach the tops of the arms on each side in the same direction as the trumpet. Glue the hands to the trumpet. Attach the wings to the back and dry.

Painting and finishing

Paint the arms, legs and face flesh colour (see page 52). Add a little more cadmium red and blend this into the cheeks, fingertips and toes.

Paint the gown and wings white. Add a little ultramarine to make pale blue. Blend this into the ends of the wings while they are damp. Mix white and alizarin crimson and blend into the wing tips. Use pale blue to paint the eyes. Paint the decoration on the gown and wings, trumpet and hair with gold. Varnish with spirit-based acrylic varnish or oil-based clear gloss polyurethane varnish.

Christmas Labels

Varnish and dry the back of the dough, then stick on self-adhesive labels on which to write messages.

¼ quantity basic dough, see page 44
plastic ruler
thick plastic drinking straw
small holly leaf cutter
small bird cutter
small leaf cutter
cocktail stick (toothpick)
small primrose cutter
modelling tool
stamens
about 30cm (12in) narrow ribbon or decorative string

1 Roll out half the dough to 6mm (¼in) thick. Flour a plastic ruler well and use it as a guide for cutting out two 6.5x4cm (2¼x1¼in) rectangles of dough with a sharp knife. Trim one end of both rectangles to a point to make a label shape and then, using a plastic straw, make holes for the ribbon in the pointed ends.

2 Roll out some thinner dough and cut out two holly leaves. Indent a central vein in both with the back of a knife and fix them end to end on one label, leaving enough room for the robin. Make three small balls of dough to represent holly berries and place in the middle of the leaves.

3 Use a small bird cutter to cut out the robin and sit him on top of the holly berries. Make a wing with the small leaf cutter and notch one side slightly to represent feathers. Mark the robin's eye with a cocktail stick (toothpick).

4 For the second label, cut out and mark veins on five more holly leaves, then arrange them in a ring, with their ends pointing inwards. Make five small balls of dough for holly berries and pile these up in the middle of the leaves.

5 Cut out a Christmas rose using a small primrose cutter and press out the petals with the rounded end of a modelling tool (see page 48). Fix the rose close to the holly and push four small stamens into the middle.

6 Bake the labels in a preheated oven at 145°C (290°F/Gas 1½) for about 1 hour. Look at them repeatedly during baking and if they show any signs of bubbling, either prick them with a needle or lay something heavy, like the metal handle of a knife, on them.

Painting and finishing

Paint all the holly leaves with olive green and all the berries with spectrum red. Continue using the red to paint the robin's chest and a line all around the top of both labels. Encircle the hole with another line of red and decorate the sides of the label with dots in the same colour.

Paint the rest of the robin with raw umber, adding a yellow eye and beak.

Use pure permanent white to paint the Christmas rose and, while this is still wet, wash a watery mixture of olive green and lemon yellow into the middle of the flower.

Finish the labels by brushing a little gold onto the ends of the leaves and by painting a gold line just inside the red one.

Varnish and when this is dry, thread coloured ribbon or string through the holes.

Christmas puddings

Simple balls of basic dough (see page 44), are placed on circles of dough to make these tree decorations. Fix a hanging hook in the top of them.

CANDELABRA

Most candelabras are metal, so you could paint this one silver or gold, but as it is so richly ornamented I thought it would look more interesting and exciting with a verdigris finish. Please remind your family that you must not light the candles on this plaque.

1¼ quantities basic dough, see page 44
retracted ballpoint pen
cocktail stick (toothpick)
modelling tool
ivy leaf cutter
2–3 fine floristry wires
2 hanging hooks, see page 48
gold spray paint
clear gloss polyurethane varnish
9 small white candles

1 Roll about a quarter of the dough into a fairly thick 34cm (13½ in) long rope. Lay this horizontally on a baking sheet and lightly mark the middle point on the rope.

2 Make a second, slightly thicker, 10cm (4in) long rope and butt it up to the middle of the first one at right angles. Fix the ropes together with a little water.

3 Make three, short, finger-thick ropes, 6.5cm (2½in), 7.5cm (3in), and 10cm (4in) long. Fix these horizontally, in order of size so that they form a graduated pedestal, at the base of the vertical rope.

4 Make two pencil-thin 20cm (8in) ropes. Take one of these and trim one end diagonally before fixing it to the upright column about 5cm (2in) down from the intersection with the

horizontal rope. Lay the rest of the rope across one of the corners made by the intersection and fix it 5cm (2in) along the horizontal bar, then coil the remainder of the rope back on itself. Secure the coil in position to resemble an ornamental bracket. Use the second 20cm (8in) rope to make a similar bracket for the other side.

5 Make a very thin rope and fix it around the join between the top rope of the pedestal and the upright column. Decorate the three ropes that make the pedestal with stars of David and marks made with the retracted ballpoint pen. I have also added a few little balls of dough and indented their middles with the cocktail stick (toothpick).

6 Make ten walnut-sized balls of dough. Flatten one of these slightly, then fix it on top of the horizontal rope, in the middle.

7 Use the rounded end of a modelling tool to hollow out the other nine balls so that they resemble little round pots. Place one of these on top of the centre ball and fix the others evenly along the horizontal rope so that there are four on either side.

8 Roll nine very thin ropes, about 7.5cm (3in) long, and fix one of these around the top of each pot to make a lip. The pots should stay open while they are baking, but if you are concerned that they might collapse inwards, prop them open with wads of cooking foil. Decorate the centre pot with a line of marks made using the retracted ballpoint pen and use the cocktail stick to make similar marks on the others.

9 Roll out half of the remaining dough to 3mm (⅛ in) thick and cut out about 20 ivy leaves. Mark a central vein on the leaves and put them to one side while you roll several dozen little balls to represent grapes. Build up bunches of grapes, with leaves attached, down the column and along the cross bar.

10 Cut some floristry wires into 5cm (2in) lengths and wind these around a pencil to make tendrils. Push one end of these into the dough where you have a bunch of leaves and grapes.

11 Push a hanging hook into the back of each of the end pots and bake in a preheated oven at 145°C (290°F/Gas 1½) for about 3 hours.

Painting and finishing

Give the candelabra two or three thin coats of gold paint. When completely dry, mix viridian and, working quickly, completely cover the gold with this colour. While damp blend a mixture of white and viridian into some areas: mainly in the nooks and

crannies around the pots, and between the leaves and grapes, but do not overdo this. When the paint is almost dry, take a soft, lint-free cloth and rub some of it away to reveal the gold. This will look most authentic if you rub back some of the decorative raised areas. Do not rub back so far as to show the dough.

When you are satisfied with the effect, allow the paint to dry and add a coat of clear gloss polyurethane varnish. The gold will gleam if you apply two or three coats of varnish; remember to leave 24 hours between applications.

Shave the bases off the candles and arrange them in the holders.

Cherubs

Winged Head Cherub

If you want a rosy cherub, like the one illustrated, give the dough a coating of egg glaze (see page 45), before baking and tint the cheeks, knees and feet with some watery pink paint while the glaze is still wet.

1 quantity basic dough, see page 44
leaf cutters
modelling tool
garlic press
hanging hook, see page 48

1 Make an 18cm (7in) rope from a quarter of the dough (see page 46). Taper the ends and flatten the rope with a rolling pin, then place on a baking sheet, tilting the tapered ends up slightly.

2 Roll out the remaining dough and cut out several leaves in all sizes. Mark veins on the leaves using the back of a knife and arrange them on the rope, overlapping each other with the smallest leaves at the tapered ends and the largest ones towards the middle. Leave a space about 4cm (1½ in) across in the centre and towards the base of the rope.

3 Mould a large, slightly flattened ball of dough for the head and place it in the space on the rope. Tuck two large leaves under the head on either side of the chin. Lay two medium leaves on top, then add two very small leaves on top of those.

4 Mould a small ball of dough for the nose and place it in the middle of the face. Mark the mouth with the end of the modelling tool. Arrange two small, flattened balls of dough on the face for cheeks. Smooth the cheek edges with the modelling tool and a damp brush.

5 Push several short lengths of dough through a garlic press to represent hair. Fix a hanging hook in the dough at the back and bake in a preheated oven at 145° (290°F/Gas 1½) for about 2 hours.

Painting and finishing

Leave the dough natural adding a little watery rose madder to the cheeks, mouth and chin. Paint two permanent white lozenge shapes for eyes, remembering to paint the left one first if you are right-handed and vice versa. While this is drying, paint the wings white. Make pale blue by mixing ultramarine and white, add some pink by adding a little rose madder to white. Tip all the feathers with a little of each while the white is still damp. Use the pale blue to paint an iris in each eye. When the wings are quite dry edge the feathers with gold and paint the hair with the same colour. Finish by putting a black dot in the centre of the iris and by outlining the eyes and the eyebrows.

Garlanded Cherub

½ quantity basic dough, see page 44
wing template, see below
thin card
modelling tool
small holly leaf cutter
blossom plunger cutter

1 For the legs, roll two finger-thick ropes each about 6.5cm (2½ in) long, from a small handful of dough (see page 46). Trim one end of each rope diagonally and fix the two diagonal cuts side-by-side, shortest sides inwards, on a baking sheet. Trim feet-ends on the slant, with the longest sides together in the middle. Make four small cuts into the trimmed edges to represent toes.

2 Trace the wing template, then cut it out in thin card. Roll out one-third of the remaining dough and press the template down on it to leave a clear impression when removed. Carefully cut around the imprint, then transfer the wings to the baking sheet, above the legs.

3 Dampen the wings and leg tops. Mould a piece of dough into the shape of a large smooth egg and press this down on the wings and the tops of the legs to represent the body. Mark a belly button using the modelling tool. Fix a small flattened ball of dough halfway up each leg for knees.

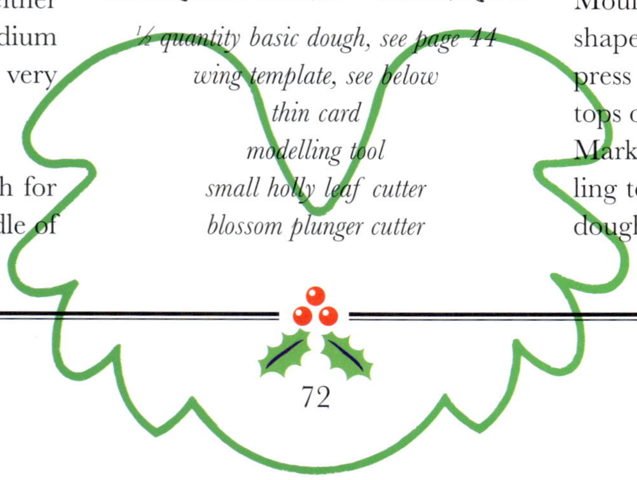

4 Roll two pencil-thin, 7.5cm (3in) long ropes of dough and flatten one end of each to make hands (see page 47). Trim the other end of the dough diagonally and fix to the shoulders. Dampen the inside of the hands and lay these on the body.

5 Mould a ball of dough for the head in proportion to the body and mark a smiling mouth using the modelling tool. Flatten a small ball of dough on either side of the mouth to represent the cheeks and add a very small ball of dough for a nose. Mark the eyes with the modelling tool. Fix the head on the body and wings, then decorate with small coils of dough to represent hair.

6 Make the garland with small holly leaves and blossoms, adding a few very small balls of dough for holly berries. Fix a hanging hook on the side so that the cherub appears to be flying when he is hung up. Bake in a preheated oven at 145°C (290°F/ Gas 1½) for about 1 hour.

Painting and finishing

If you did not make your cherub rosy before baking, take some very watery rose madder and add a little wash to the cheeks, mouth, toes and knees.

Paint the holly leaves with thin olive green and the berries with spectrum red. Use permanent white to paint the wings and add a little pale blue, made by mixing ultramarine and white, to the edges while still wet. Edge the blue with a rose madder and white mix, then finish by just tipping the edges with a little gold and adding a few decorative gold dots. Paint the hair gold. Paint the little blossoms white, adding pale green in the centre.

CHRISTMAS FLOWER PROJECTS

Joanna Sheen

Introduction

Christmas is not only a time for families and celebrations, but also for flowers and decorations. Whether you are spending Christmas in a small apartment or a big family house, you can always find a place for a decoration or two. In this section there are ideas for making all sorts of arrangements from holly rings to topiary trees, all of which will add extra sparkle, as well as for packaging parcels and decorating crackers.

Christmas is a time for sharing and several of these projects could be made by younger flower arrangers, but with plenty of adult supervision, of course!

Whether you are planning your floral decorations for Christmas well in advance or looking for last-minute ideas, I hope you enjoy the projects and are inspired to think of other creative ideas and designs.

Preparing For Christmas

Planning ahead

Many of the items used in these projects can be bought all year round, but some may need a little advance preparation. Think ahead during the summer days and harvest flowers and seed heads for drying at the right time, and store them away in a warm, dark place.

The projects using dried or preserved items can be made in advance and stored. Make sure, however, that you pack them away carefully – preferably in the dark.

Fresh ingredients such as blue spruce and holly can be cut a little while before Christmas, but make sure they are kept cool and damp. Spruce lasts very well if it is kept outside with the occasional rain shower keeping it watered!

Spraying with gold and silver paint

Spraying plant material, such as dried seed heads, with gold or silver paint can add a truly festive touch to arrangements. There is no need to stop at seed heads or other dried flower bits and pieces when you are thinking of things to spray. Artificial fruit looks wonderful with a coat of gold or silver – and that includes the cheapest, most unrealistic plastic specimens that you never thought would be at all useful. Bargain baskets and containers that were a hideous colour originally look quite transformed when they are given a liberal coating of gold or copper metallic spray.

Spraying with gold paint can be a very messy affair. The easiest way is to lay the items you want to spray in a large shallow fruit box – the sort used by supermarkets. Spray one side and then once they have dried off a little, turn them over and spray the other. If you decide to take items out in the garden to spray, do take care to protect your hands and shoes. The spray drifts quite a lot and I have ruined a couple of pairs of shoes with the addition of gold paint speckles!

Making a wreath base

As a change from using shop-bought wreath bases, you might consider making your own wreaths or rings. You could try using lengths of vine or clematis stems, but for a really sturdy wreath I have found the trimmings from a willow tree the most successful material.

Make up a board with nails placed in the pattern as shown in the diagram opposite. The size of the board will depend on the finished size you want your wreath to be. Wind the stems in and out of the nails on the board making a good circular shape, easing each piece around the bends. Continue with plenty of stems until you have a sturdy wreath. As the depth of the ring increases, try to wind some of the stems through the others to make the wreath even more secure. Once you feel that you have a ring of the shape and size that you are happy with, slide

some lengths of wire under the ring in various places around the circle and knot or twist the wire so that it holds the depth of the ring in shape.

Leave your wreath on the board to dry in a really warm place, such as a boiler cupboard, until the stems have dried completely. This will take varying amounts of time depending on the variety of plant material used and the dampness.

Making bows

Bows always feature largely in Christmas arrangements and packaging, and making wired bows is much easier than it looks and is a technique worth trying. The diagrams on the right illustrate two types of bow. To make the top one, take a length of ribbon and wrap it around like wrapping a shawl around your shoulders. Gather up the middle, making a bow and tails and bind the middle with some wire. To make the bottom one, loops of ribbon are bound together with wire as shown. The wires can be hidden by tying a small piece of ribbon around them or by covering them with flowers or other decorations.

The overall effect at Christmas should be one of abundance and cheerfulness. So don't worry too much about the technical side of your ideas or arrangements, just have fun, rope as many of the family in as possible and make the house look happy and friendly.

Collect an assortment of useful Christmas decorations for your arrangements (above).
Make a wired bow in two ways, and a board for a wreath base (below).

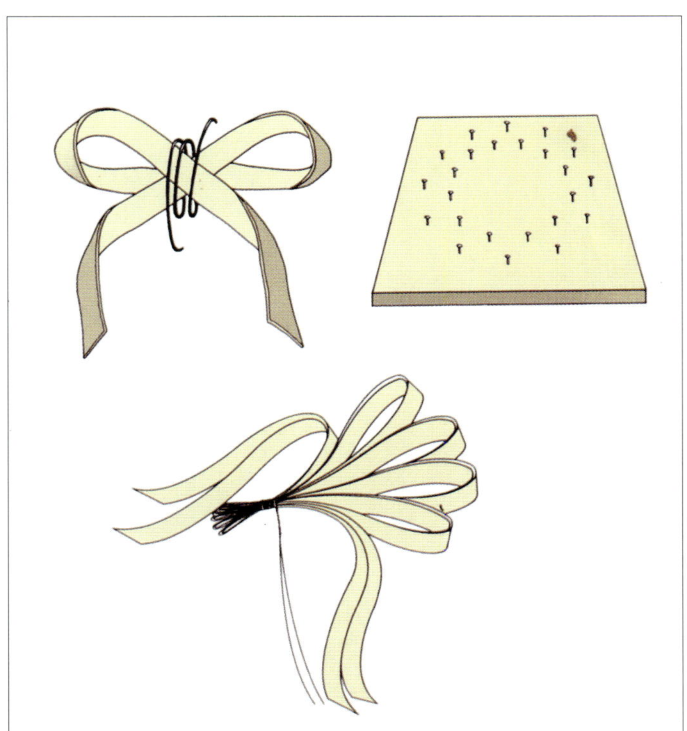

Holly and Ivy Ring

Christmas wreaths and rings are a welcome sight on doors during the festive season. This idea is a little different with the golden eggs adding an extra sparkle. The basic ring can be made at home or you can use a commercial one as the base.

Holly and Ivy Ring

A traditional holly ring always looks pretty at Christmas and will last well against the elements. This combination of holly and ivy will stay fresh for quite some time and the feature of the twigs and gilded eggs adds an unusual twist to a very popular Christmas decoration. You will need plenty of sprays of holly and some very long trails of ivy. The eggs are emptied of their contents by piercing them at each end with a large needle, waggling the needle inside the egg to break down the white and yolk, and then blowing gently through one end. Once the eggs are empty, rinse the shells well with clean water to make sure all the contents have been removed and leave them to drain overnight.

glue gun and glue
holly and ivy, see above
a twiggy ring, 30cm (12in) in diameter
a bundle of lichen-covered twigs
5 eggs
gold spray paint

1 Glue the sprays of holly all around the ring, covering it evenly but not so densely that you cannot see the twiggy ring underneath. Both plain holly and variegated holly look very attractive, or you could use a mixture of them both. If you cannot find any holly, any other evergreen leaf – preferably with a similar texture – could be substituted.

2 Wind the trails of ivy around the ring, bending them through the holly leaves and in and out of the centre of the ring. This will hold them securely enough, but you could glue each end to keep them in a particular position. Make sure the ivy has been given a long drink in water before using it to help the ring stay fresh for as long as possible.

3 Glue the lichen-covered twigs in position. You could either add the twigs to a central point or offset to one side. Spray the eggs with gold paint and, when dry, glue them to the ring cluster. Place a few ivy leaves between each of the eggs to complete the festive decoration.

I COME A MOTLEY PAGE TO SAY
GREETINGS TO YOU ON NEW YEARS DAY

Fireside Basket

This unusual display of bay leaf balls and fresh orange pomanders adds a lovely spicy aroma to the room. The arrangement also looks attractive when dried. Extra essential oil can be rubbed into the balls or pomanders. Christmas pot pourri (page 86) is another fragrant idea.

FIRESIDE BASKET

Whether you have a real log fire or just a radiator, the warmth will help release the lovely natural perfume of these pomanders. The bay leaf balls are a little fiddly to make but last well and can be enjoyed for ages after they have been made. The orange pomanders can be enjoyed while they are drying out and then arranged with fruit or as a decoration on their own. You will need a carrier bag full of fresh bay leaves – more than you might think, as many may well be damaged. The oranges also take quite a few cloves so it is best to buy a large pack or two from a herb supplier.

bay leaves
0.71mm (22 gauge) stub wires
assorted florists' foam balls, 7cm (2 ¾ in) and 9cm (3 ¼ in) in diameter
glue
cloves
oranges

1 Sort out the bay leaves, discarding any that are damaged. Cut the wire into roughly 5cm (2in) lengths and bend each in half to make a 'hairpin'. Use these hairpins to pin the bay leaves onto each foam ball, so the entire surface is covered. The patterns you create are up to you – you can start from the top or middle, so long as the leaves overlap each time.

2 Continue to cover the ball until the foam is completely covered. Cover the joins between the rows of leaves by changing direction and pinning leaves across each other. The last few leaves can be stuck on with a small amount of glue to prevent the wires being seen.

3 Tip the cloves onto a flat surface and press them one by one into the skin of each orange. You can make many different patterns with the cloves – swirls and stripes or patches, circles and sections. Place the decorated oranges in a basket together with the bay leaf balls.

Christmas Pot Pourri

Memories of Christmas are as much about scents and aromas as they are of tastes and sights. Spiced wine mulling in a large pan, aromatic cinnamon and tangy oranges – all of these bring Christmas memories to mind. A festive pot pourri can encapsulate many of these fragrances. For this recipe, you will need ten slices of dried orange, ten cinnamon sticks, ten nutmegs, a cup each of dried marigold flowers, dried green leaves, rose hips and costus flowers or small pine cones. For the essential oils, I used a mixture of cinnamon, ginger and orange.

dried ingredients, see above
bowl and metal spoon
15g (½ oz) orris root
2 teaspoons essential oils of your choice
large plastic bag and elastic band
container for pot pourri

1 Assemble all the ingredients; put aside some orange slices and cinnamon sticks to decorate the top, but cut or break the rest. Put the ingredients in a bowl, add the orris root and essential oils, and mix well with a metal spoon.

2 Tip the mixture into a large plastic bag and shake well. Secure the top with an elastic band and store for at least a week for the perfumes to mature and blend. Then tip the pot pourri into the container and decorate with the reserved orange slices and cinnamon sticks.

The Compliments of the Season
For Auld Lang Syne.
A Happy New Year

Floral Parcels and Decorated Crackers

Beautifully giftwrapped parcels need not take hours to do or cost a lot. These floral giftwrap ideas are inexpensive and make a parcel truly special. Christmas crackers, too, can look really sumptuous, simply by adding extra decorations.

FLORAL PARCELS

Half the fun of receiving presents at Christmas is looking at them under the tree or appreciating the wrapping before you open the gift. Anticipation is certainly one of the best parts of any celebration! You can add small floral decorations very simply to Christmas and other gifts and it makes the present mean so much more. There are three different ideas featured here, but you will be able to think of many more once you have the flowers to hand together with a box of 'useful bits' that you have saved throughout the year. To make these decorations you will need two yellow roses, two sprays of carnation, a spray of golden rod (*solidago*) and spruce for the first design, two or three long strands of ivy for the second and a small piece of spruce and a poinsettia flower for the third.

wrapping paper
flowers and foliage, see above
assorted wires
1m (1⅛ yd) orange chiffon ribbon (1st design)
glue
3m (3¼ yd) gold curling ribbon (2nd design)
50cm (2in) thick red and gold cord (3rd design)

1 After wrapping the parcel, make a small bunch with the roses and spray carnations and wrap some wire firmly around them. Add the spruce at the back of the bunch and some pieces of golden rod at the sides. Wire the whole bunch securely. Tie the ribbon around the bunch in a pretty bow. Fix the bunch to the parcel by either gluing it down or tying it firmly in position with ribbon.

2 Wrap the parcel firmly, making the corners as neat as possible. Tie a long strand of ivy around one side of the parcel. Using small strands, tie those in to the first strand so that they come out at various angles. Cut the curling ribbon in half, then tie it in the middle of the ivy and curl by winding it around a pencil.

3 Take a piece of spruce as a backing and wire it together with a poinsettia flower. Once the wire is bound tightly around the flower, trim away any excess and tie the piece of cord into a bow around the posy. Attach to the parcel either with a little glue or by tying it on.

Decorated Crackers

Most crackers are bought for their decorative value rather than for their contents. Sometimes the jokes can liven up a rather quiet gathering but usually you can only rely on finding plastic animals, so the youngest child present gradually collects the contents of all the crackers! These crackers may well be no improvement inside but the outside can be helped along with a little flower know-how! You will need some commercial crackers, ones that have a basically nice paper base but they do not need to have very special decorations. You will also need some gold-sprayed fern (*pteris*) leaves or other dried foliage, cinnamon sticks, small pine cones and dried orange slices. Obviously the exact quantities will depend on how many crackers you are decorating.

crackers
glue gun and glue
flowers, foliage and spices, see above
gold-wired cord

1 Remove all the commercial trimmings from the crackers, unless they blend with the decorations you are adding, like a twist of gold tinsel or something similar. Cut two or three small sprays of gold leaves and carefully glue them onto the centre of the cracker – use the minimum amount of glue so that it does not show.

2 Add two or three small pieces of cinnamon stick, gluing them on individually. Then place a few small pieces of orange between the cinnamon and the cracker, leaving room for the small pine cones.

3 Glue into position on the cracker two or three very small pine cones, or you could use costus flowers which look very similar. Loops of gold-wired cord can be added to give a stylish finishing touch. You could substitute many other ingredients for the decorations, depending upon the oddments you have available.

Yuletide Table Centrepiece

All that glitters can easily be sprayed gold! Gold materials look very effective in Christmas displays and when combined together, as in this arrangement, they make an excellent focal point.

Yuletide Table Centrepiece

The main thing to aim for with a Christmas table is a bright, cheerful centrepiece that will add some festive sparkle. The table is always crowded with glasses, plates and other dishes so it is best to keep any floral decorations fairly compact. Most of the items in this arrangement have been sprayed with gold paint which adds a special glow to the display. You will need some preserved oak foliage, five cardoon heads, fifteen gilded pine cones, fifteen natural walnuts and nine golden mushrooms.

glue
a plastic 'frog' fixing
25 x 20cm (10 x 8in) oval cork base
half-block of dried florists' foam
secateurs
foliage, etc, see above
0.71mm (22 gauge) stub wires
1m (1⅛ yd) bronze chiffon ribbon

1 Glue the green frog fixing to the cork base. Once it is firmly fixed in position, impale the dried foam over the prongs of the frog. Cover the surface of the foam with sprays of gold oak leaves, keeping the oval shape of the arrangement. If the foam seems too high, cut some off the top with a knife to make the arrangement slightly shallower.

2 Push the gilded cardoon heads into the foam, making sure they are well spaced and not too close together. You will need very short stem lengths on these or they will stick out too far. Wire up the pine cones by winding some wire around the base petals of the cone, then bend down the wire and use as a stem. Add them to the arrangement.

3 Fill in the arrangement with wired walnuts (if you prefer you could glue them into position) and wired golden mushrooms. Take some chiffon ribbon and make a few loops, holding the base of the loops between your thumb and forefinger. Then wrap wire around the base to secure (see diagram on page 77), bend down the wire and press into the arrangement. Place loops on both sides of the table centrepiece.

Traditional Arrangement

This very traditional combination of poinsettias, holly and conifer sprigs always looks attractive at Christmas time. But if you prefer a larger version, the poinsettias could be used in their pots rather than in foam.

Although it is fun to make modern or unusual flower arrangements and come up with new ideas as often as possible, it is also very satisfying to make a really traditional Christmas arrangement. This particular idea reminds me of many Christmas cards I have received over the years and I like the comforting feel of an arrangement one almost seems to recognize! For the foliage, I used a mixture of blue spruce and variegated holly, about nine stems of each, and three large red poinsettia flowers.

half-block of fresh florists' foam
long shallow container, about 20 x 10cm (8 x 4in)
3 candle holders
3 ivory candles
foliage and flowers, see above
2m (2¼ yd) red ribbon, 2.5cm (1in) wide
2 stub wires, 0.71mm (22 gauge)

1 Soak the foam in water until it is saturated. Wedge the foam into the container. Press the three candle holders into the foam wherever you would like them. Trim two of the candles so that they are all differing heights. Fix the candles into the candle holders. Place 15cm (6in) long sprays of both foliages into the arrangement.

2 Cut the poinsettia stems to a suitable length and add them to the arrangement. Keep them spaced well apart so that they do not look too crowded.

3 Make two wired bows from the ribbon (see page 77) and place them at either side of the arrangement so that the display can be viewed from both sides. Take care never to leave the arrangement unattended when the candles are alight as indoor bonfires are most unwelcome!

TOPIARY TREE AND INDOOR WREATH

The little apple and cranberry topiary tree is a pretty and unusual decoration which is simple enough for children to make. The wreath is an idea for indoors as the ingredients are definitely not weather-proof.

KIND

Topiary Tree

There are many different designs for topiary trees but this one uses the unusual combination of fruit and foliage instead of flowers. As most of the ingredients are dried it should last well; the cranberries will shrivel or go mouldy after a while but they can be replaced by fresh or artificial berries. The clear glass container makes a change from a terracotta base but a basket or pot could be used if you prefer. You will need about 60 apple slices to include the base, a pack of fresh cranberries, a bunch of preserved beech leaves and some hazelnuts.

half-block of dried florists' foam
knife
glass base, about 12.5cm (5in) square
fruit and foliage, see above
chunky cinnamon stick for trunk
7cm (2¾ in) florists' foam ball
assorted wires

1 Cut the foam to size using a sharp knife, leaving room for the apple slices, and insert in the glass base. Camouflage the foam on all sides with apple slices; arrange them so that they overlap or touch. Choose a fairly chunky cinnamon stick, about 20–23cm (8–9in) long, and push this into the centre of the foam.

2 Cover the surface of the base with hazelnuts. Impale the foam ball onto the cinnamon stick and cover it with sprays of beech leaves. If necessary, wire together bunches of individual leaves if the ends of the sprays are not bushy enough.

3 Wire the remaining apple slices individually and then push the wires into the foam tree, placing them evenly among the beech foliage throughout the arrangement. Cut shorter pieces of wire for the cranberries. Insert one end of the wire into a cranberry and the other into the tree. As before, dot the cranberries among the foliage. Finally, sprinkle some cranberries among the hazelnuts at the base of the tree for extra colour.

Indoor Wreath

Many people have a welcome ring or wreath on their front door at Christmas. This design is intended for indoor use as the dried flowers would simply not survive the elements. It could be hung in a hallway or on an inside door, depending on where you have a space. Again, some of the ingredients have been sprayed gold and it is interesting to see how well they blend with the naturally coloured materials. To make this indoor ring, you will need a bunch of eucalyptus and some blue spruce, a bunch of gilded poppy heads, a bunch of preserved and gilded foliage, such as box, and 20 pink roses.

twiggy ring, about 30cm (12in) in diameter
flowers and foliage, see above
glue
1.5m (1⅔ yd) ribbon, 7.5cm (3in) wide
assorted wires

1 Cover the ring roughly with blue spruce and glue firmly into position. Add pieces of eucalyptus to thicken up the background. Make a wired bow with the ribbon (see page 77).

2 Glue the bow firmly onto the ring. Add in the gilded poppy heads and box, following the curve of the circle and covering about three-quarters of the ring.

3 Finally, glue the pink roses onto the ring. These are best placed in groups of three or five in between the gilded poppy heads and box. This design would look equally pretty if the poppies and box were sprayed silver instead of gold.

FESTIVE GARLAND

This luxurious spruce garland can be made at home for a fairly reasonable price. Although it takes a little while to make, it does look wonderful!

Festive Garland

Spruce is a very attractive foliage to use at Christmas and it has the added benefit of lasting very well. It will not drop like some conifers or traditional Christmas trees – it just dries and turns a greyish-blue instead of bluish-green. It will take a reasonable amount of spruce to make this garland – about 50 sprigs to make a 1.5m (5ft) garland. It is hard to be accurate about the exact number required as it depends on the quality and density of the spruce.

1.8m (2yd) twisted paper ribbon
a reel of binding wire
spruce, see above
1m (1⅛yd) wired ribbon, 6.5–7.5cm (2½–3in) wide
glue gun and glue
assortment of gilded poppy heads, cinnamon sticks, walnuts, dried orange slices, pine cones and gilded lotus heads
spray gloss varnish

1 Bend some twisted paper ribbon over at both ends and wire firmly to make a hanging loop at each end of the garland. Twist a small piece of wire in the middle of the garland to remind you where the centre is. Starting from one end, place a 10cm (4in) sprig of spruce over the loop and wire it onto the twisted paper ribbon. Keep adding pieces of spruce, fanning them out so the garland is fairly flat rather than chunky. Continue until you reach the marked central point, then turn the garland around and start from the other end.

2 Once you reach the central point, cut some smaller pieces of spruce and place them at right angles to the ribbon and wire to fill the gap in the middle. Use plenty of wire as it is more important to have a secure garland than a neat one, and the glued-on bits and pieces will cover most wiring problems. Make a large bow with the ribbon (see page 77) and attach it to the centre with glue.

3 Glue on all the bits and pieces you have chosen. Place larger pieces like the lotus heads on first, and the cinnamon sticks through the centre of the bow and at intervals along the garland. Once you have all your nuts and cones glued on, give them a coat of spray gloss varnish as this will highlight their colours and give the nuts in particular an attractive shine.

Christmas Tree Decorations

We all have favourite Christmas tree decorations which come out every year. Here are some new ideas using fresh flowers and foliage.

Christmas Tree Decorations

We all have many beloved family tree decorations that have been around for years – some may be very special as they were made by the children. Although there are always new, different and exciting commercially made tree decorations on the market, these homemade decorations are a little bit different, and something perhaps the whole family could make together a couple of days before Christmas. You will need some sea lavender, golden rod (*solidago*), spray carnations, one or two roses, and any fresh foliage from the garden.

gold wire or cord
terracotta flowerpots, 2.5cm (1in) in diameter
fresh florists' foam
flowers and foliage, see above
silver rose wire
cellophane
curling ribbon

1 Thread two loops of gold wire or cord through the whole in the base of each flowerpot to act as hanging loops for the decoration. Fill the pots with foam that has first been soaked in water and make a miniature arrangement with foliage, sea lavender and golden rod. The ingredients can be altered according to what is available.

2 Make some small bunches of carnations or roses with sea lavender or golden rod, and wire into a small posy. Add a wrapping of cellophane and secure with curling ribbon, adding a loop to hang them from the tree.

DRAMATIC TABLE CENTRE

In complete contrast to the traditional red, green and gold Christmas colour schemes, these orchids look absolutely stunning in this unusual table centre arrangement. The twigs can be found lying on the ground under trees in the countryside or even in city parks.

Dramatic Table Centre

The colouring of this arrangement is by no means traditional, but it is certainly dramatic and would be ideal for a New Year's Eve celebration. Although it looks very impressive, the actual arrangement is very easy and will only take a short while to make. The list of ingredients is quite short – you will need two small bunches of mauve Singapore orchids, a selection of lichen-covered twigs and some hellebore leaves.

1 Soak the foam in water until it is saturated and fill the tin with it. Lay the twigs in position if you are arranging the flowers in situ; if not, lay them on the table and add the container with flowers after step 3.

2 Insert the hellebore leaves into the foam, making the arrangement long or round, depending on the shape of your table. If you cannot obtain hellebore leaves, any other large, dark leaves would be suitable.

fresh florists' foam
small baking tin or other container, about 15cm (6in) wide
flowers and twigs, see above

3 Next add the sprays of Singapore orchids. If they are very long, break them in half and add both halves towards the centre of the display. These orchids are also readily available in other colours so the arrangement could be varied simply by replacing with cream or peach orchids, for instance.

Creative Christmas Cakes

Joanna Farrow

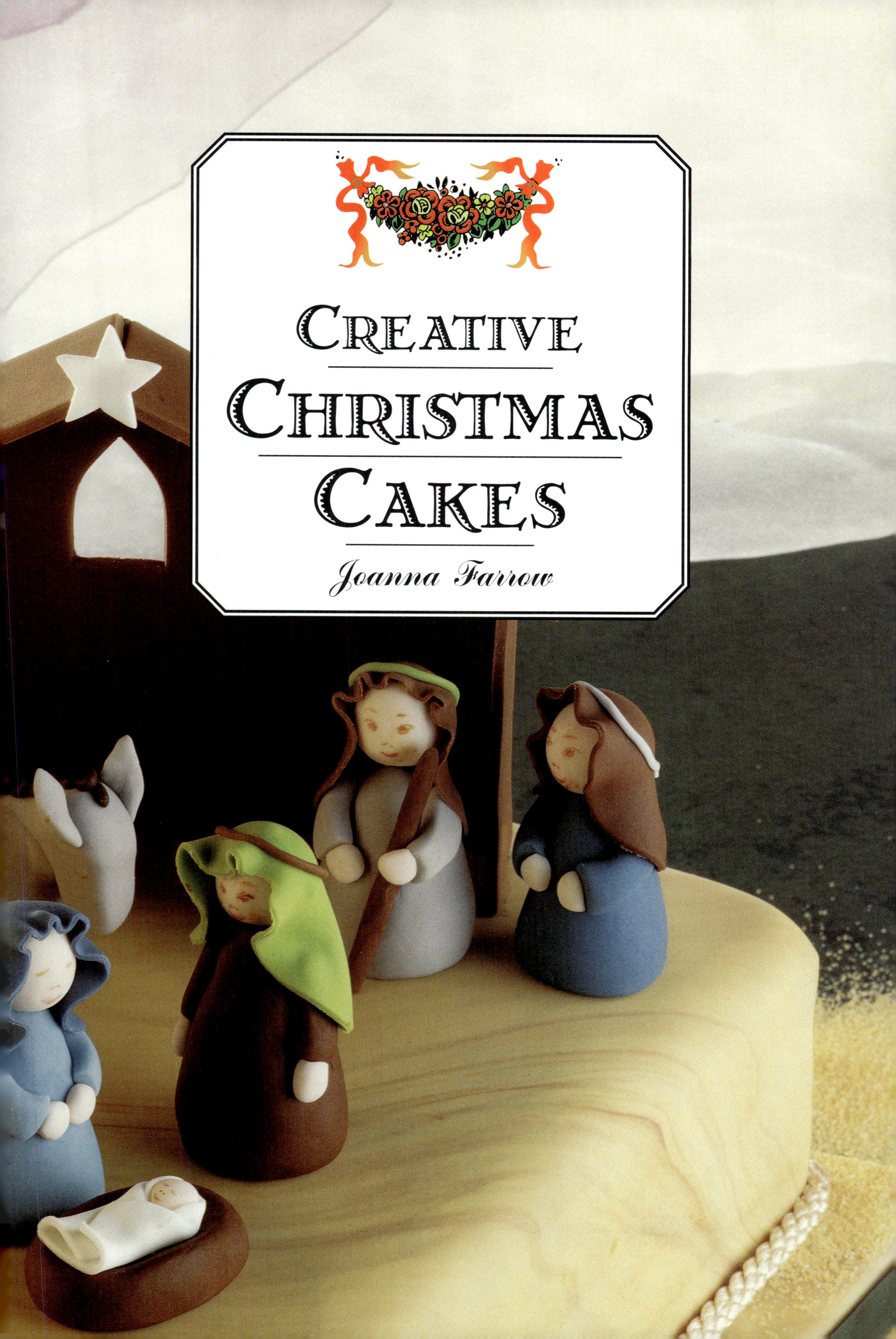

INTRODUCTION

No Christmas is complete without a beautifully decorated cake to grace the tea table, and whether you are a novice cake decorator or quite an expert, you will find plenty of inspiration in the wide range of designs featured in this section. Simple but imaginative ideas, such as the pretty Chocolate Box Cake spilling over with luscious truffles, can be attempted by anyone. Both Winter Wonderland and the Christmas Rose Cake will appeal to more experienced cake decorators looking for designs that will show off their skills.

Children can be enlisted to help to decorate some of the novelty cakes. They may well prove to be very competent at modelling sugarpaste – for example, making candy canes for the Holly Garland Cake or the brightly coloured teardrops for the Jewelled Boxes.

Recipes for both a rich and a light fruit cake are given. Either type can be used for all the cakes in this section. There are also recipes for sugarpaste and royal icing as well as detailed information on the basic techniques and many helpful tips.

Whatever design you choose, make sure that you have all the necessary equipment to avoid a frenzied shopping expedition on Christmas Eve!

BASIC CAKE RECIPES

RICH FRUIT CAKE

For ingredients, tin sizes and baking times, see the chart opposite. This cake stores well for several months in a cool, dry place. Leave the lining paper on and wrap in plenty of foil. If liked, drizzle the cake with brandy before storing.

1 Preheat the oven to 140°C (275°F/Gas 1). Grease and line the required tin.

2 Cream together the softened butter or margarine and sugar. Lightly beat the eggs and gradually beat into the creamed mixture, adding a little of the flour to prevent curdling. Sift together the remaining flour with the spice and fold into the mixture.

3 Gradually add the mixed fruit, cherries and almonds, stirring until evenly blended. Transfer to the prepared tin and level the surface.

4 Bake in the oven for the time stated in the chart. (The time will vary considerably, depending on the type of oven.) Use the chart as a guide and test towards the end of the stated time. A skewer inserted into the centre should come out clean. Leave the cake to cool in the tin. Wrap and store.

LIGHT FRUIT CAKE

This is ideal for those who find rich fruit cake a little too heavy. It still contains plenty of fruit but has a more spongy texture. Make up to 1 month before Christmas and store, wrapped in its lining paper, in plenty of foil. For ingredients, tin sizes and baking times, see the chart opposite.

1 Preheat the oven to 140°C (275°F/Gas 1). Grease and line the required tin.

2 Place the mixed dried fruit, peel and apricots in a bowl. Add the brandy and leave for 2–3 hours.

3 Cream together the softened butter or margarine and the sugar. Lightly beat the eggs and gradually add to the creamed mixture, adding a little of the flour to prevent curdling. Sift together the remaining flour and spice and fold into the mixture.

4 Gradually add the fruit mixture and stir until evenly combined. Transfer to the prepared tin and make a deep depression in the centre. Bake in the oven for the time stated in the chart or until a skewer, inserted into the centre, comes out clean. Leave the cake to cool in the tin. Wrap and store.

Rich Fruit Cake Quantities Chart

Round tin	18cm (7in)	20cm (8in)	23cm (9in)	25cm (10in)	28cm (11in)
Square tin	15cm (6 in)	18cm (7in)	20cm (8in)	23cm (9in)	25cm (10in)
Butter or margarine	150g (5oz/ ⅔ cup)	200g (6½oz/¾ cup)	280g (9oz/1 cup)	410g (13oz/1⅔ cups)	470g (15oz/2 cups)
Dark soft brown sugar	150g (5oz/ ¾ cup)	200g (6½oz/ 1 cup)	280g (9oz/1½cups)	410g (13oz/ 2¼ cups)	470g (15oz/3 cups)
Eggs	3	3	4	6	8
Plain (all-purpose) flour	180g (6oz/1½ cups)	250g (8oz/2 cups)	375g (12oz/3 cups)	500g (1lb/4 cups)	625g (1¼lb/5 cups)
Ground mixed (apple pie) spice	1 teaspoon	1½ teaspoons	2 teaspoons	1 tablespoon	4 teaspoons
Mixed dried fruit	625g (1¼lb/4 cups)	875g (1¾lb/6 cups)	1.1kg (2¼lb/7½cups)	1.5kg (3lb/10 cups)	1.8kg (3¾lb/12 cups)
Glacé (candied) cherries, chopped	60g (2oz/½ cup)	90g (3oz/½ cup)	100g (3½oz/ ⅔ cup)	150g (5oz/¾ cup)	250g (8oz/1⅓ cups)
Almonds, chopped	30g (1oz/¼ cup)	45g (1½oz/⅓ cup)	60g (2oz/½cup)	90g (3oz/¾ cup)	125g (4oz/1 cup)
Baking time	2–2¼ hours	3–3¼ hours	3½–3¾ hours	4 hours	4½–4¾ hours

Light Fruit Cake Quantities Chart

Round tin	18cm (7 in)	20cm (8in)	23cm (9in)	25cm (10in)	28cm (11in)
Square tin	15cm (6in)	18cm (7in)	20cm (8in)	23cm (9in)	25cm (10in)
Mixed dried fruit	440g (14oz/2¾ cups)	500g (1lb/3¼cups)	750g (1½lb/5 cups)	1kg (2lb/6½cups)	1.25kg (2½ lb/8 cups)
Mixed peel	30g (1oz/¼ cup)	30g (1oz/¼cup)	60g (2oz/ ⅓ cup)	90g (3oz/½cup)	125g (4oz/¾cup)
Dried apricots, chopped	60g (2oz/½cup)	125g (4oz/1 cup)	180g (6oz/1½cups)	250g (8oz/2 cups)	315g (10oz/2½cups)
Brandy	2 tablespoons	2 tablespoons	3 tablespoons	3 tablespoons	4 tablespoons
Butter or margarine	250g (8oz/1 cup)	315g (10oz/1¼cups)	440g (14oz/1¾cups)	525g (1lb 1oz/2¼cups)	625g (1¼lb/2½ cups)
Light soft brown sugar	250g (8oz/1⅓cups)	315g (10oz/1¾cups)	440g (14oz/2½cups)	525g (1lb 1oz/3¼cups)	625g (1¼lb/3¾ cups)
Eggs	4	4	5	6	7
Plain (all-purpose) flour	315g (10oz/2½cups)	375g (12oz/3 cups)	500g (1lb/4 cups)	625g (1¼lb/5 cups)	750g (1½lb/6 cups)
Ground mixed (apple pie) spice	1½teaspoons	2 teaspoons	1 tablespoon	4 teaspoons	5 teaspoons
Baking time	2–2¼ hours	3–3¼hours	3½–3¾hours	4 hours	4½–4¾ hours

Lining Tins

For a round tin, place the tin on a piece of greaseproof paper (parchment) and draw around it, then cut out just inside the line. Cut a strip of paper that is as long as the circumference of the tin and 2.5cm (1in) deeper. Make a 2.5cm (1in) fold along one long edge of the strip and snip the folded portion from the edge to the fold at 2.5cm (1in) intervals. Position the strip around the inside of the greased tin with the snipped edge flat on the base. Place the paper in the base, then grease the paper.

Lining the sides of a round tin.

For a square tin, use the same method as for a round tin, although the folded portion will only need snipping in the corners.

For a star-shaped tin, draw and cut around the tin as for a round tin. For the sides, cut strips as before, then snip into the points of the star.

For a ring tin, place the tin on a piece of greaseproof paper and draw around the inside and outside edge of the ring. Cut out the paper ring and press into the base of the greased ring tin. Line the sides with rectangles of paper, generously snipping the paper so that it fits in the curves.

Apricot Glaze

This is used to moisten the surface of the cake and secure the marzipan (almond paste) to it. Put the apricot jam into a saucepan (see chosen recipe for amount required), adding 1 teaspoon water for each tablespoon of jam. Heat gently until the jam has melted, then press the mixture through a sieve to remove any pieces.

Marzipan (Almond Paste)

Before covering a cake with sugarpaste or royal icing, it is important to create a good, smooth base. This is done by applying a covering of marzipan (almond paste), now readily available in both supermarkets and cake-decorating shops. Before covering, trim the cake to the shape required (see chosen recipe) and fill any small holes or gaps with marzipan. Brush with apricot glaze.

To cover a cake with marzipan

1 Lightly knead the marzipan to soften it. Roll out two-thirds on a surface dusted with icing (confectioner's) sugar to a round or square 5cm (2in) larger than the diameter of the cake.

Invert the cake onto the marzipan, press marzipan into the gap, then cut off the excess with a sharp knife.

2 Place the marzipan on a sheet of greaseproof paper (parchment). Invert the cake onto it and press the excess marzipan into the gap left between the cake and the marzipan. Using a sharp knife, cut off the excess. Invert the cake onto the board and remove the greaseproof paper from the top of the cake.

To cover the sides, cut a strip of marzipan to the required size, roll it up, then unroll around the cake.

3 To cover the sides of a round cake, measure the circumference of the cake with a piece of string. Roll out the remaining marzipan to a strip slightly longer than the string and deeper than the cake. Using the string as a guide, cut the strip to the exact circumference of the cake, and then to the exact depth. Roll up the marzipan and unroll around the sides of the cake.

4 Lightly smooth the marzipan around the join and top edge of the cake. Use the same method to cover a square cake, but use four strips of marzipan, each the exact measurement of the cake sides.

ICING RECIPES

SUGARPASTE

You can use either bought or homemade sugarpaste (also known as rolled fondant) for the cakes in this section. Bought sugarpaste has a similar taste to homemade and is slightly easier to work with. If you are making several cakes, it is worth buying ready-coloured sugarpaste. Strong colours such as red, blue, green and black are particularly good and save you the trouble of kneading in colour. Supermarket sugarpastes vary slightly in quality. Some are very soft and become easier to manage if you work in a little icing (confectioner's) sugar before using. Both homemade and bought sugarpaste should be wrapped tightly in cling film (plastic wrap) when not in use as they quickly develop a dry crust. Store in a cool, dry place. Check 'best before' dates on bought sugarpastes.

MAKES 500G (1LB)

1 egg white
2 tablespoons liquid glucose (available from chemists)
about 500g (1lb/2½ cups) icing (confectioner's) sugar
icing sugar, for dusting

1 Put the egg white and liquid glucose in a bowl. Gradually beat in the icing sugar until the mixture becomes too stiff to stir.

2 Turn it out onto a surface heavily dusted with icing sugar and knead until it forms a stiff, smooth paste. Wrap in several layers of cling film until needed. Keeps for one week.

Tips

★ If homemade sugarpaste is sticky when rolled, work in more icing sugar. If too dry and crumbly, work in a little water.

★ Most recipes list icing sugar and cornflour (cornstarch) for dusting. Icing sugar should be used for rolling and applying marzipan and sugarpaste; cornflour only for smoothing sugarpaste and decorations.

To cover a cake with sugarpaste

Lift the sugarpaste onto the cake with the aid of a rolling pin, then smooth into place with the hands.

1 Lightly knead the required amount of sugarpaste on a surface dusted with icing sugar. Roll out the paste to a round or square a good 7.5cm (3in) larger than the diameter of the cake. Lift the sugarpaste on a rolling pin and lay it over the top of the cake.

2 Dust the palms of the hands lightly with cornflour and smooth the sugarpaste over the top and down the sides of the cake, easing it gently to fit around the sides of the cake.

3 Trim off any excess paste around the base of the cake. For the most professional results use an icing smoother, a flat-sided tool available from cake-decorating shops. Work it in a circular action over the cake, for a beautifully flat surface.

Colouring sugarpaste

Lightly knead the sugarpaste on a surface dusted with icing sugar. Using a cocktail stick (toothpick), dot the paste with colour. Gradually knead it into the paste until evenly coloured, adding more if necessary.

Tip

Partial kneading in colour gives a streaked, marbled appearance, which can be effective.

To colour sugarpaste, add dots of colouring with a cocktail stick, then knead until evenly mixed.

Royal Icing

Royal icing can be applied to a cake in a smooth 'flat-iced' layer, or, more traditionally on Christmas cakes, as peaked 'snow'. This is particularly easy to do, and does not require the patience, skill and equipment of flat icing. In this section smaller quantities of royal icing are also used for piping, spreading and making decorative runouts. The quantities below are sufficient for most decorative work.

Makes 250g (8oz)
1 egg white
250g (8oz/1⅓ cups) icing (confectioner's) sugar, sifted

1 Lightly whisk the egg white in a bowl. Gradually beat in the icing (confectioner's) sugar, beating well after each addition until the icing forms soft peaks.

2 Cover the surface of the icing with cling film (plastic wrap), then a damp cloth and further cling film to prevent a crust forming. Well sealed, the icing will store in a cool place for several days.

Covering a cake with peaked royal icing

1 Using a palette knife, spread the top and sides of the marzipan-covered cake with royal icing, repeatedly smoothing the knife over the icing until covered in an even layer.

2 Clean the palette knife. Press the palette knife flat onto the icing, then pull away sharply to form a peak. Repeat all over the cake.

Tips

★ Royal icing firms up slightly during storage. Before use beat well to soften, adding a little water or beaten egg white if necessary. For spreading and peaking, royal icing should be softly peaking.
★ When piping, remember that the smaller the tube (tip), the thinner the consistency of the icing must be. If you find piping lines hard work, the icing probably needs thinning down a little.

Royal Icing Techniques

Making a paper piping bag

Homemade paper piping bags are far easier to use than bought ones as they are less bulky and can simply be discarded after use. It is worth making several at a time so you always have some at the ready.

1 Cut a 25cm (10in) square of greaseproof paper (parchment), then cut the square in half diagonally to make two long triangles. Holding one triangle with its longest side away from you, fold the right-hand point over to meet the bottom point, as shown in the above photograph, curling the paper to shape a cone.

2 Fold the left-hand point over the cone and bring all three points together. Fold over several times to secure the bag.

3 Cut 12mm (½in) off the tip if fitting a piping tube.

Royal icing quantities chart

Use this chart as a guide for covering a marzipan-covered cake with peaked icing.

Round cake	18cm (7in)	20cm (8in)	23cm (9in)	25cm (10in)	28cm (11in)
Square cake	15cm (6in)	18cm (7in)	20cm (8in)	23cm (9in)	25cm (10in)
Royal icing quantities	2 egg whites	3 egg whites	4 egg whites	5 egg whites	6 egg whites

Making royal-iced runouts

The Winter Wonderland cake (see page 131) is finished with iced runouts which are piped onto paper, left to harden and then carefully transferred to the cake. This technique can be used equally well using your own designs such as Christmas stockings, stars, candles and other festive shapes, traced from cards, books or drawn by hand. Avoid making them too complicated.

Place your traced design beneath a sheet of non-stick parchment. Pipe over the outline.

1 Trace the chosen design onto greaseproof or non-stick parchment paper. Place the traced design under a sheet of non-stick parchment paper. Using a little royal icing in a piping bag fitted with a fine or medium writing tube (tip), pipe over the outline.

Fill in the outline with thinned-down royal icing, easing it into the corners with a cocktail stick (toothpick).

2 Thin a little more royal icing with beaten egg white or water until it becomes completely level when left to settle in the bowl for 10 seconds. Place in a paper piping bag and snip off 3mm ($^1/_8$ in) from the tip. Gradually fill the outline with the icing, easing around the edges and into corners with the tip of a cocktail stick (toothpick).

3 Leave for about 48 hours until completely hardened, then carefully peel the paper away from the icing. If liked, the runouts can be painted with food colourings diluted with clear alcohol (gin or vodka).

Basic Techniques

Covering a cakeboard with sugarpaste

This gives a professional-looking finish to a stylish or novelty cake.

1 Lightly dampen the surface of the cakeboard. Thinly roll white or coloured sugarpaste to a curved strip, slightly wider than the board area to be covered. Trim the inner edge of the strip with a knife.

2 Lift the strip around the cake so that the trimmed edge rests against the side of the cake. Smooth out the icing using hands dusted with cornflour (cornstarch), then trim off the excess around the edges. On larger cakes it is easier to cover the board in two sections.

When covering a large cakeboard it is often easier to apply the sugarpaste in two sections.

Cutting around templates

Rolled sugarpaste, shaped and left to harden, makes effective three-dimensional designs, particularly on novelty cakes. Make them well in advance so they have ample time to harden.

1 Roll out the sugarpaste on a surface lightly dusted with cornflour (cornstarch) to 3mm ($^1/_8$ in) thickness, or as stated in the chosen recipe.

2 Lay the cut-out template over the icing and cut around it with a small, sharp knife. Carefully transfer to a sheet of greaseproof or non-stick parchment and leave to harden. (For large templates, lay the icing on the paper before cutting out, as the shape might become distorted if transferred afterwards.)

Lay the template over the sugarpaste and, keeping it very still, cut around it with a sharp knife.

Making holly leaves

Cut-out holly leaves make an effective decoration on a simple 'snow'-covered cake, or as part of a more involved decoration. Bought holly cutters come in various sizes but the most realistic looking leaves are made using the wide base of a piping tube (tip).

Cut out semi-circles from the edge of the holly leaf with the wide base of a writing tube (tip).

1 Thinly roll a little green sugarpaste on a surface dusted with cornflour (cornstarch). Cut out a rough leaf shape about 7.5cm (3in) long and 4cm (1½ in) wide. Using the wide base of a writing tube dipped in cornflour, cut out semi-circles from around the shape to create holly leaves.

2 Lightly mark veins with the back of a knife. Transfer to a sheet of crumpled foil and leave for at least 24 hours.

Tip

Secure the holly leaves to the cake with a dot of royal icing, propping them up with balls of foil or absorbent kitchen paper until set in position. Add tiny balls of red icing for berries.

Painting sugarpaste

This is best done when the sugarpaste has hardened as you can gently rest your hand against the cake without denting the surface. Freehand painting can be applied directly to the cake. Simpler designs can be made by impressing festive shapes into soft sugarpaste, then filling in with colour once the icing has hardened. Use a size of brush appropriate to the area to be covered.

Impress the soft sugarpaste with shapes. Leave to harden before filling the outline with colour.

1 Dilute the chosen food colouring with clear alcohol (gin or vodka) to give the required density. (Test on a little spare sugarpaste or white paper first.)

2 Use light brush strokes to cover the area.

Making bows

Pretty bows make perfect decorations on Christmas cakes, whether used large or small.

1 Thinly roll the chosen colour on a surface dusted with cornflour (cornstarch). Cut out one long strip, then cut the strip into two rectangles. Dampen the ends, then fold the rectangles over to form loops. Position on the cake, leaving a small gap between the loops and tucking rolls of absorbent kitchen paper inside the loops to hold them in shape until they are set.

2 Cut more long strips of the same thickness for bow ends. Finish the ends that will trail neatly with a knife. Pinch the other ends together and secure between the loops. Cut a square of sugarpaste doming it slightly in the centre. Secure over the centre of the bow to hide all the ends. Remove the absorbent kitchen paper once the bow has hardened.

3 If liked, the bows can be further decorated by painting the edges with gold or silver, or painting random dots of contrasting colour.

Tip

If doing a lot of decorative sugarpaste work, cut a 12cm (5in) square of muslin (cheesecloth) and spoon a little cornflour (cornstarch) into the centre. Bring the edges over the cornflour and tie with an elastic band or string. 'Pat' the cornflour onto the surface when rolling the sugarpaste to give an even and economical dusting.

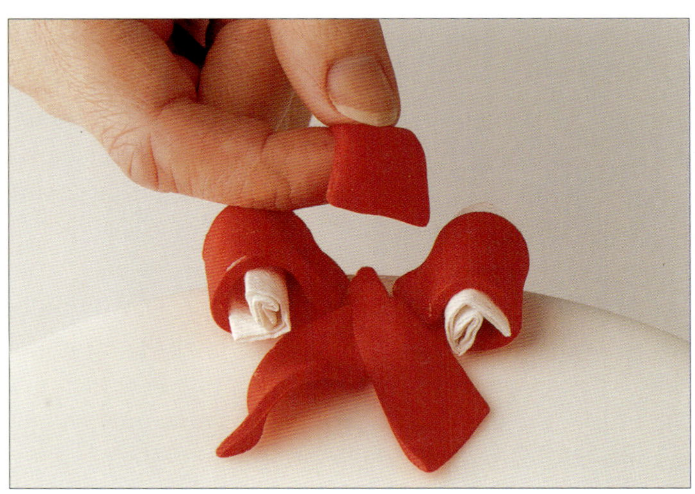

Tuck pieces of absorbent kitchen paper into the loops of the bow until hardened.

Chocolate Box

Covered with star-embossed sugarpaste and finished with trailing curling ribbons and chocolate truffles, this effective cake combines simplicity with speed.

Cake and decoration
two 15cm (6in) square rich or light fruit cakes
4 tablespoons apricot glaze
1kg (2lb) marzipan (almond paste)
1kg (2lb) sugarpaste
icing (confectioner's) sugar and cornflour (cornstarch), for dusting
burgundy food colouring
2m (2¼ yd) green ribbon, 12mm–2cm (½–¾in) wide (alternatively, use two or three contrasting ribbons)
60g (2oz/⅓ cup) icing (confectioner's) sugar
gold-coloured foil
about 500g (1lb) selection of chocolate truffles
1m (1⅛yd) ribbon for board edge

Equipment
20cm (8in) square gold cakeboard
small, medium and large star cutters
paper piping bag

TIP

The gold foil can be saved from bars of dark chocolate.

1 Trim any excessive domes from the surfaces of the cakes. Brush one cake top with apricot glaze and invert the other cake onto it. Fill any gaps left around the edges with pieces of marzipan (almond paste). Place the cake on the board and brush with the remaining apricot glaze.

Secure the ribbon loops to the top edge of the cake, then stick foil over the ends.

2 Roll out the marzipan and use to cover the cake, one side at a time. Colour the sugarpaste burgundy. Roll out a little and use to cover the top of the cake, trimming off the excess around the edges. Roll out the remaining sugarpaste and use to cover the sides. If preferred, cover one side at a time and smooth out the joins using hands dusted with cornflour (cornstarch).

3 Dip the cutters in a little cornflour, then impress them gently into the sides of the cake, spacing the stars randomly and overlapping some.

4 Cut the ribbon into varying lengths between 20cm (8in) and 30cm (12in). Mix the icing (confectioner's) sugar with a little water to make a fairly thin paste. Place in the piping bag and snip off the tip.

5 Use the icing in the bag to secure the ribbon lengths around the top edges of the cake, so that the loops or ends trail down the sides. Tear the gold-coloured foil into pieces and secure over the ribbon ends to resemble opened wrappings.

6 Arrange the chocolates over the top of the cake, piling them up in the centre. Secure the ribbon around the edges of the board.

CAROL SINGERS

The appeal of this cake lies in its strong Christmassy colours and simple details. The basic colours can, however, be easily adjusted to suit personal taste.

CAKE AND DECORATION
23cm (9in) round rich or light fruit cake
3 tablespoons apricot glaze
1kg (2lb) marzipan (almond paste)
icing (confectioner's) sugar and cornflour (cornstarch), for dusting
2kg (4lb) sugarpaste
red, dark green, light green, yellow, blue and black food colourings

EQUIPMENT
30cm (12in) round silver cakeboard
medium Christmas tree cutter
cocktail sticks (toothpicks)
fine paintbrush

1 Brush the cake with apricot glaze and cover with marzipan (almond paste). Place on the cakeboard. Colour 1.25kg (2 ½ lb) of the sugarpaste red and use to cover the cake.

Place a 12.5cm (5in) diameter bowl or saucer on the centre of the cake. Cut around it and then lift out the red sugarpaste from the centre. Re-roll the red trimmings and use to cover the cakeboard. Reserve the trimmings for the figures.

2 Thickly roll 180g (6oz) of the white sugarpaste and cut out a 12.5cm (5in) round using the bowl or saucer. Lay the white sugarpaste in the centre of the cake, then smooth out gently with the palms of the hands. Reserve the trimmings.

3 Colour the remaining sugarpaste, 180g (6oz) dark green, 125g (4oz) light green, 60g (2oz) yellow, 60g (2oz) blue, 30g (1oz) pale pink (using a dash of red colouring), and colour the remainder black.

4 Thinly roll half the dark green sugarpaste and cut out a 38x5cm (15x2in) rectangle. Thinly roll half the light green sugarpaste and cut out several Christmas trees using the cutter. Lay the trees over the dark green strip, then gently roll with the rolling pin so that the trees are secured to the sugarpaste. Trim the edges of the strip. Lightly moisten one side of the

sugarpaste along the edge. Repeat on the other scarf end.

6 To make a character, shape a small pair of boots from black sugarpaste. Mould a rounded cone shape for the body and mark a line down the front. Position the body over the boots and secure together by pressing a cocktail stick (toothpick) right through to the base of the boots so that the figure stands upright. Add moulded arms, gloves and scarf. Roll a ball of sugarpaste and position for the head, adding a tiny ball for the nose. Shape a hat and gently press into position.

cake and wrap the rectangle around it, pinching the ends together around the front to create a 'tie' in the scarf. Shape and secure another rectangle around the other side of the cake. Shape two smaller scarf rectangles and secure to the front of the cake for the scarf ends.

5 Roll more light green sugarpaste under the palms of the hands to 7.5cm (3in) lengths. Bend the lengths and make knife-marks to resemble threads of wool. Secure to one scarf end and finish with flattened balls of

Assemble the boots and body of each character first, then add the other components.

7 Shape the other figures in the same way, varying their clothes and colours. Position them on the cake. Dilute a little red and brown food colouring with clear alcohol (gin or vodka) and use to paint the faces. Press the figures into the cake, then sprinkle lightly with icing (confectioner's) sugar to simulate snow.

FATHER CHRISTMAS IN BED

This jolly cake provides a golden opportunity to play at modelling and painting. Older children can also have fun with the small decorative features.

CAKE AND DECORATION

20cm (8in) square rich or light fruit cake
2kg (4lb) sugarpaste
icing (confectioner's) sugar and cornflour (cornstarch), for dusting
light and dark green, red, brown, yellow, blue and black food colourings
3 tablespoons apricot glaze
750g (1½lb) marzipan (almond paste)
1.2m (1⅓yd) ribbon for board edge

EQUIPMENT

36cm (14in) round silver cakeboard
small piece of foam sponge
greaseproof paper (parchment)
large paintbrush
black icing pen

1 Cut off 4cm (1½in) from one side of the cake to give the bed shape. Lightly dampen the cakeboard. Thinly roll 375g (12oz) of the sugarpaste and use to cover the board. Trim off the excess sugarpaste around the edge of the board. Mix together a little of the light green and dark green colourings and dilute with clear alcohol (gin or vodka). Dip the piece of sponge in the colour, then use to stipple the surface of the cake lightly. (Practise on a little white paper or spare white icing first.)

2 Brush the cake with apricot glaze. Reserve 180g (6oz) of the marzipan (almond paste). Roll out the remainder and use to cover the cake. Use half the remaining marzipan to shape a pillow, pressing it down in the centre. Roll the remainder into strips and lay over the bed to create folds. Position the cake on the cakeboard. Colour 500g (1lb) of the sugarpaste light green, 375g (12oz) red, 60g (2oz) pink (using a dash of the red colouring), 60g (2oz) black, 125g (4oz) blue and 250g (8oz) a soft brown, using a mixture of brown and yellow colourings. Leave the remainder white.

3 Trace the 'Father Christmas in bed' template on page 150 onto greaseproof paper (parchment) and cut it out. Roll out the soft brown sugarpaste. Lay the template over the sugarpaste and cut around it. Carefully transfer to a piece of greaseproof paper. Mark the decorative edges with the tail-end of a paintbrush. Leave for 48 hours to harden.

4 Roll out the light green sugarpaste to a 27cm (10½ in) square. Take small balls of white sugarpaste and press them lightly into the green. Dust a rolling pin with cornflour (cornstarch) and roll it gently over the sugarpaste so that the white sugarpaste forms dots over the green. Carefully, lift the sugarpaste over the cake, so that it just covers the pillow area at the head-end of the bed and falls down the sides of the cake.

5 Colour a little white sugarpaste dark green and cut out small holly leaves (see pages 120–121). Dampen the underside of the leaves and secure to the bedhead. Decorate with small ribbons of blue sugarpaste and tiny red berries. Secure small pieces of white sugarpaste to the marzipan at the top end of the bed. Lightly dampen, then press the bedhead gently into position.

6 Shape a ball of pink sugarpaste for the head. Add a small nose, then chubby cheeks and closed eyelids. Secure a small smiling mouth, made from red sugarpaste. Shape the remaining pink sugarpaste into hands and feet.

7 Position a large ball of white sugarpaste on the bed for Father Christmas's body. Shape and position chubby arms and legs from red sugarpaste. You will need about 60g

10 Position all the prepared accessories. Roll a long thin strip of white sugarpaste and lay loosely over the sack. Using the icing pen, write a ticked list on the sugarpaste and outline Father Christmas's eyes. Dilute a little red food colouring with clear alcohol (gin or vokda) and add a blush to his cheeks, hands and feet. Use a little black food colouring diluted with clear alcohol to make 'coal' marks on his knees and arms. Secure the ribbon around the edge of the board.

(2oz) for each leg and 30g (1oz) for each arm. Position the head, hands and feet. Thinly roll out more red sugarpaste and cut out a jacket, first positioning the strip below the waist and then two sections above, cutting and trimming to fit.

8 Roll and secure a black belt and buttons. From the remaining sugarpaste, shape a selection of items such as slippers, hat, Christmas cards, empty sack, glass of beer, snack, pencil and books. For the books, wrap coloured sugarpaste around rectangles of white.

9 For Father Christmas's hair, thinly roll a little white sugarpaste and cut into pieces. Lightly dampen the head, then position the hair in sections. Finish with a small beard and moustache.

WINTER WONDERLAND

This beautiful cake, depicting a winter snow scene, takes a little more time to make than most, but the results are well worth the time and effort involved.

CAKE AND DECORATION
double quantity of 18cm (7in) round rich or light fruit cake mixture
4 tablespoons apricot glaze
1kg (2lb) marzipan (almond paste)
1.5kg (3lb) sugarpaste
icing (confectioner's) sugar and cornflour (cornstarch), for dusting
double quantity royal icing
blue and pearlized or white dusting powder (petal dust/blossom tint)

EQUIPMENT
two 15cm (6in) round cake tins
33cm (13in) petal or round silver cakeboard
non-stick paper
paper piping bags
fine writing tube (tip)
wooden cocktail sticks (toothpicks)
large soft paintbrush

1 Line the round cake tins (see page 116). Divide the cake mixture between the tins and bake for the time stated in the quantities chart (see page 115). Leave to cool in the tins. (If you only have one 18cm (7in) tin, bake one cake at a time.)

2 Level off the domes on top of the cakes if excessive. Brush the cakes with apricot glaze, then position one cake over the other, filling in the gaps left around the middle with marzipan (almond paste). Place the cake in the centre of the board. Use three-quarters of the marzipan to cover the sides of the cake. Use the remainder to cover the top.

3 Roll out 1kg (2lb) of the sugarpaste on a surface dusted with icing (confectioner's) sugar to a 38cm (15in) round. Lay over the top of the cake and ease around the sides. Cut off any excess bulk of sugarpaste around the sides, then smooth the sugarpaste with the palms of the hands to eliminate the creases. Trim off the excess around the base.

4 Position small mounds of the remaining sugarpaste on the board around the cake, varying them in height and diameter. Roll out half the remaining sugarpaste to a long curved strip. Trim the inner edge of the strip. Dampen the base of the cake around the mounds, then lay the strip in position so that the trimmed edge rests against the sides of the cake. Cover the other half of the board in the same way, smoothing out the joins and trimming off excess around the edge.

5 To make the trees, trace five of each tree template (see page 150) onto non-stick paper. Beat some of the royal icing, adding a little water or lemon juice so that it just holds it shape. Place in a piping bag fitted with the writing tube (tip). Lay a large sheet of non-stick paper over the large template and pipe over the outline. Move the templates under the paper and trace 35 more trees. Use the same technique for the other trees, making about 60 of the medium size and 40 of the small.

6 Thin more of the royal icing with water until the surface is smooth and level when left to settle for several seconds. Place in a piping bag and snip of the merest tip. Pipe the icing into the tree outlines, easing the icing into the corners with a cocktail stick (toothpick). Leave to set for 48 hours.

7 Mix together a little blue and pearlized or white dusting powder (petal dust/blossom tint). Using the large soft brush, gently dust the sides of the cake, making the colour slightly more dense near the base. (Practise on a little spare icing first to check that the blue is not too deep.)

8 Pipe small dots of royal icing over the top and sides of the cake to resemble snow, making the dots more dense near the base of the cake. Carefully peel the paper lining away from the icing tree shapes. To assemble the trees, pipe a line of icing along the straight edge of a large tree shape. Gently secure the shape to the cake, letting the shaped edge stand slightly away from the cake. Position another tree section against the cake so that the straight edges almost meet. Build up the tree with three more sections. Repeat at intervals around the cake using large and medium sections.

9 For the trees that stand away from the cake, pipe a dot of royal icing where the tree is to stand. Secure two tree sections together and position on the icing. Gradually build up the tree with more sections. (You will need six to seven for each tree.) Continue adding trees to the cake, arranging some in clusters. Use a medium-size tree to decorate the top of the cake. If any of the trees will not stand unsupported, prop them up with a crumpled piece of absorbent kitchen paper until set. Once set in position, dust the trees with a little sifted icing sugar to simulate snow.

Christmas Storybooks

Christmas story characters, like Father Christmas's elves and chubby snowmen, all come together on this jolly cake. It is a cake for enthusiasts, as shaping both the books and the characters takes a little time.

Cake and decoration

25cm (10in) square rich or light fruit cake
6 tablespoons apricot glaze
1.5kg (3lb) marzipan (almond paste)
icing (confectioner's) sugar and cornflour (cornstarch), for dusting
2.5kg (5lb) sugarpaste
yellow, black, orange, red, green, brown and black food colourings
1 quantity royal icing
gold dusting powder (petal dust/ blossom tint)
clear alcohol (gin or vodka)
small piece of rice paper
white edible glitter
1.5m (1⅔yd) ribbon for board edge

Equipment

30cm (12in) square silver cakeboard
12.5cm (5in) square silver cake card
large writing tube (tip)
paper piping bag
fine paintbrush

1 Cut any dome off the top of the cake so that it is completely flat. Using a large serrated knife, carefully cut the cake in half horizontally using a sawing action to make two thin slabs of cake. Cut a 2.5cm (1in) slice off one side of one slab. (The large rectangle forms the largest book.) Cut a third off the other slab and halve this widthways. (This will form the

opened book.) Halve the remaining rectangle of this slab to shape the middle two books.

2 Trim the edges of one long side from the three largest cakes to shape the spine. Place the largest cake on the board at an angle and brush with apricot glaze. Thinly roll some marzipan (almond paste). Cut strips to cover the straight sides of the cake, then cover the top and spine side with another piece.

3 Colour the sugarpaste as follows: 500g (1lb) yellow, 375g (12oz) black, 375g (12oz) orange, 375g (12oz) red, 60g (2oz) green and 60g (2oz) pale pink (using a little red food colouring). Leave the remaining 750g (1½ lb) white. Use about half the red sugarpaste to cover the cakeboard, trimming off the excess around the edge.

4 Thinly roll a little white sugarpaste and use to cover three sides of the cake. Using the blade of a long knife, gently impress the 'pages'. Thinly roll a long strip of yellow sugarpaste and cut out a long thin strip.

Secure a strip around the base of the white-iced sides, mitring the corners to neaten.

5 Roll out more yellow sugarpaste to a rectangle measuring the width of the book, including the spine, and the depth. Carefully lay the sugarpaste over the cake so that it only just comes over the white sides, and fits around the spine. If the sugarpaste has stretched a little while lifting, ease it to fit and if necessary, trim off the excess with a sharp knife.

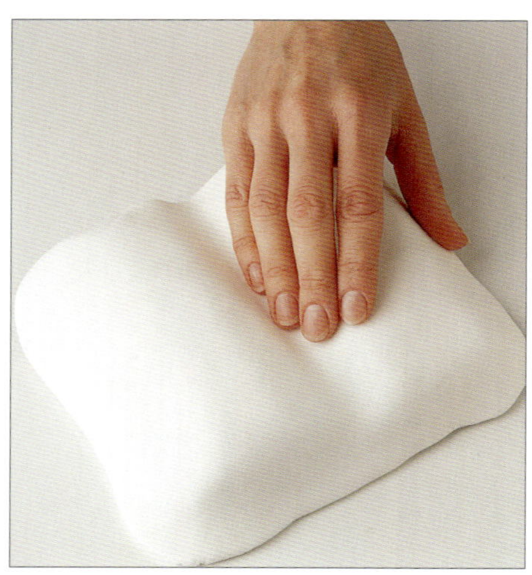

TIP

If preferred, paint some simplified sheet music onto the open book, or paint a simple Christmas poem or rhyme. This is best done with an icing pen once the sugarpaste has hardened.

6 Position another cake over the first, changing the angle. Glaze, cover with marzipan and white sugarpaste as before, then use black sugarpaste for the cover. Assemble the third cake, using orange sugarpaste for the cover. For the open book, lay the shaped cake on the cake card and cover with marzipan. Thinly roll out more white sugarpaste and lay over the cake, easing around the sides to fit.

7 Press the sugarpaste into the centre, then gently press with the back of a knife to give a deep groove. Impress more page markings with a knife. Place the opened book cake in position at a different angle and finish the edges with a band of black sugarpaste. Using diluted food colouring, paint decorative designs onto the pages of the open book.

8 Place the royal icing in the piping bag fitted with the writing tube (tip). Use to pipe decorative borders on the

Pinch the sugarpaste to make the hat fall over the elf's face.

covers. Leave the piped icing to harden for several hours. Mix a little dusting powder (petal dust/blossom tin) with clear alcohol (gin or vodka) until the consistency of thin paint. Use to paint the borders.

9 To make an elf, mould red, green, pink and brown sugarpaste into the shapes shown in the photograph, assembling them on the cake as they are moulded, stretching and bending the limbs. Arrange the hat so that it falls down over the elf's face.

10 To shape the snowman, take 60g (2oz) white sugarpaste. From this mould a small head. Use the remainder to mould and cut a body. Secure to the cake, bending one leg up on a book and the other on the board. Add a small crumpled hat, buttons, eyes, mouth and carrot nose.

11 Assemble Father Christmas, starting with the boots, then adding trousers, tunic, head, arms and hat. Use the royal icing in the piping bag to pipe wiggly lines of hair, moustache, cuffs and bobble on the hat.

12 Shape a simple angel using a cone-shaped base. Add more piped royal icing for the angel's curly hair. For the wings, trace and cut out the template on page 150, and secure to the back of the body. Paint the piped icing with gold colouring.

First, roll a ball for the snowman's head, then mould and cut the body shape as shown.

13 Using the remaining sugarpaste, shape and secure more Christmas characters such as Scrooge, choirboys or carol singers. Dilute a little brown food colouring with clear alcohol (gin or vodka) and use to paint features on the characters. Scatter the cake with the edible glitter. Secure ribbon around the edge of the board.

WHITE IVY CAKE

Generously 'embroidered' with a pretty selection of leaves and trimmed with pearls, this festive cake is both classic and stylish.

CAKE AND DECORATION

25x20cm (10x8in) oval rich or light fruit cake, made using mixture for a 23cm (9in) round tin
3 tablespoons apricot glaze
1kg (2lb) marzipan (almond paste)
1.5kg (3lb) sugarpaste
icing (confectioner's) sugar and cornflour (cornstarch) for dusting
1 quantity royal icing
45cm (18in) pearlized beading for top of cake
1m (1⅛yd) pearlized beading for base of cake
pearlized white dusting powder (petal dust/blossom tint)
clear alcohol (gin or vodka)
white candles
1m (1⅛yd) ribbon for board edge

EQUIPMENT

30x25cm (12x10in) oval silver cakeboard
greaseproof paper (parchment)
dressmaker's pins
paper piping bags
fine writing tube (tip)
small, medium and large ivy leaf cutters
medium and large holly cutters
leaf veiner
fine paintbrush

1 Brush the cake with apricot glaze and cover with marzipan (almond paste). Place on the cakeboard. Reserve 500g (1lb) of the sugarpaste. Use the remainder to cover the cake. Use a little more sugarpaste to cover the edge of the cakeboard.

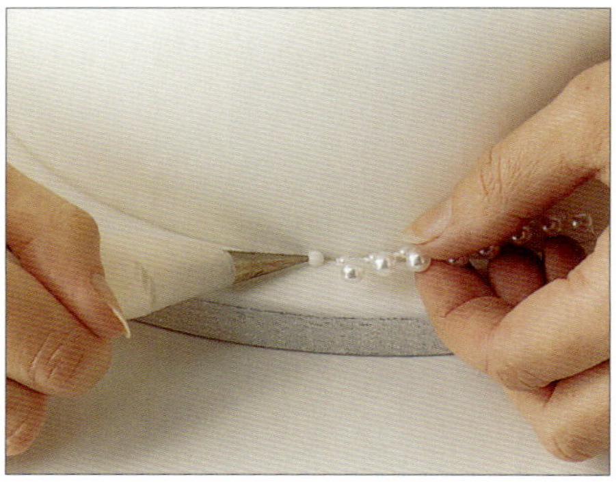

2 Draw an oval template measuring 15x10cm (6x4in) onto a piece of greaseproof paper (parchment) and cut it out. Lay it on the centre of the cake and mark the outline with a pin. Beat the royal icing, adding a little water or lemon juice until it is softly peaking. Place in the piping bag fitted with the writing tube (tip). Trim the beading for the top of the cake so that it fits neatly over the marked line. Press it gently down, securing the ends with a dot of icing. Arrange the beading around the cake base, securing the ends as above.

3 Roll out a little of the sugarpaste and cut out ivy and holly leaves in various sizes. Mark each with a veiner or knife, then secure to the cake, bunching two or three holly leaves together and graduating the strings of ivy leaves from small to large.

4 Pipe a fine outline around all the leaves, then add decorative loops and trails of royal icing around the ivy leaves, particularly where there are large gaps between them.

5 Roll small balls of sugarpaste to represent holly berries and secure with a little royal icing to the holly leaves. Mix a little of the dusting powder (petal dust/blossom tint) with enough clear alcohol (gin or vodka) to give the consistency of thin paint. Use to paint over the holly berries. Gently press the white candles into the top of the cake. Secure the ribbon around the edge of the board.

TIP

If you do not have an oval cake tin, and cannot hire one from a cake-decorating shop, this cake can be made equally successfully using a 23cm (9in) round tin. Use a 12.5cm (5in) circle to mark the position for the beading on the top of the cake.

Christmas Rose Cake

A ring of Christmas roses and a rich collar of festive ribbon transform a simple royal-iced cake into something really special.

CAKE AND DECORATION
20cm (8in) round rich or light fruit cake
3 tablespoons apricot glaze
1kg (2lb) marzipan (almond paste)
125g (4oz) sugarpaste
optional triple quantity royal icing
60g (2oz) bought petal paste
yellow dusting power (petal dust/blossom tint)
white stamens
0.75m (28in) firm gold ribbon, about 5cm (2in) wide
2m (2¼yd) fine green or red wired ribbon
1m (1⅛yd) fine ribbon for board edge

EQUIPMENT
28cm (11in) round gold cakeboard
palette knife
foil
medium rose petal cutter
cocktail sticks (toothpicks)
piece of foam sponge
soft paintbrush
paper piping bag

1 Brush the cake with apricot glaze and cover with marzipan (almond paste). Place on the cakeboard. Cover the edges of the board with the sugarpaste if liked. Reserve 4 tablespoons of the royal icing. Spread the remainder over the top and sides of the cake until covered in one even layer. Work the palette knife around the sides of the cake, then over the top to neaten. Leave to set.

2 To make the Christmas roses, roll some strips of foil, then shape into rounds about 5cm (2in) in diameter. Place on a sheet of greaseproof paper (parchment). You will need 11 altogether, allowing one spare. Take a little petal paste and roll as thinly as possible. Cut out five petals with the cutter. Roll a cocktail stick (toothpick) over the edges of the petal to give a delicate, lightly curled edge. Press each petal onto a piece of sponge to cup it lightly.

3 Lightly dampen one side of each of the five petals. Arrange the petals, slightly overlapping, inside a foil ring so that the rose is supported by the foil. Make the nine remaining roses in the same way and leave to harden for 24 hours.

4 Using the soft paintbrush, lightly colour the centre of each rose with dusting powder (petal dust/blossom tint). Place the reserved royal icing in the piping bag and snip off the tip. Pipe a dot of icing into the centre of a rose. Cut about a dozen stamens down to 12mm (½in) depth and press several at a time into the royal icing. Finish the remainder in the same way.

5 Secure the roses in a ring around the edge of the cake with a dot of royal icing. Tie the firm gold ribbon around the cake and secure with a dot of icing. Loosely pleat the wired ribbon concertina-fashion between the fingers and thumbs. Secure over the gold ribbon around the top edge of the board.

TIP

If more convenient, sugarpaste can be used instead of petal paste to make the roses. However, the results will not be as delicate.

Christmas Nativity

The design of this cake is effective in its simplicity. Both the stable and figures are exceptionally easy to shape.

Cake and Decoration

25cm (10in) square rich or light fruit cake
4 tablespoons apricot glaze
1.25kg (2½ lb) marzipan (almond paste)
icing (confectioner's) sugar and cornflour (cornstarch), for dusting
2.5kg (5lb) sugarpaste
brown, purple, red, black, dark and light blue, green and yellow food colourings
125g (4oz/⅔ cup) icing (confectioner's) sugar
1.5m (1⅔ yd) cream cord
2m (2¼ yd) ribbon for board edge

Equipment

30cm (12in) square silver cakeboard
non-stick paper
small star cutter
4 and 5 cm (1½ and 2in) plain pastry cutters
cocktail stick (toothpick)
paper piping bag
fine paintbrush

1 Brush the cake with apricot glaze and cover with marzipan (almond paste). Place on the cakeboard. Colour 250g (8oz) of the sugarpaste dark brown. Trace and cut out the stable templates on page 151 onto non-stick or greaseproof paper. Thinly roll the brown sugarpaste and lay on a sheet of non-stick paper. Lay the templates over the sugarpaste and cut around them, then carefully peel away the excess sugarpaste. (You will need two roof templates and two side templates.) Roll out and cut a small star from white sugarpaste. Leave the star and stable components to harden for 48 hours.

2 Colour the remaining sugarpaste as follows: 90g (3oz) purple, 90g (3oz) red, 90g (3oz) pale pink (using a dash of red colouring), 90g (3oz) grey (using a little black colouring), 60g (2oz) light blue and 30g (1oz) green. Leave 30g (1oz) white, then colour the remainder yellow.

3 Reserve 90g (3oz) of the yellow sugarpaste. Roll the remainder to a

thick sausage. Dot with 30g (1oz) of the brown icing. Fold the ends of the sugarpaste into the centre and roll again so that the yellow sugarpaste becomes marbled with the brown. Continue rolling and folding until the colours are fairly evenly distributed. Roll out the sugarpaste and use to cover the cake and board. Trim off the excess sugarpaste around the edges of the board.

The simple figures consist of cone-shaped bodies with balls for heads and hands and circular cloaks.

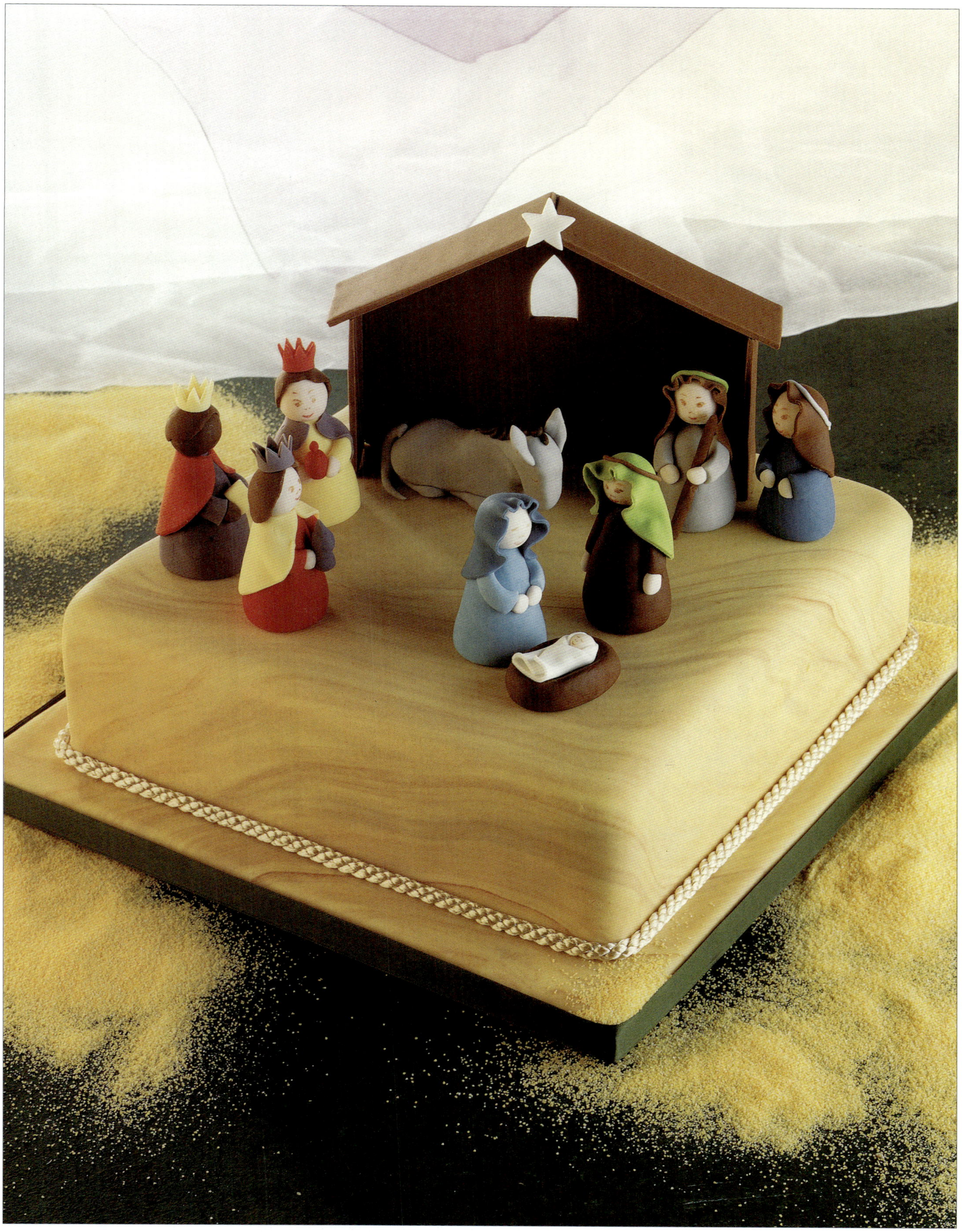

4 To shape a 'king', make a small piece of sugarpaste into a cone shape. Shape two curved sections for the arms and secure to the cone. Shape head and hands from pink sugarpaste. For the cloak, cut a 5cm (2in) circle of contrasting sugarpaste using the large cutter. Cut away an area for the neck, and position around the body. Shape a small circle of brown sugarpaste for the hair, then add the crown and gifts. Shape two more kings in the same way. Shape 'Mary' as above draping a 4cm ($1\frac{1}{2}$in) circle of dark blue sugarpaste over her head.

5 Shape the remaining characters in the same way, using a cocktail stick (toothpick) for the centre of the shepherd's crook. For Jesus in the manger, shape a simple base of brown sugarpaste. Roll a tiny ball of flesh-coloured sugarpaste for the head and lay it on a thinly rolled square of white sugarpaste. Wrap the white sugarpaste around the head and lay it on the base. For the donkey, shape the grey sugarpaste as shown above and assemble it so that the donkey is in a sitting position.

6 Mix the icing (confectioner's) sugar with a little water to make a paste. Colour it dark brown and place in a piping bag. Snip off the tip. Pipe a little icing down one side of the stable back. Secure one side-piece to the back and position on the cake. Position the other side-piece and then the roof sections in the same way. Pipe another line of icing around the base of the stable.

7 Use a little more icing to pipe the donkey's mane. Secure the star to the stable roof. Using a little brown colouring diluted with clear alcohol (gin or vodka), paint simple features onto the faces, then position the figures on the cake. Tie the cord around the cake and secure at the back with a little icing. Secure the ribbon around the edge of the board.

HOLLY GARLAND CAKE

Simple decorations such as holly leaves, candy canes, baubles and presents are cleverly combined on this cake for traditionalists who are looking for something a little different.

CAKE AND DECORATION
25cm (10in) round quantity rich or light fruit cake mixture, baked in a 25cm (10in) petal-shaped tin
4 tablespoons apricot glaze
1.25kg (2½lb) marzipan (almond paste)
icing (confectioner's) sugar and cornflour (cornstarch), for dusting
2kg (4lb) sugarpaste
red, dark green and blue food colourings
silver dusting powder (petal dust/blossom tint)
90g (3oz/½ cup) icing (confectioner's) sugar
1m (1⅛yd) fine cord

EQUIPMENT
33cm (12in) petal-shaped silver cakeboard
large and small holly cutter
crumpled foil
fine paintbrush
paper icing bag

1 Brush the cake with apricot glaze and cover with marzipan (almond paste), pressing it into the flutes of the petal shape. Trim off the excess. Cover the cake with 1.3kg (2¾lb) of the sugarpaste.

2 From the remaining sugarpaste colour 180g (6oz) red, 250g (8oz) green and 60g (2oz) blue, leaving the remainder white. Use the red sugarpaste to cover the cakeboard, trimming off the excess around the board edge. Reserve the trimmings.

To make the candy canes, roll strips of white and red sugarpaste together.

3 Thinly roll a little green sugarpaste and cut-out eight large holly leaves. Mark the central veins with a knife, then lay them over the crumpled foil to set in curved positions. To make the candy canes, roll a little white sugarpaste very thinly under the palms of the hands. Roll a little red sugarpaste to the same thickness. Twist the rolls together. Cut into 3cm (1¼in) lengths and bend over the tops. You will need about 12 altogether. Make four or five thicker, longer canes in the same way for the top of the cake.

4 From the blue sugarpaste shape 12 small cubes, about 6mm (¼in) in size. Roll out the red sugarpaste trimmings very thinly and use to shape ribbons for the larger parcels. From the remaining white sugarpaste roll 48 tiny balls and 10 larger balls, about 12mm (½in) in diameter. Leave all the decorations to harden for 24 hours.

5 Roll out some green sugarpaste under the palms of your hands to a sausage, a scant 12mm (½in) thick. Cut a section of the sugarpaste and secure around one petal of the cake, so that the end is 12mm (½in) from the top edge of the cake and the lowest part about 2cm (¾in) from the base. Secure with a dampened paintbrush. Repeat around all sections of the cake.

6 Roll out more green sugarpaste thinly and cut out holly leaves using the small cutter. Mark the central veins with a knife. Dampen the underside of the leaves, then secure them to the green ropes around the sides of the cake to make a garland.

7 Lightly brush the small and large baubles with silver dusting powder (petal dust/blossom tint). Mix the icing (confectioner's) sugar with a little water to make a fairly thin paste. Place in the paper piping bag and snip off the tip. Use to secure the small baubles, candy canes and parcels to the garlands around the sides.

8 Use the larger decorations to make an attractive arrangement on the top of the cake, first securing the leaves and parcels, propping them up on small balls of foil until set in position. Then arrange the candy canes and baubles. Arrange the cord around the base of the cake, securing with a little icing.

Dampen the backs of the holly leaves and secure, at an angle, across the green ropes.

JEWELLED BOXES

These pretty cakes, resembling little trinket boxes, make lovely presents for those who would have no need for a large cake. Choose your own colour scheme to suit the recipient – rich and bold or delicate and pretty.

CAKE AND DECORATION

18cm (7in) round quantity rich or light fruit cake mixture
4 tablespoons apricot glaze
1kg (2lb) marzipan (almond paste)
1.5kg (3lb) sugarpaste
icing (confectioner's) sugar and cornflour (cornstarch), for dusting
red, blue and green food colourings
piping jelly
1 quantity royal icing
gold dusting powder (petal dust/blossom tint)
clear alcohol (gin or vodka)

EQUIPMENT

6 empty, clean 440g (14oz) food cans with both ends removed
6 x 10cm (4in) round gold cake cards
paper piping bags
medium writing tube (tip)
fine paintbrush

1 Place the food cans on a baking sheet and line with greaseproof paper (parchment) as you would a round cake tin (see page 116). Divide the cake mixture evenly between the cans and bake for about 1 hour or until a skewer, inserted into the centres, comes out clean. Leave to cool in the cans.

2 Brush the cakes with apricot glaze. Roll out 250g (8oz) of the marzipan (almond paste) and use to cover the

tops of the cakes. Roll out the remaining marzipan and cut out six rectangles, each the circumference and depth of the cakes. Use to cover the sides of the cakes as shown above, then position them on the cake cards.

3 Divide 1kg (2lb) of the sugarpaste into six portions. Use a portion to cover each cake, trimming off excess icing around the bases. From the remaining sugarpaste, colour 250g (8oz) red, 125g (4oz) blue and 125g (4oz) green. Shape pea-sized balls of the colours into small teardrop shapes. Use to decorate the top and sides of the cake, pressing down gently and leaving small gaps between the decorations. Leave the top centre area of each cake clear to allow for the ribbons.

4 Place the royal icing in a piping bag fitted with the writing tube (tip). Use to pipe a border around each coloured shape. Leave for several hours or overnight to harden.

5 Mix a little gold dusting powder (petal dust/blossom tint) with clear alcohol (gin or vodka) until the consistency of thin paint. Using a fine paintbrush, carefully paint over the piped icing. Lightly beat the piping jelly, then paint it over the coloured icing to give a glazed appearance.

6 To make a bow, thinly roll some red sugarpaste and cut out long strips about 3cm (1¼ in) wide. Use to assemble the bows on the tops of the cakes (see page 121). Prop up the bows with small pieces of absorbent kitchen paper until they harden. To add a touch of glamour, paint thin lines of gold along the edges of the ribbons to finish.

TIP

There are many other simple ways to decorate small cakes prettily. The white sugarpaste can be impressed with small festive cutters and then painted. Alternatively, decorate the cakes with coloured cut-out shapes.

Cake Templates

The templates shown here are actual size, and can be reduced or enlarged on a photocopier.

FATHER CHRISTMAS IN BED

page 127

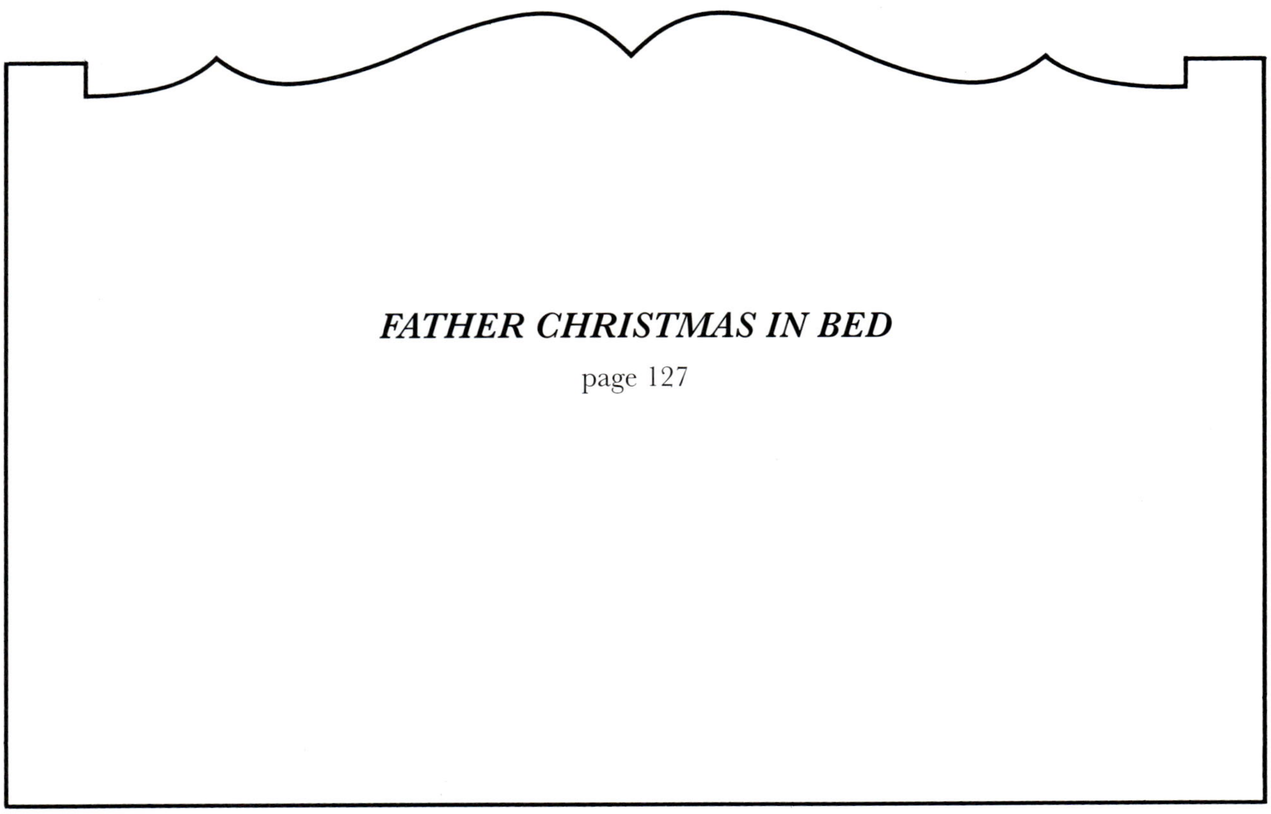

WINTER WONDERLAND

page 131

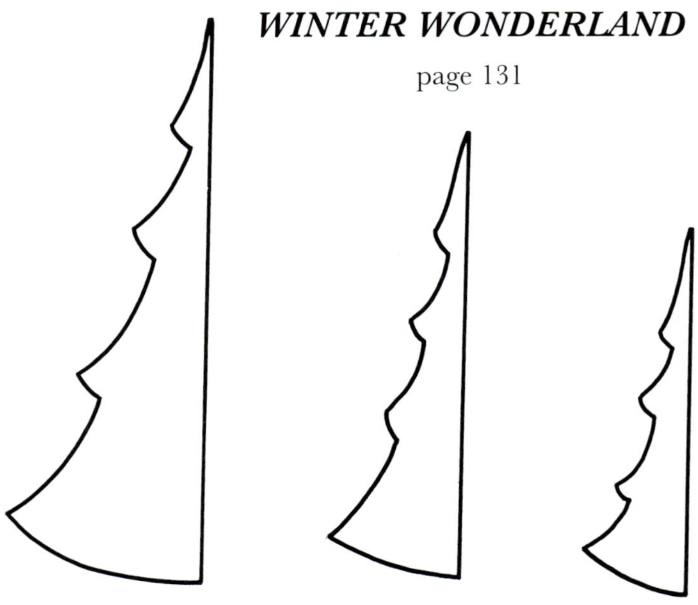

CHRISTMAS STORYBOOKS

page 134

ANGEL'S WING
(cut 2)

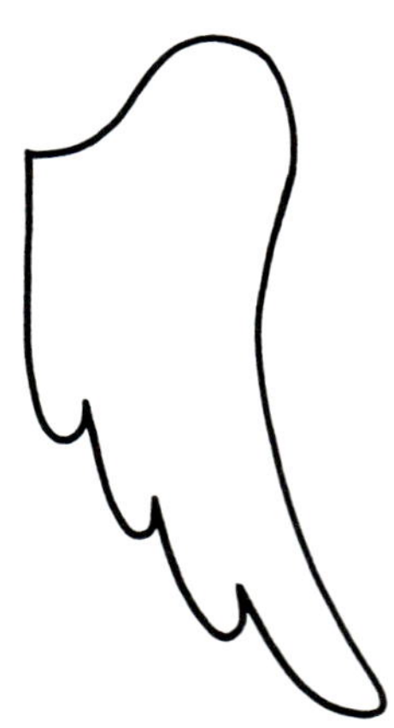

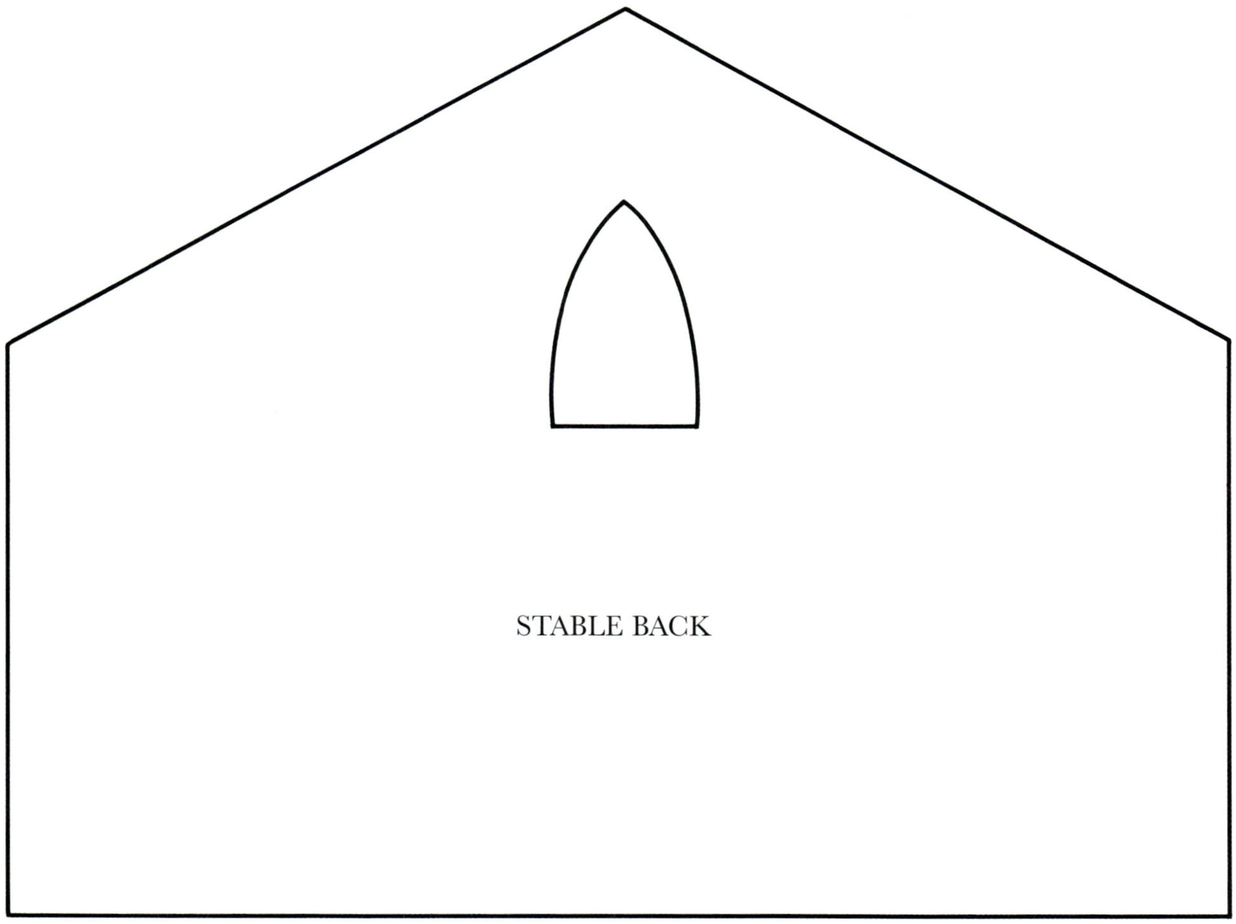

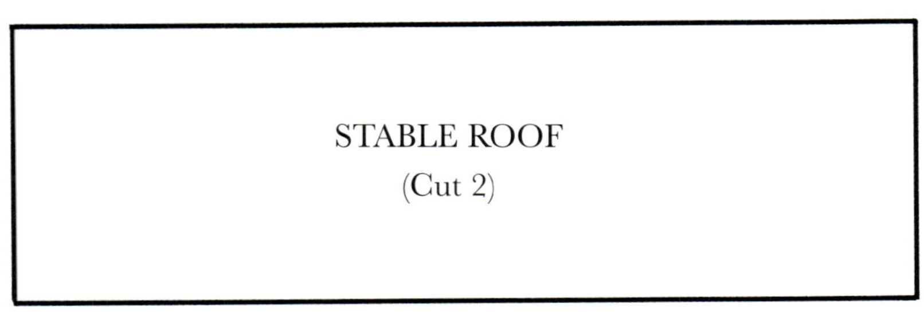

CHRISTMAS NATIVITY

page 142

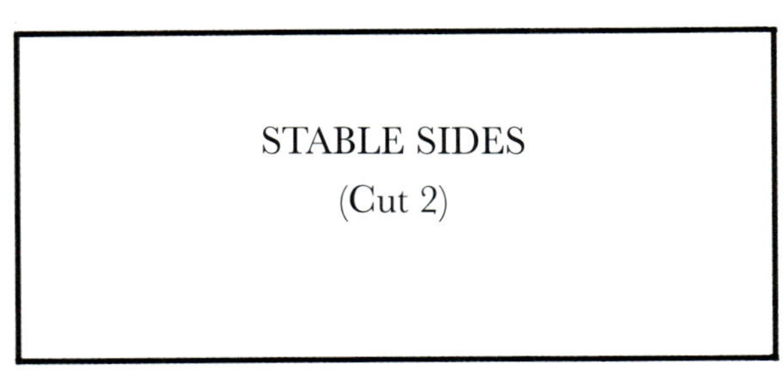

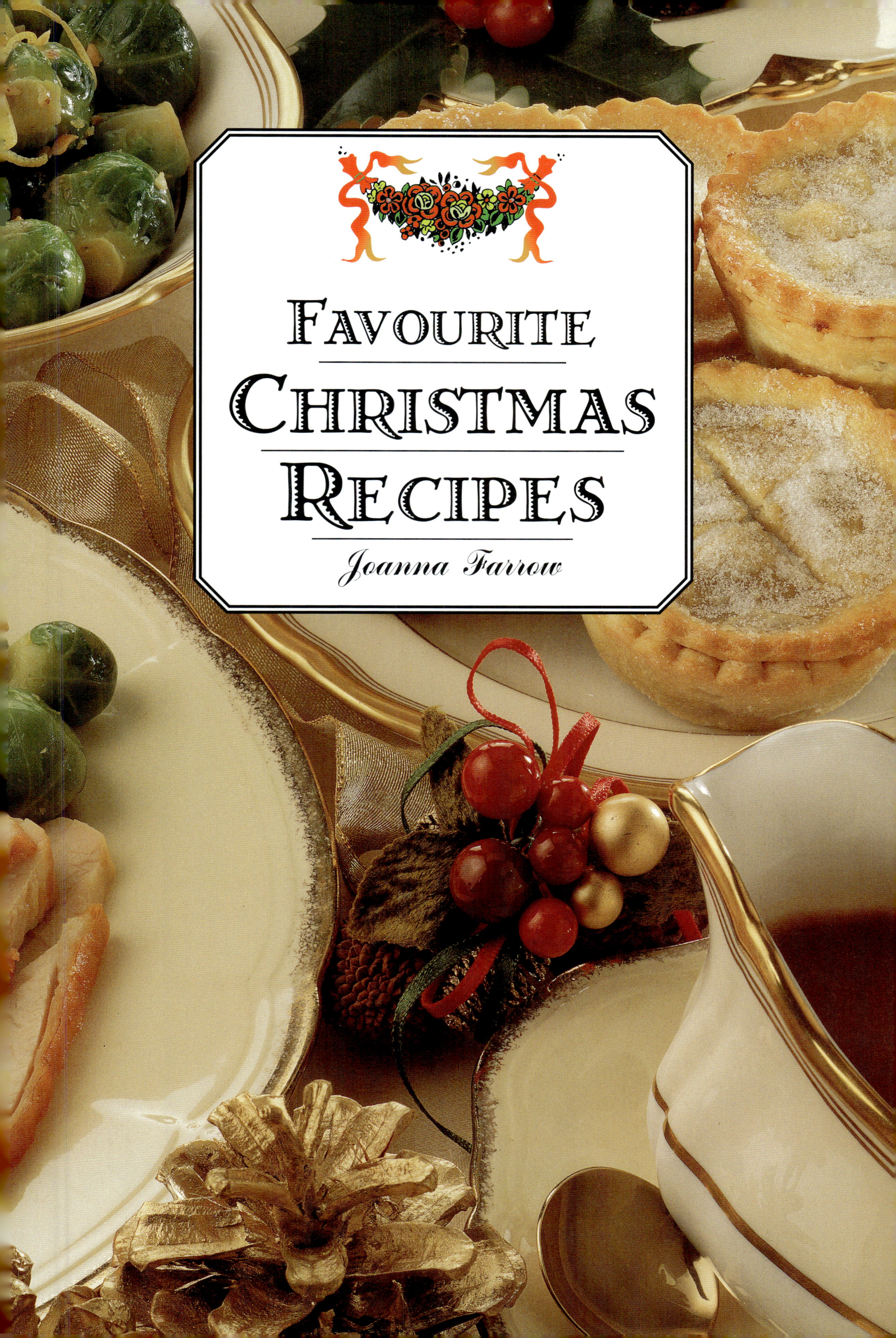

Favourite Christmas Recipes

Joanna Farrow

INTRODUCTION

Christmas is a wonderful time for indulging in all the foods we love, and possibly the one occasion when we splash out on special treats. However, while most of us can simply look forward to the oncoming feast, there's plenty of planning and preparation for the cook. This collection of classic and unusual recipes will make light work of the culinary arrangements for both beginners and experienced cooks.

Planning and cooking can start several weeks in advance to ease last-minute pressure. First make a list of the chosen dishes with any ingredients you will need to buy. Follow this by making the puddings, cakes and dishes for freezing.

To kick off Christmas dinner in style, serve a light starter, such as a smooth, creamy soup or pretty salad, that won't overload the cook or overfill the guests. Traditionalists can tuck into a perfectly roasted turkey with all the trimmings. For those who prefer something a little different, goose, duck and pheasant are increasingly popular alternatives. With these recipes and suggestions for accompaniments, even those tackling them for the first time can do so with confidence. If fish is a firm favourite, there are several recipes, from dishes for small gatherings to a spectacular salmon, and for vegetarians, an impressively festive pie. To complete the feast, there are rich puddings, iced desserts, sumptuous gâteaux and chocolates.

If you are planning a party over the holiday, follow the buffet ideas which focus mainly on salads or if you have friends dropping in for drinks, the savoury nibbles. There are recipes and menu ideas here to suit every taste and occasion.

Starters

Smoked Salmon with Dill Pancakes

SERVES 4

125g (4oz/1 cup) self-raising flour
pinch of salt
½ teaspoon caster (superfine) sugar
1 egg
1 tablespoon olive oil
150 ml (¼ pint/⅔ cup) milk
1 teaspoon wholegrain mustard
2 tablespoons chopped fresh dill
vegetable oil, for frying
250g (8oz) smoked salmon
4 tablespoons soured cream
paprika
lime wedges and dill sprigs, to garnish

1 Sift the flour and salt into a bowl. Stir in the sugar.
2 Beat the egg and mix with the olive oil, milk, mustard and dill. Pour into the flour and whisk, gradually incorporating the flour to make a smooth batter. Transfer to a jug.
3 Heat a little oil in a large frying pan. Pour in a little batter mixture to make a pancake about 6cm (2½ in) in diameter. Make several more.
4 Cook for 1–2 minutes until golden. Turn over and cook for a further 1–2 minutes. Keep warm while cooking the remaining batter.
5 Arrange the smoked salmon on one large or four individual plates. Add a spoonful of soured cream to each pancake and sprinkle with paprika. Serve garnished with lime wedges and dill sprigs.

Mushroom Salad with Garlic Crumbs

SERVES 6

1 small radicchio or red chicory
½ an iceberg lettuce
handful of chopped flat-leaved parsley
8 tablespoons olive oil
salt and pepper
250g (8oz) button mushrooms
250g (8oz) oyster mushrooms
250g (8oz) shiitake mushrooms
4 rashers of streaky bacon
2 slices day-old bread
3 garlic cloves, thinly sliced
grated rind of 1 lemon

1 Tear the salad leaves into small pieces and put in a bowl. Add the parsley, 2 tablespoons of the oil, salt and pepper and toss well together. Spoon onto plates.
2 Cut any large mushrooms in half. Remove the rind from the bacon and finely chop the flesh. Crumble the bread into small pieces.
3 Heat another 2 tablespoons of the oil in a large frying pan. Add the bacon, bread and garlic and fry for about 5 minutes, stirring, until golden. Remove from the pan.
4 Add the remaining oil to the pan with the mushrooms and lemon rind and fry for 3 minutes, stirring.
5 Spoon the mushrooms over the salad and sprinkle with the bacon mixture.

Watercress and Blue Brie Soup

SERVES 6

2 onions
1 large potato
2 tablespoons vegetable oil
600ml (1 pint/2½ cups) vegetable stock
150g (5oz) watercress
250g (8oz) blue brie cheese
salt and pepper
150ml (¼ pint/⅔ cup) double (heavy) cream
watercress, to garnish (optional)

1 Roughly chop the onions. Cut the potato into chunks. Heat the oil in a large pan. Add the onions and fry gently for 5 minutes. Stir in the potato, stock and 600ml (1 pint/ 2½ cups) water. Bring to the boil. Cover and simmer gently for 10 minutes.

2 Add the watercress and cook for 3 minutes, then remove from the heat. Cut 6 very thin slices from the firm end of the cheese and reserve. Roughly chop the remaining cheese and add to the soup. Blend in a food processor until smooth.

3 Return to the pan and season lightly with salt and pepper. Pour in half the cream.

4 Ladle into soup bowls and swirl in the remaining cream. Garnish with the reserved cheese, chopped, and watercress sprigs, if desired.

Seafood Rillettes

SERVES 4-6

1 spring onion (scallion)
180g (6oz/ 1½ cups) peeled prawns (shrimp)
150g (5oz) smoked trout
1 tablespoon chopped fresh tarragon
pepper
125g (4oz/½ cup) butter
tarragon sprigs, to garnish
soda bread or oatcakes, to serve

1 Roughly chop the spring onion (scallion), put in a food processor with the prawns (shrimp) and blend until finely chopped. Transfer to a bowl.

(Alternatively finely chop the onion and prawns by hand, put in a bowl and mash together.)

2 Flake the trout with a fork and add to the prawn mixture with the tarragon and pepper.

3 Melt the butter and stir about half into the fish mixture. Lightly pack into a 600ml (1 pint) pâté or soufflé dish. Cover with the remaining butter and chill for several hours.

4 Spoon scoops onto serving plates and garnish with tarragon. Serve with toasted soda bread or oatcakes.

COOK'S TIP

Fresh salmon can be used in place of the smoked trout.

Melon and Pawpaw Salad

SERVES 6

1 small charentais melon
small Ogen or honeydew melon
2 pawpaws
2 figs
1 piece of stem ginger, plus 4 teaspoons of the syrup
grated rind and juice of 1 lime
6 tablespoons fresh orange juice
mint leaves, to garnish

1 Cut the melons in half and remove the seeds with a teaspoon. Scoop out the flesh from both the melons using a melon baller.

2 Halve the pawpaw and remove the seeds. Cut away the skin and thinly slice the flesh. Cut each fig into six wedges.

3 Put the prepared melons, pawpaws and figs in a bowl. Very thinly slice the stem ginger and add to the bowl.

4 Mix together the lime rind and juice, ginger syrup and orange juice and pour over the salad. Toss together lightly.

5 Spoon into serving dishes and garnish with mint leaves.

COOK'S TIP

When scooping out the melon balls, save any juice and add it to the salad.

The Main Event

Perfect Gravy

SERVES 8

pan juices from cooked turkey
2 tablespoons plain (all-purpose) flour
600ml (1 pint/2½ cups) giblet stock (see last recipe, step 1)
150ml (¼ pint/⅔ cup) red wine
salt and pepper

1 Pour the turkey cooking juices from the foil into the roasting tin. Drain off all but about 1 tablespoon of the fat layer, leaving the juices.

2 Add the flour and cook stirring, for 2 minutes. Whisk in the stock, then add the red wine.

3 Bring to the boil and simmer gently for 3–4 minutes, until smooth. Season with salt and pepper.

Bread Sauce

SERVES 8

1 onion
8 whole cloves
900ml (1½ pints/3¾ cups) milk
3 bay leaves
180g (6oz/2½ cups) fresh breadcrumbs
60g (2oz/¾ cup) butter
salt and pepper
3 tablespoons double (heavy) cream

1 Skin the onion and stud with cloves. Put in a pan with milk and bay leaves. Bring to the boil, then remove from heat and leave for 30 minutes.

2 Remove the bay leaves and onion. Stir in the breadcrumbs and return to the heat. Simmer gently for 4–5 minutes, until the sauce thickens. Stir in the butter, salt and pepper.

3 Just before serving, reheat gently and stir in the cream.

Chestnut, Leek and Sage Stuffing

Enough to stuff a 5.5kg (12lb) turkey and make plenty of stuffing balls.

two 410g (13oz) cans peeled whole chestnuts
3 leeks
60g (2oz/¼ cup) butter
5 tablespoons chopped fresh sage or 4 teaspoons dried
grated rind of 1 lemon
125g (4oz/2 cups) fresh breadcrumbs
salt and pepper
1 egg

1 Finely chop the chestnuts in a food processor. (Alternatively, finely chop by hand.)

2 Finely chop the leeks. Melt the butter in a large pan. Add the leeks and fry for 3 minutes, stirring. Add the chestnuts, sage, lemon rind, breadcrumbs, salt and pepper.

3 Beat the egg, add and mix until thoroughly combined. Cover and chill until ready to use.

Traditional Roast Turkey

SERVES 8

5.5kg (12lb) oven-ready turkey, thoroughly thawed if frozen
1 onion
2 carrots
2 bay leaves
1 quantity stuffing (see page 168 or above)
180g (6oz/¾ cup) butter
salt and pepper
bacon kebabs (see page 168)
fresh herbs, to garnish

1 Remove the giblets from the turkey as soon as possible. Put in a pan with the onion, carrot, bay leaves and 600ml (1 pint / 2½ cups) water. Bring to the boil, then simmer for about 1 hour. Strain, cool and reserve.

2 Preheat the oven to 190°C (375°F)/ Gas 5). Spoon some stuffing into the neck end of the turkey. Form the remaining stuffing into small balls. Tuck the skin under the bird and truss it with the wings folded under the body and the legs tied together. Soften the butter and spread over the breast. Season with salt and pepper.

3 Line a large roasting tin with strong, wide foil. Place the turkey in the tin. Cover with the foil, tucking under the rim. Cook for 3¾–4 hours.

4 Uncover the turkey. If room, tuck the bacon kebabs and stuffing balls around the turkey. If not, cook in a separate dish. Cook for a further 30 minutes until brown.

5 Test to see if the turkey is cooked (see page 162). Lift the turkey from the roasting tin, tipping slightly to allow juices to run out. Place on a large warmed serving dish and cover with foil. Leave to stand for up to 30 minutes while preparing gravy (see left).

6 Garnish the turkey with the bacon kebabs, stuffing balls and herbs.

Thawing

Frozen turkeys must be completely thawed before cooking. Leave in the bag, opened, place on a large plate or tray to catch juices and thaw at room temperature for the time stated in the chart opposite. Remove the giblets as soon as they can be released and use for making stock. To see if the bird is thawed, check there are no ice crystals inside the body cavity. The legs should feel flexible, rather than rigid. Rinse the turkey, cover loosely and store in the refrigerator. Once thawed, the turkey should be cooked as soon as possible.

Stuffing

Only stuff the neck cavity of the turkey, being careful not to pack it too tightly. Fold over the neck skin, then truss the turkey with the wings folded under the body and the legs tied together. Any excess stuffing can be rolled into small balls and roasted around the turkey for the last 25–30 minutes of cooking time. Alternatively, put it into a separate dish and cook for 1 hour.

If liked, put 2–3 onions and a handful of herbs into the body cavity to give extra flavour.

Cooking

Once stuffed, weigh the turkey and calculate the cooking time, see the chart opposite. (You'll need to allow 30 minutes for the bird to rest before carving and serving.) Cover the breast with softened butter, then season with salt and pepper.

Line the roasting tin with foil, bringing the edges up around the rim. Place the turkey on the foil, then cover with another sheet of foil, tucking the edges under the rim. Roasting the turkey in a tent of foil helps keep the meat moist and prevents over–browning. Roast at 190°C (375°F/Gas 5) for the calculated cooking time. Fold back the foil about 30 minutes before the end of cooking time to brown the skin.

Testing

To test if the turkey is cooked, insert a skewer into the thickest part of the thigh. If the juices run clear, it is ready; if not, roast a little longer.

Resting

Transfer the turkey to a large warmed serving dish, cover with foil and leave to rest for about 30 minutes. This allows the flesh to firm up, making carving easier.

Leftovers

Once carved, leave the turkey until cold, then cover with foil and refrigerate for up to 2 days. Serve reheated leftovers piping hot.

If freezing leftovers, slice the meat from the bones and freeze in small quantities. Alternatively, cover with stock, gravy, tomato or white sauce. Reheat thoroughly and do not refreeze.

Making Stock

The turkey carcass and bones can be made into a delicious stock for flavouring soups and stews.

Put the bones in a large saucepan. Add 2 roughly chopped onions, carrots and celery sticks, a bouquet garni, bay leaves or thyme. Cover with cold water and bring to the boil. Reduce heat and simmer for about 1½ hours. Cool, strain and refrigerate for up to 2 days or freeze.

Carving

Turkey is easy to carve provided you have a large, sharp knife and fork to hold the bird steady on the dish. Loosen the legs from the body so that the breast can be reached easily. On large turkeys the leg meat can be sliced from the bone.

Turkey Timetable

Oven-ready weight	Thawing at room temperature	Cooking time at 190°C (375°F/Gas 5)	Servings (allowing for cold next day)
up to 2.5kg (5½ lb)	10–15 hours	1½–2 hours	3
2.5–3kg (5½–6½lb)	15–16 hours	2–2½ hours	4
3-3.1kg (6½–6¾lb)	16–17 hours	2½–3 hours	5
3.1–3.6kg (6¾–8lb)	17–18 hours	3–3¼ hours	6
3.6–5kg (8-11lb)	18–22 hours	3¼–3¾ hours	7
5–6kg (11–13lb)	22–25 hours	3¾–4 hours	8
6–6.8kg (13–15lb)	25–30 hours	4–4¼ hours	8–10
6.8–8.2kg (15–18lb)	30–35 hours	4¼–4½ hours	10–15
8.2–10kg (18–22lb)	35–40 hours	4½–5 hours	15–20

Christmas Countdown

Six to eight weeks ahead Make traditional Christmas pudding (if using).

One week before Christmas Calculate thawing time of turkey if using frozen. Make light Christmas pudding (if using) and mince pies.

23rd December Make chosen sauces to accompany turkey and Christmas pudding.

Christmas Eve Make starter from pages 158–159, if chosen. Prepare batter if using starter on page 156. Make stuffing, bacon kebabs and giblet stock for gravy. Prepare vegetables and refrigerate in plastic bags. Peel potatoes and cover with cold water. Lay table. Chill white wine.

Christmas Day Preparation and cooking times are for a 6kg (13lb) turkey. Adjust timetable for a smaller or larger bird. The following times plan for lunch at 2.00pm (or dinner at 8.00pm).

9.15am (3.15pm) Preheat the oven to 190°C (375°F/Gas 5). Stuff turkey and prepare for cooking.

9.45am (3.45pm) Put the turkey in the oven. Drain and blanch the potatoes, ready for roasting.

11.30am (5.30pm) Steam the pudding.

12.15pm (6.15pm) Put the potatoes in the oven to roast. Pour any cold sauces, butters and cream into serving containers. Put the mince pies on a baking sheet ready to reheat.

12.45pm (6.45pm) Unwrap the turkey. Cook the bacon kebabs and stuffing. Warm the plates and serving dishes. Open the red wine.

1.15pm (7.15pm) Prepare and take the cold starter to the table.

1.30pm (7.30pm) Test the turkey and keep covered with foil. Make the gravy and cook the vegetables. Reheat the bread sauce and soup, if serving. Cook the starter on page 156, if using.

2.00pm (8.00pm) Serve the starter. Turn off the pudding. Keep the vegetables warm. Reheat the mince pies.

Roast Potatoes with Garlic and Rosemary

SERVES 8

1.5kg (3lb) small baking potatoes
salt
3 garlic cloves
6 rosemary sprigs
6 tablespoons olive oil
coarse sea salt, to sprinkle
rosemary sprigs, to garnish

1 Preheat the oven to 190°C (375°F/Gas 5). Peel and halve the potatoes and put in a saucepan. Cover with water, add salt and bring to the boil. Reduce the heat and simmer for 2 minutes. Drain well.

2 Slice the garlic as thinly as possible. Chop the rosemary finely.

3 Make deep cuts in the potatoes, 6mm (¼in) apart. Tuck the garlic slices into some of the cuts.

4 Place the potatoes in a roasting tin and sprinkle with the chopped rosemary and oil. Bake for about 1¼ hours, turning occasionally, until crisp and golden brown.

5 Transfer to a warmed serving dish, sprinkle with coarse salt and garnish with rosemary sprigs.

COOK'S TIP

The potatoes are roasted at a lower temperature than usual as they are being cooked at the same time as the turkey. If roasting at a higher temperature, reduce the cooking time.

Sauteed Leeks and Carrots

SERVES 8

750g (1½lb) carrots
750g (1½lb) small leeks
salt and pepper
4 tablespoons olive oil
2 tablespoons sesame seeds

1 Peel the carrots and cut diagonally into 6mm (¼ in slices). Trim the leeks and cut diagonally into 12mm (½in) slices.

2 Cut the carrots in boiling salted water for 2 minutes. Add the leeks and cook for a further 1 minute. Drain the vegetables thoroughly.

3 Heat the oil in a large frying pan. Add the carrots and leeks and cook,

stirring frequently, for 4–5 minutes until beginning to colour. Season with salt and pepper.

4 Transfer to a warmed serving dish and sprinkle with the sesame seeds.

Brussels Sprouts with Hazelnut Butter

SERVES 8

1.25kg (2½lb) Brussels sprouts
60g (2oz/½ cup) blanched hazelnuts
60g (2oz/¼ cup) butter
salt and pepper
shredded rind of 1 lemon

1 Trim the Brussels sprouts and pull off any damaged or discoloured outer leaves. With a sharp knife, make a cross in the stalk end of each one. Although time-consuming, it is important to do this as it allows the thick part to cook as quickly as the leaves.

2 Toast the hazelnuts under a grill (broiler) for a few minutes, stirring frequently, until golden, then chop finely.

3 Melt the butter in a saucepan and mix with the hazelnuts.

4 Cook the Brussels sprouts in boiling salted water for about 8 minutes, until just tender. Drain and return to the pan.

5 Add the hazelnut butter, lemon rind and a little salt and pepper. Toss the ingredients lightly together and transfer to a warmed serving dish.

Cranberry Sauce

SERVES 8

250g (8oz) fresh or frozen cranberries
90g (3oz/½ cup) light soft brown sugar

1 Put the cranberries, sugar and 150ml (¼ pint/⅔ cup) water in a pan. Simmer for 10 minutes, until soft.

2 Leave to cool, then transfer to a small dish. Cover and chill.

COOK'S TIPS

If liked, spice up the sauce with ½ teaspoon cinnamon or finely chopped fresh root ginger. The addition of the grated rind of an orange or lemon, or a splash of port also tastes good.

Roast Chicken with Ginger

SERVES 4

8 small onions
4cm (1½ in) piece of fresh root ginger
4 spring onions (scallions)
2–3 sprigs of fresh thyme
4 garlic cloves
250g (8oz) mascarpone cheese
salt and pepper
30g (1 oz/2 tablespoons) butter
½ teaspoon cornflour (cornstarch)
150m (¼ pint/ ⅔ cup) ginger wine
fresh herbs, to garnish

1 Preheat the oven to 180°C (350° F/Gas 4). Cut off the root ends from the onions so they sit flat. Leave unpeeled but pull away any loose layers. Cook in boiling water for 3 minutes, then drain.

2 Peel and grate the ginger. Trim and finely chop the spring onions (scallions). Pull the leaves from the thyme stalks. (You'll need 4–5 teaspoons.) Crush the garlic. Mix the ginger, spring onions, thyme and garlic with half of the mascarpone cheese and a little salt and pepper.

3 Tuck your fingers between the skin and flesh of the chicken to loosen the skin over the breast and thighs. Using a teaspoon, push the cheese mixture between the skin and flesh. Press the stuffing down until evenly distributed.

4 Place the chicken and onions in a large roasting tin. Soften the butter and dot on the onions. Roast for 1½ hours until the chicken and onions are golden. Baste the chicken after 45 minutes and cover with foil if sufficiently browned. To test if the chicken is cooked, pierce the thickest part of the thigh with a skewer, the juices should run clear.

5 Transfer the chicken and onions to a warmed serving dish and keep warm. Skim off the fat left in the roasting tin. Stir the cornflour (cornstarch) into the juices left in the pan. Blend in the ginger wine, remaining mascarpone cheese and 5 tablespoons water. Bring to the boil, stirring until thickened. Garnish the chicken with thyme and serve with the gravy.

COOK'S TIPS

For extra flavour, tuck an onion and a bunch of thyme inside the chicken before cooking. If the chicken has giblets, use to make stock and use instead of the water in the gravy.

Cucumber Saute

SERVES 4

1 large cucumber
2 tablespoons capers
2–3 dill cucumbers or gherkins
2 tomatoes
30g (1oz/2 tablespoons) butter
1 tablespoon olive oil
salt and pepper

1 Peel the cucumber and halve lengthways. Scoop out the soft centres, then cut widthways into 12mm (½ in) slices.

2 Finely chop the capers. Thinly slice the dill cucumbers or gherkins. Put the tomatoes in a bowl, cover with boiling water for about 40 seconds, then plunge into cold water. Peel off the skins. Halve, scoop out the seeds and dice the flesh.

3 Melt the butter with the oil in a pan. Add the cucumber and fry for 2–3 minutes, until just softened.

4 Stir in the capers, dill cucumbers or gherkins, diced tomato, salt and pepper. Cook, stirring, for 1 minute.

Spiced Chicken Roulade

Chicken breasts, stuffed with spicy apricots and beans, make an ideal meal if just serving two or three people. For a more traditional dish, replace the spicy stuffing with a half quantity of the stuffing on page 160 or the recipe on this page. Accompany with festive trimmings such as bacon kebabs and cranberry sauce.

SERVES 2–3

2 large chicken breasts
2.5cm (1in) piece of fresh root ginger
90g (3oz) French (green) beans
1 teaspoon coriander seeds
1 teaspoon cumin seeds
90g (3oz/¾ cup) no-soak dried apricots
4 no-soak dried prunes
1 onion
1 garlic clove
60g (2oz/¼ cup) butter
45g (1½ oz/¾ cup) fresh breadcrumbs
60g (2oz) sausagemeat
1 tablespoon beaten egg
salt and pepper
4 rashers of streaky bacon
150ml (¼ pint/⅔ cup) dry white wine
4 tablespoons double (heavy) cream
fresh coriander (cilantro), to garnish

1 Preheat the oven to 180°C (350°F/Gas 4). Using a sharp knife, cut horizontally almost through each chicken breast. open out, place between two sheets of damp greaseproof paper (parchment) or cling film (plastic wrap), then beat with a rolling pin to flatten.

2 Peel and grate the ginger. Cook the beans in boiling water for 1 minute, then drain. Lightly crush the coriander and cumin seeds. Chop the apricots and prunes.

3 Chop the onion finely and crush the garlic. Melt 30g (1oz/2 tablespoons) of the butter in a saucepan. Add the onion and garlic and fry for 3 minutes. Stir in the ginger, crushed spices, breadcrumbs, sausagemeat, egg, salt and pepper. Beat the ingredients well together until thoroughly combined.

4 Lay a third of the stuffing down the centre of one chicken breast. Cover with half the beans and another third of the stuffing. Cover with the remaining beans and stuffing. Lay the second chicken breast over the stuffing and bring up the sides to form a roll. Remove the rind and any bones from the bacon and lay over the chicken.

5 Tie the roll with string, at 2.5cm (1in) intervals. Lay the chicken in an ovenproof dish in which it fits snugly. Dot with the remaining butter and spoon over the white wine.

6 Cover with foil and bake for 30 minutes. Uncover and bake for a further 30 minutes.

7 Leave to stand for 5 minutes, then remove the string and transfer to a warmed serving dish. Keep warm.

8 Pour the juices from the chicken into a saucepan and stir in the cream, salt and pepper. Heat through gently.

9 Slice the roulade and garnish with coriander (cilantro). Serve with the hot sauce.

Bacon Kebabs

SERVES 8

8 rashers of streaky bacon
8 chipolata sausages
8 apricots
8 prunes

1 Remove the rind and any bones from the bacon rashers. Twist each sausage into three and separate.

2 Thread each rasher onto a wooden skewer, tucking a piece of sausage, apricot, sausage, prune and remaining sausage between the folds of the bacon.

3 Cook with the turkey for the last 30 minutes of cooking time, or until crisp and golden. Arrange around the turkey to serve.

Oatmeal and Orange Stuffing

Enough to stuff a 5.5kg (12lb) turkey and make plenty of stuffing balls.

60g (2oz/⅓ cup) wild rice
125g (4oz/1 cup) medium oatmeal
500g (1lb) onions
60g (2oz/¼ cup) butter
grated rind of 2 oranges
90g (3oz/½ cup) raisins
180g (6oz/3 cups) fresh breadcrumbs
salt and pepper
1 egg

1 Cook the wild rice in boiling water for 30 minutes, until tender. Drain well.

2 Toast the oatmeal under a grill (broiler) for a few minutes, stirring frequently, until golden. Finely chop the onions. Melt the butter in a large saucepan, add the onions and fry for 3 minutes.

3 Stir in the rice, oatmeal, orange rind, raisins, breadcrumbs, salt and pepper.

4 Add the egg and mix until thoroughly combined. Cover and chill in the refrigerator until ready to use.

Roast Goose with Spiced Apples and Figs

SERVES 8

5–6kg (11–13lb) oven-ready goose
1 medium and 1 large onion
1 carrot
1 celery stick
375g (12oz/2½ cups) dried figs
60g (2oz/¼ cup) butter
180g (6oz/3 cups) fresh breadcrumbs
1 egg
2 tablespoons chopped fresh parsley plus sprigs, to garnish
2 tablespoons chopped fresh thyme plus sprigs, to garnish
salt and pepper
1 small loaf of bread
8 small apples
16 whole cloves
3 tablespoons light soft brown sugar
½ teaspoon ground mixed (apple pie) spice

1 Remove the giblets from the goose and put in a saucepan, removing the liver (see Cook's Tip). Cut the medium onion in half and add to the pan with the carrot, celery and 1.1 litres (2 pints/4½ cups) water. Bring to the boil, reduce the heat and simmer gently for 1 hour. Strain the giblet stock and reserve.

2 Preheat the oven to 180°C (350°F/Gas 4). Chop the large onion. Chop the figs. Melt half of the butter in a pan and fry the onion for 3 minutes. Remove from the heat and add 250g (8oz/1¾ cups) of the figs, the breadcrumbs, egg, chopped parsley and thyme. Season lightly with salt and pepper and mix together well.

3 Pack half the stuffing into the neck end of the goose. Tuck the flap of skin under the bird and truss it with the wings folded under the body and the legs tied together with string. Place the goose on a rack standing over a roasting tin. Shape the remaining stuffing into 2.5cm (1in) balls.

4 Remove the crusts from the loaf of bread and push the bread into the body cavity of the bird to absorb the fat during roasting. Cook the goose in the oven for 2¾ hours.

5 Meanwhile, core the apples and cut a thin slice off the top of each. Stud each apple with 2 whole cloves. Stand in a roasting tin. Mix the remaining figs with the sugar and spice and pack into the apples, letting the excess stuffing rest on top of the apples. Melt the remaining butter and pour over the apples.

6 Thirty minutes before the end of the goose roasting time, place the apples and stuffing balls in the oven, basting the apples frequently.

7 To test if the goose is cooked, pierce the thickest part of the thigh with a skewer, the juices should run clean. If not cooked, return to the oven for a little longer.

8 Transfer the goose to a large, warmed serving dish and surround with the spiced apples and stuffing balls. Keep warm.

9 Pour off all the fat from the roasting tin. Add 600ml (1 pint/2½ cups) reserved giblet stock, making up with water if necessary. Bring to the boil and season lightly with salt and pepper. Strain into a warmed gravy boat or jug.

10 Garnish the goose with sprigs of parsley and thyme.

COOK'S TIPS

If liked, chop the goose liver finely and add to the stuffing, frying it with the onions. Roast potatoes are delicious cooked in goose fat. Add them to the roasting tin about 1 hour before the end of cooking time.

Baked Potatoes and Parsnips

SERVES 4

750g (1½ lb) parsnips
500g (1lb) small baking potatoes
salt and pepper
1 small onion
5 tablespoons hot chicken or vegetable stock
60g (2oz/¼ cup) butter
rosemary sprigs, to garnish

1 Preheat the oven to 180°C (350°F/Gas 4). Peel and thinly slice the parsnips and potatoes.

2 Put the potatoes in a saucepan of cold salted water. Bring to the boil and cook for 2 minutes with the lid off. Drain well.

3 Layer half the potatoes and parsnips in an ovenproof dish. Slice the onion finely and add three-quarters to the dish. Cover with the remaining potatoes and parsnips.

4 Pour over the hot stock, then sprinkle with the remaining onions. Melt the butter, pour over the onions and season lightly with salt and pepper.

5 Bake for 1¼ –1½ hours until golden. Garnish with rosemary sprigs.

COOK'S TIP

Don't be tempted to prepare this dish too far in advance as both the potatoes and the parsnips tend to discolour if left too long before cooking. Once cooked, it will keep well without spoiling.

Creamy Celeriac Puree

SERVES 8

1.5kg (3lb) celeriac
30g (1oz/2 tablespoons) butter
1 tablespoon wholegrain mustard
4 tablespoons double (heavy) cream
salt and pepper
snipped fresh chives, to garnish

1 Peel the celeriac and cut into small chunks. Immediately put in a saucepan of water and bring to the boil. Cook for 20 minutes or until softened. Drain well.

2 Mash the celeriac with the butter and mustard until completely smooth.

3 Return to the pan and reheat gently. Stir in the cream, salt and pepper. Transfer to a warmed serving dish and garnish with snipped chives.

Creamy Onion Sauce

SERVES 8

375g (12oz) onions
30g (1oz/2 tablespoons) butter
450ml (¾ pint/2 cups) milk
freshly grated nutmeg
60g (2oz/1 cup) fresh breadcrumbs
2 tablespoons chopped fresh parsley
4 tablespoons double (heavy) cream
salt and pepper

1 Chop the onions finely. Melt the butter in a saucepan, add the onions and fry gently for 3 minutes.

2 Add the milk, ¼ teaspoon grated nutmeg and the breadcrumbs. Bring to the boil, reduce the heat and simmer gently for 6-8 minutes, until pulpy.

3 Stir in the parsley, cream, salt and pepper and heat through gently. Transfer to a warmed sauceboat and sprinkle with grated nutmeg.

COOK'S TIP

This classic accompaniment to roast goose, is also good with roast turkey. It can be made in advance and stored in the refrigerator for several days. If necessary, thin down with a little cream or milk when reheating.

Stir-fried Cabbage with Crispy Bacon

SERVES 8

1 medium cabbage
4 rashers of streaky bacon
2 tablespoons olive oil
2 tablespoons sunflower seeds
salt and pepper

1 Shred the cabbage, discarding the central core. Dice the bacon finely.

2 In a large frying pan, fry the bacon in its own fat, until turning golden. Add the remaining ingredients.

3 Fry for 3–4 minutes, stirring, until crisp. Transfer to a warmed dish.

Roast Duck with Cranberries and Clementines

SERVES 4

2.5kg (5lb) oven-ready duckling
½ teaspoon ground allspice
salt and pepper
1 orange
4 clementines
30g (1oz/2 tablespoons) butter
2 cinnamon sticks, halved
180g (6oz) fresh or frozen cranberries
5 tablespoons light soft brown sugar
2 teaspoons white wine vinegar
2 tablespoons Cointreau
flat-leaved parsley, to garnish

1 Preheat the oven to 220°C (425°F/Gas 7). Using a fork, pierce the duckling all over, except the breast area. Rub the skin with allspice and sprinkle with salt and pepper. Place the duckling on a rack, over a roasting tin. Cook for 15 minutes. Reduce the oven temperature to 190°C (375°F/Gas 5) and cook for a further 1 hour.

2 Pare thick strips of rind from the orange. Squeeze the juice and reserve. Peel the clementines, leaving them whole. Melt the butter in a small saucepan. Add the orange rind, cinnamon sticks and whole clementines and cook for 1 minute. Place the clementines and orange rice around the duckling and pour over the remaining butter. Return to the oven for a further 45 minutes.

3 Pour the reserved orange juice and the cranberries into the butter pan. Simmer gently for about 10 minutes, until the cranberries pop.

4 Transfer the duckling, clementines and orange peel to a warmed serving dish and keep warm. Drain off the fat from the roasting tin, then add the cranberries and juice, sugar, vinegar and Cointreau. Bring to the boil, stirring constantly. Season with salt and pepper to taste.

5 Spoon the cranberries around the duckling and garnish with parsley. Serve with the gravy.

COOK'S TIPS

When serving duckling, carve it in the same way as you would a chicken or turkey, first removing the legs and then taking thin slices from the breast. Although there's not as much flesh on a duckling, the meat is richer so portions needn't be large.

Glazed Turnips with Beans

SERVES 4

750g (1½ lb) baby turnips
salt and pepper
125g (4oz) French (green) beans
30g (1oz/2 tablespoons) butter
2 teaspoons caster (superfine) sugar
flat-leaved parsley, to garnish

1 Trim the ends from the turnips and peel. Cut each turnip into four or six wedges, depending on size. Cook in boiling salted water for about 5 minutes, until almost tender, then drain. Cut the beans into 5cm (2in) lengths and cook in boiling salted water for 2 minutes, then drain.

2 Melt the butter in a heavy-based frying pan. Add the turnips and sprinkle with the sugar.

3 Fry over a moderate heat, stirring, until the turnips begin to colour and turn glossy. Add the beans and heat through for 1–2 minutes.

4 Season lightly with salt and pepper and turn into a warmed serving dish. Serve garnished with parsley.

Sweet Potato Cake

SERVES 4

1kg (2lb) sweet potatoes
1 ripe pear
60g (2oz/¼ cup) butter
3 tablespoons honey
salt and pepper

1 Cook the potatoes in their skins, in boiling water for 30–40 minutes, until tender, then drain.

2 Preheat the oven to 200°C (400°F/Gas 6). Grease and base-line a 20cm (8in) sandwich (layer cake) tin with greaseproof paper (parchment).

3 Peel and slice the potatoes as thinly as possible. Peel, core and very thinly slice the pear.

4 Pack half the potato slices into the tin. Cover with the pear slices, then the remaining potato.

5 Melt the butter and mix with the honey, salt and pepper. Pour over the potatoes. Cover with foil and bake for 45 minutes.

6 Invert onto a flameproof plate and remove the paper. Cook under a hot grill (broiler) for 2–3 minutes, until brown. Serve cut into wedges.

SWEET POTATOES

Sweet potatoes, with their rough, reddish skins and misshapen appearance, are readily available throughout the winter. Boiled just like ordinary potatoes, their creamy white flesh mashes well. Their sweet, earthy taste is delicious in this layered vegetable accompaniment and is perfect with any rich game dish.

Roast Pheasant

SERVES 4

2 oven-ready pheasants
6 rashers of smoked streaky bacon
3 onions
2–3 bay leaves
salt and pepper
500g (1lb) red cabbage
15g (½ oz/1 tablespoon) butter
2 tablespoons olive oil
45g (1½ oz/⅓ cup) pistachio nuts
5 teaspoons redcurrant jelly
1½ teaspoons cornflour (cornstarch)
5 tablespoons port
150ml (¼ pint/⅔ cup) chicken stock
bunches of fresh herbs, to garnish

1 Preheat the oven to 200°C (400°F/Gas 6). Rinse and dry the pheasants and remove any stray

feathers. Lay 3 rashers of bacon over each and place in a roasting tin. Halve 1 onion and tuck half inside each bird with the bay leaves. Season lightly with salt and pepper.

2 Roast the pheasants for 1 hour, basting frequently during cooking. Meanwhile, shred the red cabbage, discarding the core. Slice the remaining onions.

3 About 20 minutes before the pheasants are cooked, melt the butter with the olive oil in a saucepan. Add the red cabbage, onions and pistachio nuts and cook gently for about 8 minutes, stirring frequently, until softened but retaining some texture.

4 Stir 3 teaspoons of the redcurrant jelly into the red cabbage and stir until melted. Season lightly with salt and pepper.

5 Transfer the pheasants to a warmed serving dish and keep warm. Drain off all but 1 tablespoon of the fat layer, retaining the juices. Stir the cornflour (cornstarch) into the juices, then blend in the port, the remaining redcurrant jelly and the stock.

6 Bring to the boil and simmer for 2 minutes, until thickened. Season lightly with salt and pepper and pour into a warmed sauceboat or jug. Garnish the pheasant with fresh herbs and serve with the red cabbage and gravy.

COOK'S TIP

Roast pheasants, because like all game birds they lack fat, have a tendency to be dry. To overcome this, always roast them in a jacket of fatty bacon. This will help to maintain their succulence and also crisp and flavour the skin.

PHEASANT

Fresh pheasant makes a perfect choice for a small festive gathering as one pheasant will generously serve two people. Most supermarkets sell oven-ready pheasants, over the Christmas season, which have sufficient flavour for most tastes. If, however, you prefer a more gamey taste, you might prefer to order them in advance from a good butcher or poulterer who sells hung pheasants as these have a stronger flavour. Traditionally, pheasant is served with game chips (thinly sliced and deep-fried potatoes) but the sweet potato cake opposite, makes a delicious alternative accompaniment.

Glazed Baked Ham

A beautifully presented joint of ham not only makes a delicious addition to a traditional Christmas roast but is also a delicious meal on its own.

SERVES 8

2.5kg (5lb) smoked or unsmoked middle gammon (ham butt)
1 onion
whole cloves
1 carrot
1 celery stick
1 bouquet garni
2.5cm (1in) piece of fresh root ginger
3 tablespoons light soft brown sugar
5 teaspoons orange juice
1 tablespoon honey
12 kumquats
bay leaves, to garnish

1 Soak the gammon (ham butt) for 12 hours or overnight in a bowl of cold water, then drain.

2 Place the gammon in a saucepan. Skin and stud the onion with 10 cloves. Add to the pan with the carrot, celery and bouquet garni. Cover with cold water and bring to the boil. Reduce the heat, cover with a lid and simmer for 1¼ hours. Leave to cool slightly in the pan, then drain.

3 Meanwhile, peel and grate the ginger. Mix in a bowl with the sugar, orange juice and honey.

4 Preheat the oven to 200°C (400°F/Gas 6). Loosen one corner of the gammon skin with a knife. Pull the skin away from the fat and discard.

5 Using the tip of a sharp knife, score wavy lines diagonally across the fat, 2.5cm (1in) apart.

6 Slice the kumquats thinly. Press a clove through the centre of a kumquat slice and press into the gammon fat. Continue adding more cloves and kumquat slices to garnish the fat, spacing them about 4cm (1½ in) apart.

7 Line an ovenproof dish or roasting tin with foil. Place the gammon in the dish or tin and brush all over with some of the glaze. Bake for 30–40 minutes, basting frequently with more glaze, until golden.

8 Serve hot or cold, garnished with bay leaves.

COOK'S TIP

I suggest using a middle cut piece gammon as it looks spectacular and is very easy to carve.

Baked Potatoes with Soured Cream

SERVES 8

8 medium baking potatoes
½ teaspoon curry powder
1 tablespoon vegetable oil
30g (1oz/2 tablespoons) butter
300ml (½ pint/1½ cups) soured cream
2 tablespoons wholegrain mustard
salt and pepper

1 Preheat the oven to 200°C (400°F/Gas 6). Scrub the potatoes and prick all over with a fork. Mix together the curry powder and oil and brush over the potatoes.

2 Bake the potatoes for 1–1¼ hours, until they feel soft when squeezed.

3 Cut each potato in half and lightly fluff up the flesh with a fork. Dot the potato halves with butter.

4 Mix together the soured cream, mustard, salt and pepper. Spoon over the potatoes and serve immediately.

Courgettes and Corn with Garlic

SERVES 8

4 courgettes (zucchini)
250g (8oz) baby corn
30g (1oz/2 tablespoons) butter
3 garlic cloves
1 tablespoon vegetable oil
salt and pepper

1 Cut the courgettes (zucchini) diagonally into chunks. Bring a saucepan of water to the boil. Add the corn and cook for 30 seconds. Add the courgettes and cook for a further 30 seconds, then drain well.

2 Thread the courgettes and corn onto metal or wooden skewers and arrange on a grill (broiler) rack.

3 Melt the butter. Crush the garlic, add to the butter with the oil, salt and pepper and mix together. Brush over the vegetables.

4 Cook under a moderate grill (broiler) for about 5 minutes, turning frequently and brushing with more garlic butter, until golden. Serve hot.

COOK'S TIP

If you haven't any skewers, arrange the vegetables in a single layer on a foil-lined grill rack. Cook as above, turning and brushing frequently.

Spiced Fruit Compote

SERVES 8

250g (8oz) onions
5 tablespoons white wine vinegar
3 tablespoons redcurrant jelly
375g (12oz) kumquats
8 ripe plums
4 tablespoons port
4 tablespoons orange juice
1 tablespoon Worcestershire sauce
½ teaspoon paprika
½ teaspoon cornflour (cornstarch)

1 Slice the onions and put in a pan with the vinegar and redcurrant jelly.

Cover and cook gently for 10 minutes, until softened.

2 Prick the kumquats with a fork, add to the pan and cook for 5 minutes, stirring frequently, until the kumquats are softened.

3 Meanwhile, cut the plums in half and remove the stones (pits). Add the plums, port, orange juice, Worcestershire sauce and paprika to the kumquats and cook for a further 2 minutes.

4 Blend the cornflour (cornstarch) with a little water, then add to the pan. Bring to the boil, stirring. Spoon into a serving dish and serve hot or cold.

Shredded Cabbage with Orange and Caraway

SERVES 8

1 small cabbage
30g (1oz/2 tablespoons) butter
2 teaspoons olive oil
1 teaspoon caraway seeds
grated rind of ½ an orange
salt and pepper
shredded orange rind, to garnish

1 Roughly shred the cabbage, discarding the stalk. Cook in boiling salted water for 2 minutes, then drain thoroughly.

2 Melt the butter in the cleaned saucepan with the olive oil. Add the caraway seeds and grated orange rind and stir.

3 Add the cabbage and cook gently for 1–2 minutes, until heated. Season lightly with salt and pepper.

4 Transfer to a warmed serving dish and serve garnished with shredded orange rind.

COOK'S TIPS

Use cabbage with deep green leaves. Fennel, sesame, sunflower or pumpkin seeds can be used too.

Baked Salmon with Spices

Fish makes an excellent alternative to the traditional meats at Christmas, especially if you cook it in an interesting way. A whole baked salmon looks particularly impressive and is very easy to prepare. Serve it with the spicy hollandaise sauce and accompaniments on the following pages.

SERVES 4–6

60g (2oz/¼ cup) butter
1–1.5kg (2–3lb) whole salmon, cleaned
150ml (¼ pint/⅔ cup) white wine
salt
1 teaspoon black peppercorns
2 teaspoons coriander seeds
2 teaspoons mustard seeds
2 teaspoons fennel seeds
sliced limes, fresh coriander (cilantro) and bay leaves, to garnish

1 Preheat the oven to 150°C (300°F/Gas 2). Melt the butter. Spread a double thickness of foil, large enough to wrap the salmon, with some of the melted butter.

2 Lay the salmon on the foil, then bring up the sides of the foil loosely to make a container. Pour the wine over the salmon and sprinkle with a little salt. Secure the foil together so that the parcel is tightly sealed but leaves space around the salmon. Place on a large baking sheet and cook for 1–1¼ hours until tender. To test if the salmon is cooked, push a knife into the thickest part of the flesh near the backbone. The flesh in the centre should have turned opaque. If necessary, re-wrap and cook for a little longer.

3 Meanwhile, grind the peppercorns, coriander, mustard and fennel seeds in a coffee grinder or pestle and mortar until fairly fine.

4 Remove the salmon from the oven and fold back the foil. Raise the oven temperature to 200°C (400°F/Gas 6). Transfer the salmon carefully to a chopping board. Using a sharp knife, cut through the skin around the head and tail, and down the back of the fish. Carefully peel away the skin and any dark brown flesh.

5 Brush the pink flesh with melted butter and coat with half the spice mixture.

6 Carefully turn the fish over and skin the other side. Brush with the remaining butter and coat with the remaining spice mixture. Turn the fish back to the original side and place on a clean piece of buttered foil.

7 Bake for a further 5 minutes, then transfer to a warmed serving dish. Surround with plenty of sliced limes, coriander (cilantro) and bay leaves and serve hot.

COOK'S TIP

This is the easiest way to cook a small salmon as it requires no specialist equipment, although a fish kettle can be used if you have one. Half-fill it with water, adding a little white wine, salt and pepper. Bring to simmering point, then lower the salmon, on the rack, into the water. Return to a gentle simmer and cook for 5 minutes per 500g (1lb). Leave to drain for 5 minutes, then continue from step 4.

Buttered Rice Castles

SERVES 6

60g (2oz/⅓ cup) wild rice
salt and pepper
180g (6oz/¾ cup) brown rice
180g (6oz/¾ cup) long-grain white rice
60g (2oz/⅓ cup) split red lentils
45g (1½ oz/3 tablespoons) butter

1 Cook the wild rice in boiling salted water for 30 minutes until tender, then drain. Cook the brown rice in boiling salted water for 20–25 minutes until tender, then drain.

2 Cook the long-grain rice and split red lentils together in boiling salted water for 8–10 minutes until just tender, then drain.

3 Preheat the oven to 200°C (400°F/Gas 6). Melt the butter. Brush the bases and sides of six dariole moulds or individual pudding basins with a little of the butter.

4 Pack the long-grain rice mixture into the bases of the moulds. Spoon the wild rice into the moulds and press down lightly. Spoon the brown rice into the moulds and pack down lightly. Spoon the remaining butter over the rice.

5 Place the moulds in a roasting tin and add 12mm (½ in) depth of boiling water to the tin. Cover with foil and cook for 10 minutes.

6 Loosen the sides of the moulds with a knife, then tap the rice out onto a serving plate. Keep warm until ready to serve.

Hot Mushroom Salad

SERVES 6

500g (1lb) oyster mushrooms
180g (6oz) mange-tout (snow peas)
4 tablespoons walnut or olive oil
1 tablespoon balsamic vinegar
salt and pepper
30g (1oz/¼ cup) ground almonds

1 Halve any large mushrooms. Trim and halve the mange-tout (snow peas).

2 Heat the oil in a frying pan. Add the mushrooms and mange-tout and fry for 2 minutes, until just softened.

3 Stir in the vinegar, salt and pepper and transfer to a shallow heatproof serving dish. Sprinkle the vegetables

evenly with the ground almonds.

4 Cook under a moderate grill (broiler) until the almonds are just beginning to colour. Serve hot.

COOK'S TIP

Try to make use of the various interesting types of mushrooms available at this time of year from most major supermarkets and good greengrocers. If, however, you can only buy ordinary fresh mushrooms, add some dried mushrooms, such as porcini, to liven up the salad. These can now be found in most supermarkets. Soak the dried mushrooms in water, to soften, before use, then cook them as above. Oyster mushrooms are now available in both yellow and pink shades as well as their natural beige.

CORIANDER HOLLANDAISE

SERVES 6

180g (6oz/¾ cup) butter
3 tablespoons white wine vinegar
3 egg yolks
¼ teaspoon curry paste
5 tablespoons chopped fresh coriander (cilantro)
few drops of lime or lemon juice
salt and pepper

1 Beat the butter thoroughly until softened. Put the vinegar in a small saucepan and boil rapidly until reduced to 1 tablespoon, watching it constantly. Then pour into a large heatproof bowl and add the egg yolks and curry paste.

2 Stand the bowl over a saucepan of hot water. Add a knob of the butter to the bowl and whisk well. When melted, gradually add the remaining butter, whisking well after each addition, until the sauce is thickened.

3 Stir in the coriander (cilantro), lime or lemon juice, salt and pepper. Transfer to a sauceboat or jug.

COOK'S TIPS

Don't let the water get too hot or the sauce may curdle. If it does, beat in a tablespoon of hot water.

If this fails, start again with another egg yolk and gradually beat in the curdled sauce. Once made, Hollandaise sauce will keep, covered, for up to 30 minutes. It is best served when still tepid.

Celebration Seafood Stew

A seafood stew, comprising several different types of fish, makes a delicious meal for adventurous diners. Although there's a fair amount of preparation involved, the first nine steps can be done several hours in advance, ready for last-minute assembly. Serve with a bowl of steaming baby potatoes and a dish of rouille (see next recipe). Warn guests to take rouille cautiously! Usually half a teaspoonful is sufficient to spice up a portion of this stew.

SERVES 6

500g (1lb) red snapper or red mullet
12 tiger prawns (large shrimp)
750g (1½ lb) cod or haddock fillet
250g (8oz) scallops
500g (1lb) fresh mussels
1 onion
salt and pepper
1 teaspoon saffron strands
4 tablespoons olive oil
3 tablespoons brandy
2 leeks
4 celery sticks
4 garlic cloves
pared rind of 1 small orange
8 sprigs of fresh thyme
3 bay leaves
300ml (½ pint/1¼ cups) white wine
1 dressed crab, weighing about 180g (6oz)
150ml (¼ pint / ⅔ cup) double (heavy) cream

1 Working on a sheet of newspaper, run a knife from the tail to the head of the snapper or mullet to remove scales. Cut off the heads and tails and reserve for making the stock. Make a cut along the back of the fish, then ease the fillet away from the bone using a sharp knife and working with short, sharp strokes. Turn the fish over and remove the other fillet. Cut the fillets into large chunks.

2 Remove the heads and shells from the prawns (large shrimp) leaving the tails intact. Reserve the trimmings for the stock.

3 Skin the cod or haddock and cut the flesh into large chunks, discarding any bones. Halve the scallops if large.

4 Scrub the mussels, discarding any damaged or open shells. Put in a large bowl and, under cold running water, scrape off any sand or mud. Knock off any barnacles with a knife and tug off the beard. Rinse again and discard any that do not close when tapped sharply with a knife.

5 Put all the fish trimmings (except the rejected mussels) in a saucepan with the onion, salt, pepper and 1.1 litres (2 pints / 4 ½ cups) water. Bring to the boil, reduce the heat and simmer gently for 30 minutes. Cool slightly, then strain the stock.

6 Put the saffron in a bowl, add 1 tablespoon boiling water and leave until needed.

7 Heat 2 tablespoons of the oil in a frying pan. Add the snapper or mullet, cod or haddock and scallops and fry, stirring, for 1 minute. Add the brandy and light with a taper. When the flames die down, remove from the heat.

8 Slice the leeks thinly, slice the celery thickly and crush the garlic. Heat the remaining oil in a saucepan. Add the leeks, celery, garlic, orange rind, thyme and bay leaves and fry gently.

9 Make the strained stock up to 1 litre (1¾ pints/4 cups) with water. Add to the vegetables with the win and saffron. Bring to the boil, cover with a lid and simmer very gently for 15–20 minutes, until the vegetables are tender.

10 Add the fried fish and juices, crab and prawns to the pan. Stir in the cream, salt and pepper and bring almost to the boil. Scatter the mussels over the stew and cover with a lid. Cook for 3–4 minutes, until the mussels have opened. Discard any mussels that do not open.

11 Remove half the mussels from their shells and gently stir into the stew. Serve hot with Rouille.

COOK'S TIP

When making this seafood stew, you may need to alter the ingredients depending on the availability of the fish and also personal preference. Halibut and monkfish can be used instead of the cod or haddock, while small cockles can replace the mussels.

Cleaned squid, cut into rings, can be used instead of the scallops. Whichever you use, don't forget that fish needs very little cooking. Overcooking will produce disappointing results.

Rouille

SERVES 4–6

1 red pepper
1 red or green chilli
2 garlic cloves
5 tablespoons olive oil
30g (1 oz/½ cup) fresh breadcrumbs
salt

1 Cut the red pepper in half, discard the core and seeds, and chop the flesh roughly. Cut the chilli in half and discard the seeds.

2 Put the red pepper, chilli, garlic and oil in a food processor and blend until smooth. Add the breadcrumbs and a little salt and blend to a paste.

3 Transfer to a serving bowl. Cover and refrigerate until ready to serve.

Roasted Monkfish with Black Beans

SERVES 4

250g (8oz / 1⅓ cups) black beans
1 large monkfish tail, weighing about 1kg (2lb)
6 garlic cloves
4 tablespoons olive oil
1 red onion, sliced
2 tablespoons chopped fresh oregano
150ml (¼ pint / ⅔ cup) white wine
salt and pepper
125g (4oz) red or yellow cherry tomatoes
sprigs of oregano, to garnish

1 Wash the beans, put in a large bowl and cover with plenty of cold water. Leave to soak overnight.

2 The next day, drain the beans and put in a large saucepan. Cover with fresh cold water and bring to the boil. Boil rapidly for 10 minutes. Reduce the heat and simmer gently for about 30 minute or until just tender, then drain well.

3 Preheat the oven to 190°C (375°F/Gas 5). Remove any loose skin from the monkfish. Cut away the central bone to leave two long fillets.

4 Lay the fillets side by side, with a thick end against a thin. Using fine string, tie the fillets together at 2.5cm (1in) intervals. Slice the garlic and tuck half the slices between the fillets.

5 Heat 2 tablespoons of the oil in a frying pan, add the monkfish and fry on all sides, until just turning brown. Drain on absorbent kitchen paper.

6 Slice the onion. Heat the remaining oil in a pan. Add the onion and remaining garlic and fry for 3 minutes, until the onion is softened. Stir in the beans, oregano, wine, salt and pepper. Bring to the boil, then turn into a shallow ovenproof dish.

7 Lay the monkfish on top and season lightly with salt and pepper. Bake for 10 minutes. Cut a cross in the top of each tomato and add to the dish. Cook for a further 10 minutes or until the fish is cooked through. Test by piercing the thick end of a fillet with a sharp knife – the centre should be opaque. If it isn't, cook for a few minutes more.

8 Serve hot, garnished with sprigs of oregano.

Halibut Pithiviers

SERVES 4–6

750g (1½ lb) halibut steaks
1 large fennel head
60g (2oz/¼ cup) butter
grated rind of 1 lemon
5 tablespoons chopped fresh parsley
salt and pepper
500g (1lb) puff pastry
beaten egg, to glaze
1 red pepper
1 yellow pepper
6 pitted black olives
1 tablespoon olive oil
½ teaspoon mild chilli seasoning
440g (14oz) can chopped tomatoes
½ teaspoon caster (superfine) sugar
fresh herbs, to garnish

1 Preheat the oven to 200°C (400°F/Gas 6). Cut the four sections of flesh from each halibut steak, discarding the skin and bones.

2 Trim and slice the fennel thinly. Melt 15g (½ oz/1 tablespoon) of the butter in a small saucepan. Add the fennel and fry gently for 5 minutes, until softened. Remove from the heat and stir in the lemon rind, parsley, salt and pepper.

3 Halve the pastry. On a lightly floured surface, roll out one half and cut out a 23cm (9in) round. Transfer to a dampened baking sheet. Arrange the fish pieces, in a single layer, over the pastry round to within 2.5cm (1in) of the edge. Season with salt and pepper.

4 Spread the fennel mixture to within 2.5cm (1in) of the edges of the fish and dot with the remaining butter.

5 Roll out the remaining pastry and cut out a 24cm (9½ in) round. Brush the edges of the pastry base with beaten egg, then cover with the larger circle. Press the edges together firmly and flute with the back of a knife. Brush with beaten egg. Using the tip of the knife, make a decorative pattern from the centre to the edges. Bake for 30–35 minutes.

6 Meanwhile, cut the peppers in half, discard the cores and seeds and dice the flesh. Quarter the olives lengthways. Heat the oil in a pan. Add the peppers, olives, chilli powder, tomatoes and sugar and bring to the boil. Simmer for 6–8 minutes, until slightly thickened.

Festive Vegetable Pie

Packed with chestnuts, stuffing balls and a feast of wintery vegetables, this delicious pie makes a perfect main dish for a special gathering.

SERVES 6–8

STUFFING BALLS
1 large onion
4 garlic cloves
4 tablespoons olive oil
60g (2oz/½ cup) freshly grated Parmesan cheese
250g (8oz/4 cups) fresh breadcrumbs
5 tablespoons chopped fresh herbs
grated rind of 1 orange
salt and pepper
1 egg, beaten
PIE
500g (1lb) leeks
500g (1lb) turnips
500g (1lb) carrots
4 tablespoons olive oil
2 tablespoons plain (all-purpose) flour
300ml (½ pint/1¼ cups) white wine
900ml (1½ pints/3¾ cups) vegetable stock
3 bay leaves
1 large parsnip
250g (8oz) button mushrooms
250g (8oz) can whole chestnuts
750g (1½ lb) puff pastry
beaten egg, to glaze

1 To make the stuffing balls, chop the onion finely and crush the garlic. Heat 2 tablespoons of the oil in a saucepan. Add the onion and garlic and fry gently for 5 minutes. Remove from the heat and stir in the cheese, breadcrumbs, herbs, orange rind, salt and pepper.

2 Leave to cool slightly, then stir in the beaten egg until evenly combined. Shape the mixture into 2.5cm (1in) balls. Heat the remaining oil in a frying pan and fry the stuffing balls for about 10 minutes, turning frequently, until golden, then drain.

3 To make the pie, trim the leeks and cut into 12mm (½in) chunks. Cut the turnips into chunks and slice the carrots thickly. Heat the oil in a large saucepan and fry the leeks, turnips and carrots for 3 minutes.

4 Stir in the flour, then gradually blend in the wine and stock. Add the bay leaves and bring to the boil. Reduce the heat, cover and simmer for 15 minutes, until the vegetables are softened.

5 Meanwhile, slice the parsnip thickly. Add the parsnip, mushrooms and chestnuts to the pan. Season with salt and pepper, then leave to cool.

6 Using a slotted spoon, transfer the vegetables to a large, deep pie dish. Arrange the stuffing balls over the vegetables. Pour over enough of the juices to two-thirds fill the dish. (Keep any remaining juices to reheat and serve separately.)

7 Preheat the oven to 200°C (400°F/Gas 6). Roll out the pastry on a lightly floured surface to a round or oval 7.5cm (3in) larger than the pie dish. Cut a 2.5cm (1in) wide strip from the outside edge of the pastry.

8 Dampen the rim of the dish and position the strip on the rim. Brush the strip with water. Position the pastry lid, pressing the edges together to seal and making a small hole in the centre of the pastry. Flute the edges decoratively. Make leaves from the pastry trimmings and use to garnish the top of the pie.

9 Brush with beaten egg and bake for 25 minutes. Reduce the oven temperature to 160°C (325°F/Gas 3). Bake for a further 30 minutes, covering the pie with a piece of foil if overbrowning. Serve hot.

Roast Lentil Patties

SERVES 4

1 large leek
2 courgettes (zucchini)
4 tablespoons olive oil
280g (9oz/1⅓ cups) split red lentils
450ml (¾ pint/2 cups) vegetable stock
90g (3oz/¾ cup) broken walnuts
2 tablespoons double (heavy) cream
1 tablespoon chopped fresh rosemary
1 egg, beaten
salt
1 tablespoon crushed peppercorns
rosemary sprigs, to garnish

1 Chop the leek finely and wash. Grate the courgettes (zucchini). Heat 3 tablespoons of the oil in a saucepan. Add the leek and courgettes and fry for 3 minutes. Add the lentils and stock and bring to the boil. Reduce the heat, cover tightly with a lid and simmer for 10–15 minutes, until the mixture is thick and pulpy. Leave to cool.

2 Preheat the oven to 200°C (400°F/Gas 6). Toast the walnuts on a sheet of foil under the grill (broiler), turning them frequently. Leave to cool, then chop roughly. Beat the walnuts, cream, rosemary, egg and salt into the lentil mixture.

3 Using lightly floured hands, shape the mixture into 12 balls and flatten them slightly.

4 Sprinkle with the peppercorns and place in a baking dish. Drizzle with the remaining oil. Bake for 20–25 minutes, until crispy. Serve hot garnished with sprigs of rosemary.

Aubergine and Feta Tart

SERVES 8

1 medium aubergine (eggplant), weighing about 315g (10oz)
2 onions
8 tablespoons olive oil
60g (2oz) sun-dried tomatoes
2 small courgettes (zucchini)
125g (4oz) feta cheese
½ teaspoon mild chilli seasoning
salt
6 sheets of filo pastry

1 Preheat the oven to 190°C (375°F/Gas 5). Cut the aubergine (eggplant) into dice. Slice the onions. Heat 4 tablespoons of the oil in a large frying pan. Add the aubergine and onion and fry gently for 8–10

minutes, until golden.

2 Chop the tomatoes and courgettes (zucchini) roughly. Add to the pan and cook for a further 2 minutes. Crumble the feta cheese lightly and stir in the chilli seasoning. Add salt to taste.

3 Line a 23cm (9in) loose-bottomed flan (quiche) tin with a sheet of the filo pastry, tucking the pastry into the corners and letting the excess overhang the edges. Brush the pastry within the tin area with a little oil.

4 Lay another sheet of pastry over the first but in the opposite direction. Brush with more oil. Continue lining the tin with the remaining filo sheets, brushing each with oil and alternating the direction of the sheets so that the pastry overhanging the edges is evenly distributed.

5 Spoon the filling into the tin and spread to the edges. Crumple the excess pastry around the edges of the tin to give an attractive border. Brush with the remaining oil.

Roast Onion Gravy

Makes 600ml (1 pint/ 2½ cups)

500g (1lb) onions
2 garlic cloves
2 tablespoons olive oil
2 bay leaves
few drops of soy sauce
750ml (1¼ pints/3 cups) vegetable stock
1½ teaspoons cornflour (cornstarch)

1 Preheat the oven to 200°C (400°F/Gas 6). Slice the onions and garlic, leaving the skins on. Put in an ovenproof dish, drizzle with olive oil. Bake for 1 hour, until lightly charred.

2 Transfer to a saucepan and add the bay leaves, soy sauce and vegetable stock. Simmer for 15 minutes.

3 Strain through a sieve, reserving a few onion slices.

4 In a saucepan, blend the cornflour (cornstarch) with a little of the strained stock. Gradually blend in the remaining stock and reserved onion slices. Bring to the boil, stirring until thickened.

Cook's Tip

It's the addition of onion skins that provide the golden colour of this vegetarian gravy – a technique worth remembering for vegetarian stocks, soups and gravy.

Polenta with Saffron Mushrooms

SERVES 4

1½ teaspoons salt
280g (9oz/2½ cups) polenta
125g (4oz/1 cup) freshly grated Parmesan cheese
3 tablespoons olive oil
1 teaspoon saffron strands
1 onion
3 celery sticks
1 red pepper
45g (1½oz/⅓ cup) pine nuts
125g (4oz) shiitake mushrooms
180g (6oz) button mushrooms
300ml (½ pint/1¼ cups) double (heavy) cream
salt and pepper
chilli tomato sauce, see opposite

1 Bring 1.1 litres (2 pints/4½ cups) water to the boil in a large saucepan. Add the salt. Gradually whisk in the polenta until thickened. When thick and pulpy, reduce the heat and cook very gently for 10 minutes, stirring frequently with a wooden spoon. Beat in half the cheese.

2 Turn the polenta into a greased flameproof dish and spread to an even layer, about 2.5cm (1in) thick. Drizzle with 1 tablespoon of the oil and sprinkle with the remaining cheese.

3 Mix the saffron strands with 1 tablespoon boiling water and set aside.

4 Slice the onion and chop the celery. Cut the pepper in half, discard the core and seeds and slice the flesh. Heat the remaining oil in a saucepan and add the onion, celery and pine nuts. Cook the mixture gently, stirring, until softened.

5 Add the red pepper and mushrooms and cook for a further 2 minutes. Stir in the saffron and liquid, cream, salt and pepper. Heat gently.

6 Cook the polenta under a moderate grill (broiler) until hot and turning golden. Cut into portions. Spoon the mushroom mixture onto warmed serving plates and top with portions of polenta. Serve with the chilli tomato sauce.

POLENTA

Polenta is a type of flour, ground from corn or maize, that is particularly popular in Italian cookery. Look for it in Italian delicatessens and large supermarkets. Polenta is not difficult to make but because it tends to spit and splutter during cooking, it is best to use a tall, heavy-based saucepan and a long-handled wooden spoon. It is also important to stir the mixture frequently to prevent lumps forming.

It is usually flavoured with cheese, herbs or garlic, then grilled and cut into wedges. It can also be served instead of pasta, rice or potatoes. Simply simmer it in the water until pulpy, then season lightly and serve plain or flavoured as above.

CHILLI TOMATO SAUCE

SERVES 6

1 red pepper
1 chilli
375g (12oz) tomatoes
1 onion
1 garlic clove
3 tablespoons olive oil
1 tablespoon tomato purée (paste)
pinch of sugar
salt and pepper

1 Preheat the oven to 200°C (400°F/Gas 6). Cut the red pepper into quarters, discarding the core and seeds. Halve the chilli, discard the core and seeds and chop the flesh roughly. Halve the tomatoes and slice the onions.

2 Put the red pepper, chilli, tomatoes, onion and garlic in an ovenproof dish and drizzle with the oil. Bake for 1 hour, until the vegetables are lightly charred.

3 Blend the vegetables in a food processor until pulpy but not completely smooth. Turn into a saucepan. Stir in the tomato purée (paste), sugar, salt and pepper and reheat gently before serving.

COOK'S TIP

Handle fresh chillies, as little as possible as the volatile oils in the flesh can make your skin burn or tingle. Rinse your hands well afterwards.

SMOKED MACKEREL AND ROCKET TERRINE

SERVES 12

375g (12oz) smoked mackerel
90g (3oz/⅓ cup) butter
1 tablespoon white wine vinegar
pepper
375g (12oz/1½ cups) cream cheese
60g (2oz) rocket (arugula)
grated rind of 1 lemon
200g (6½oz) can pimientos, drained
melba toast or toast, to serve

1 Discard the skin from the fish and flake the flesh roughly. Melt the butter. Put the fish, butter, vinegar and pepper in a food processor and blend until really smooth and creamy. (Alternatively, mash the ingredients together in a bowl.)
2 Beat the cream cheese in a bowl. Chop the rocket (arugula) finely and add to the bowl with the lemon rind, salt and pepper. Beat well together.
3 Cut three wide strips from one of the pimientos. Open out the remaining pimiento pieces.
4 Spoon half the mackerel mixture into a small rectangular terrine. Spread with half the cheese mixture. Cover with half the pimiento pieces. Spread with the remaining mackerel mixture and add the remaining pimiento pieces. Spread with the remaining cheese mixture and swirl the surface.
5 Garnish with the pimiento strips. Chill for several hours or overnight. Serve with melba toast.

COOK'S TIP

If you cannot find pimientos, use 3 red peppers. Halve, discard the cores and seeds, then simmer in water for 15 minutes.

TABBOULEH WITH NECTARINES

SERVES 8

250g (8oz / 2 cups) bulghur wheat (burgul)
1 orange pepper
2 garlic cloves
4 tablespoons chopped fresh mint
4 tablespoons chopped fresh parsley
½ teaspoon ground allspice
grated rind and juice of 1 small orange
4 tablespoons extra virgin olive oil
salt and pepper
4 nectarines
fresh herbs such as mint, parsley or bay leaves, to garnish

1 Put the bulghur (burgul) wheat in a bowl, cover with plenty of boiling water and leave to stand for 20 minutes. Drain thoroughly and transfer to a bowl.
2 Meanwhile, cut the orange pepper in half, discarding the core and seeds and chop the flesh finely. Crush the garlic.
3 Add the orange pepper, garlic, mint, parsley, allspice, orange rind and juice, oil, salt and pepper to the bulghur wheat and toss well together until thoroughly combined.
4 Halve the nectarines and remove the stones (pits). Take a slice off the rounded side of each half so that it sits flat.
5 Pile the salad mixture into the fruit halves and arrange on a serving plate. Cover loosely and chill in the refrigerator until ready to serve. Garnish with fresh herbs.

COOK'S TIP

If preferred, 2 thinly sliced necterines can be tossed gently with the other ingredients.

New Potato Salad

SERVES 8

750g (1½ lb) small new potatoes
salt and pepper
125g (4oz) sprouting broccoli
4 spring onions (scullions)
4 tablespoons pine nuts
5 tablespoons olive oil
1 tablespoon white wine vinegar
good pinch of caster (superfine) sugar

1 Wash the potatoes and put in a saucepan. Cover with boiling water, add salt and cook for about 15 minutes, until just tender.

2 Meanwhile, cut the broccoli into bite-sized pieces and lay over the potatoes. Cover and cook for a further 2 minutes, until the broccoli is tender. Drain the vegetables and set aside.

3 Slice the spring onions (scallions) finely and put in a small saucepan with the pine nuts and 2 tablespoons of the oil. Cook gently, shaking the pan until the pine nuts are toasted. Mix in a bowl with the potatoes and broccoli.

4 Mix together the remaining olive oil, the vinegar, sugar, salt and pepper. Pour over the salad and toss lightly together. Chill in the refrigerator until ready to serve.

COOK'S TIP

Even though this is a cold salad, it is best to pour the dressing over the cooked potatoes while they are still warm, as this allows the flavours to be absorbed properly.

Spiced Coleslaw with Avocado

SERVES 8

½ small onion
grated rind and juice of 1 lime
2 tablespoons roughly chopped fresh coriander (cilantro)
½ teaspoon curry paste
½ teaspoon paprika
2 tablespoons mayonnaise
375g (12oz) green cabbage
60g (2oz) Parma (prosciutto) or Serrano ham
salt and pepper
1 ripe avocado
fresh coriander (cilantro), to garnish

1 Grate the onion and put in a large bowl with the lime rind and juice, coriander (cilantro), curry

paste, paprika and mayonnaise. Mix together to make a smooth dressing.

2 Using a sharp knife, shred the cabbage finely and stir into the dressing. Tear or slice the ham into small pieces and add to the salad. Toss the ingredients together and season lightly with salt and pepper. Cover the bowl and chill in the refrigerator until ready to serve.

3 Just before serving, halve the avocado, discarding the stone (pit). Peel away the skin and slice the flesh widthways. Add to the salad, toss together and serve garnished with coriander.

COOK'S TIP

Any leftover cooked meats or diced chicken can be substituted in this recipe, for the same quantity of ham.

Pasta, Artichoke and Walnut Salad

SERVES 8

375g (12oz) penne pasta
salt and pepper
4 tablespoons walnut oil
440g (14oz) can artichoke hearts
125g (4oz) cherry tomatoes
90g (3oz / ¾ cup) broken walnuts
60g (2oz / ½ cup) black olives
grated rind and juice of 1 lemon
60g (2oz) Parmesan cheese
flat-leaved parsley, to garnish

1 Cook the pasta in plenty of boiling salted water for 8–10 minutes, until tender. Drain and toss in a bowl with 1 tablespoon of the oil.

2 Drain the artichoke hearts and cut in half. Cut the tomatoes in half and add to the pasta with the artichokes, walnuts and olives.

3 Mix the lemon rind and juice with the remaining oil, salt and pepper. Add to the bowl and toss the ingredients together lightly. Chill until ready to serve.

4 Using a potato peeler, pare the Parmesan cheese into shavings. Transfer the salad to a serving dish and sprinkle with the cheese and chopped parsley.

COOK'S TIP

Other short-cut or small pasta shapes could be used such as conchiglie, in the shape of seashells, farfalle, in the shape of bow-ties, and fusilli, spiral-shaped pasta. Never overcook pasta as it will become limp and soft.

Tomato and Pepper Salad

SERVES 8

½ a small cucumber
½ a small red-skinned onion
1 red chilli
1 tablespoon capers
1 tablespoon wholegrain mustard
2 teaspoons white wine vinegar
1 teaspoon caster (superfine) sugar
5 tablespoons olive oil
salt and pepper
2 beefsteak tomatoes
4 plum or small tomatoes
180g (6oz) cherry tomatoes
1 yellow pepper
1 red or orange pepper
parsley, to garnish (optional)

1 Dice the cucumber finely. Chop the onion finely. Halve the chilli, discarding the core and seeds and chop the flesh finely.

2 Mix together the cucumber, onion, chilli, capers, mustard, vinegar, sugar, 3 tablespoons of the oil, salt and pepper.

3 Slice the beefsteak tomatoes and arrange, overlapping, on a serving plate. Cut the plum tomatoes into wedges and halve the cherry tomatoes. Arrange the plum and cherry tomatoes on the plate.

4 Cut the peppers in half, discarding the cores and seeds and chop the flesh into small chunks. Scatter them over the tomatoes. Cover and chill in the refrigerator until ready to serve.

5 Spoon the remaining oil over the salad and season with salt and pepper. Spoon the sauce over the top and serve garnished with fresh parsley, if desired.

COOK'S TIP

To avoid last-minute preparation, chop the vegetables a day in advance and prepare the dressing, ready for assembling before serving. For a more substantial salad, scatter diced or crumbled feta cheese over the top of the salad. Alternatively, arrange slices of mozzarella cheese between the slices of beefsteak tomatoes, on the serving plate.

Sausage, Apple and Mustard Rolls

MAKES ABOUT 28

440g (14oz) pork sausagemeat
2 eating apples
2 teaspoons Dijon mustard
salt and pepper
500g (1lb) puff pastry
beaten egg, to glaze

1 Preheat the oven to 220°C (425°F/Gas 7). Grease two baking sheets lightly.

2 Beat the sausagemeat in a bowl. Peel, core and grate the apples and add to the bowl with the mustard, salt and pepper. Beat well to combine.

3 Halve the pastry. On a lightly floured surface, roll out one half to a 38 x 25cm (15 x 10in) rectangle. Cut lengthways into two strips. Divide the sausagemeat into four equal pieces. Spoon a quarter down one strip and a quarter down the remaining strip.

4 Brush the edges of the pastry with beaten egg, then bring the pastry over the filling, sealing the long edges together. Trim and flute the edges neatly.

5 Brush with beaten egg to glaze, then cut into 5cm (2in) lengths. Score the tops with a knife and transfer to baking sheets. Make more rolls with the remaining pastry and sausagemeat filling.

6 Bake for 25–30 minutes, until the pastry is risen and golden. Transfer to a wire rack to cool.

COOK'S TIPS

If preferred, these rolls can be made using shortcrust pastry. Rub 90g (3oz/⅓ cup) butter or margarine and 90g (3oz/⅓ cup) lard into 375g (12oz/3 cups) plain (all-purpose) flour, then add enough cold water to make a firm dough. Chill for 30 minutes before rolling out as above.

If made with fresh pastry and sausagemeat, these rolls can be frozen before cooking. Bake from frozen, allowing a few minutes extra.

Puddings

Rich Christmas Pudding

Makes two 1.1 litre (2 pint / 4½ cup) puddings, each serving 8–10.

125g (4oz/1 cup) blanched almonds
60g (2oz/½ cup) pecan or walnut halves
60g (2oz/⅓ cup) glacé (candied) cherries
250g (8oz/1¾ cups) dried figs or dates
60g (2oz/⅓ cup) mixed peel
180g (6oz/2½ cups) fresh breadcrumbs
250g (8oz/1⅓ cups) sultanas (golden raisins)
375g (12oz /2 cups) currants
125g (4oz/⅔ cup) shredded vegetable suet
125g (4oz/1 cup) self-raising flour
1 cooking apple
grated rind and juice of 2 oranges
3 eggs, lightly beaten
1 teaspoon ground cinnamon
1 teaspoon ground ginger
6 tablespoons ginger wine or ale

1 Lightly grease and base line two 1.1 litre (2 pint/4½ cup) pudding basins.
2 Roughly chop the almonds, pecans or walnuts, cherries and figs or dates and put in a large bowl. Add the mixed peel, breadcrumbs, sultanas (golden raisins), raisins, currants, suet and flour and stir until evenly combined.
3 Peel and grate the apple and add to the bowl with the orange rind and juice, eggs, cinnamon, ginger and ginger wine or ale. Stir well until the mixture is sticky. Divide the mixture equally between the basins and pack down lightly.
4 Pleat a piece of greaseproof paper (parchment) and foil together and lay over one basin, tying securely with string under the rim. Do the same on the other basin.
5 Stand the puddings on steaming racks or old, upturned saucers and place in large saucepans. (Alternatively use a large double saucepan.) Pour in enough boiling water to come a good third up the sides of the basins. Cover and simmer for 4 hours, topping up the water level when necessary.
6 Remove the puddings from the pans and leave to cool for 1–2 hours. Re-cover with fresh greaseproof paper and foil. Store in a cool, dark place for at least 1 month (or up to 1 year) before serving.
7 To reheat Christmas pudding, steam as above for about 2 hours.

Brandy Butter

SERVES 6–8

125g (4oz/½ cup) unsalted butter
3 tablespoons icing (confectioner's) sugar
2 tablespoons brandy

1 Soften the butter and put in a food processor with the icing (confectioner's) sugar and brandy. Mix until smooth and creamy. (Alternatively, in a bowl, beat together butter and icing sugar until evenly combined. Add brandy and mix until absorbed.)
2 Transfer to a small serving dish and chill until required.

Whipped Amaretto Butter

SERVES 6

30g (1oz) amaretti or macaroon biscuits
60g (2oz/¼ cup) unsalted butter
5 tablespoons double (heavy) cream
1 tablespoon amaretto liqueur
cinnamon, for dusting

1 Put the biscuits in a plastic bag and crush with a rolling pin until completely ground.
2 Beat the butter in a bowl until softened. Add the biscuits and beat together. Add the cream and liqueur and whip lightly until thickened.
3 Spoon into a small serving dish and dust with cinnamon. Chill until required.

Marmalade Butter

SERVES 6–8

1 slice of day-old bread
125g (4oz/½ cup) unsalted butter
3 tablespoons orange or lemon shredded marmalade
thin strips of orange or lemon zest, to decorate

1 Toast the bread and crumble into small pieces.
2 Beat the butter in a bowl until softened. Add the marmalade and beat together until well mixed.
3 Spoon into a small serving dish and chill until required. Serve sprinkled with the crumbled toast and strips of zest.

Spicy Pecan Puddings

MAKES 8–10

150g (5oz/⅔ cup) butter
180g (6oz/¾ cup) caster (superfine) sugar
¼ teaspoon ground cinnamon
¼ teaspoon ground mixed (apple pie) spice
5 eggs, separated
30g (1oz/¼ cup) plain (all-purpose) flour
2 tablespoons cocoa powder
2 tablespoons lemon juice
60g (2oz/½ cup) pecan nuts
125g (4oz/1 cup) ground almonds
60g (2oz/1 cup) fresh breadcrumbs
holly leaves, pecan nuts and cranberries, to decorate
crème fraîche or Greek yogurt and maple syrup, to serve

1 Preheat the oven to 180°C (350°F/Gas 4). Grease 10 dariole moulds or 8 individual pudding tins and line the bases with greaseproof paper (parchment).

2 Beat the butter in a bowl until softened. Add 60g (2oz/¼ cup) of the sugar, the cinnamon and mixed (apple pie) spice and beat together until fluffy. Add the egg yolks, flour, cocoa powder and lemon juice and gently stir in. Chop the pecan nuts and stir into the mixture with the ground almonds and breadcrumbs until just combined.

3 In a separate bowl, whisk the egg whites until stiff. Gradually whisk in the remaining sugar.

4 Fold a quarter into the pecan mixture to lighten. Carefully fold in the remainder until just incorporated. Three-quarters fill the prepared tins.

5 Arrange in a roasting tin and pour a 2.5cm (1in) depth of boiling water into the tin. Cover completely with the foil and bake for 30 minutes, until puddings feel firm.

6 Loosen the edges and invert onto serving plates. Decorate with holly leaves, pecan nuts and cranberries. Spoon a little crème fraîche or yogurt beside the puddings and pour over a little maple syrup.

COOK'S TIPS

For convenience, make the puddings in advance and freeze, uncooked. Bake from frozen allowing an extra 5 minutes. As an alternative to the crème fraîche or Greek yogurt, the hot apricot sauce on page 207 or the rich chocolate sauce on the opposite page, both make delicious accompaniments to the spicy pecan puddings.

Rich Vanilla Custard

SERVES 8

30g (1oz/2 tablespoons) caster (superfine) sugar
1 tablespoon cornflour (cornstarch)
2 eggs
2 teaspoons vanilla essence (extract)
600ml (1 pint/2½ cups) milk

1 Beat together the sugar, cornflour (cornstarch), eggs and vanilla essence (extract), until smooth.
2 Put the milk into a saucepan and bring just to the boil. Immediately pour over the egg mixture, stirring.
3 Return the custard to the pan and cook very gently, stirring with a wooden spoon, until the custard thickens. Do not boil. Serve hot.

SWEET SAUCES

Sweet sauces make the perfect accompaniment to various hot and cold desserts and keep well in the refrigerator for 2–3 days.

They can also be used decoratively as a base on which to serve individual portions of dessert. Spoon a little sauce onto the plates and tap or tilt the plates until the sauce is level. Using a teaspoon, drizzle a little single (light) or double (heavy) cream over the sauce and, using a cocktail stick (toothpick) or the tip of a skewer, swirl the cream into the sauce to give a pretty feathered finish. Carefully arrange the dessert on the sauce and decorate with sprigs of mint. Serve immediately.

Rich Chocolate Sauce

SERVES 6

180g (6oz/6 squares) plain (dark) chocolate
30g (1oz/2 tablespoons) unsalted butter
4 tablespoons golden (light corn) syrup
150ml (¼ pint / ⅔ cup) milk

1 Break up the chocolate and put in a small saucepan with the butter, syrup and milk.
2 Cook over a low heat, stirring, until smooth and glossy. Serve warm or cold.

COOK'S TIP

If this sauce over-thickens on cooling, beat in a little extra milk. Serve with hot puddings or vanilla ice cream.

Sugar and Spice Pavlova

SERVES 8

5 egg whites
315g (10oz/1¼ cups) caster (superfine) sugar
2 teaspoons cornflour (cornstarch)
1 teaspoon ground mixed (apple pie) spice
2 teaspoons white wine vinegar
600ml (1 pint / 2½ cups) double (heavy) cream
2 tablespoon crème de cassis
250g (8oz) cape gooseberries
3 figs
250–375g (8–12oz) mixed soft fruits such as strawberries, blueberries and raspberries
icing (confectioner's) sugar and cinnamon, to dust

1 Preheat the oven to 150°C (300°F/Gas 2). Draw a 20cm (8in) circle onto a piece of non-stick baking parchment, and an 18cm (7in) circle onto another. Use to line two baking sheets.

2 In a bowl, whisk the egg whites until stiff. Gradually whisk in the sugar, a tablespoonful at a time, whisking well between each addition until stiff and glossy. Sift in the cornflour (cornstarch) and spice and fold in with the vinegar.

3 Spread two-thirds of the meringue almost to the edge of the larger circle. Use the remainder to spread over the smaller circle.

4 Bake for 5 minutes, then reduce the oven temperature to 130°C (250°F/Gas 1/2) and bake for a further hour or until crisp. Leave to cool on a wire rack, then carefully peel off the paper.

5 Whip the cream with the crème de cassis until just beginning to stand in peaks. Remove the skins from half the gooseberries. Open out the skins on the remainder and reserve for decorating. Cut the figs into wedges.

6 Lay the large meringue on a serv-

ing plate. Spread with half the cream and cover with half of the skinned gooseberries and half of the figs.

7 Add the smaller meringue and cover with the remaining cream. Decorate with the remaining fruits. Just before serving, dust lightly with sifted icing (confectioner's) sugar and cinnamon.

COOK'S TIPS

Always use non-stick baking parchment as greaseproof paper may not always come away easily from the meringue. Avoid assembling more than 1–2 hours before serving as the pavlova will gradually soften.

Hot Apricot Sauce

SERVES 6

250g (8oz) ripe apricots
30g (1oz) caster sugar
2 teaspoons lemon or lime juice
2 tablespoons brandy

1 Halve and stone (pit) the apricots. Put in a saucepan with the sugar and 4 tablespoons water.

2 Simmer gently for about 5 minutes, until the apricots are completely soft. Cool slightly, then blend in a food processor.

3 Return to the pan and stir in the lemon or lime juice and brandy. Heat through gently and serve hot or chill and serve cold.

COOK'S TIPS

This sauce can also be made with other fruits, such as plums, gooseberries, peaches, strawberries and redcurrants, although you may need to adjust the quantity of sugar depending on the sweetness of the fruit used. If using raspberries or blackberries, after blending, press them through a sieve to remove the seeds.

Mulled Fruit Sorbet

SERVES 6

2 teaspoons powdered gelatine
500g (1lb) mixture of soft fruits such as apricots, peaches, plums, raspberries, blackberries, strawberries
1 clementine
14 whole cloves
2 cinnamon sticks, halved
grated rind and juice of 1 orange
250g (8oz/1 cup) caster (superfine) sugar
300ml (½ pint /1¼ cups) red wine
shredded orange rind, to decorate

1 In a small bowl, sprinkle the gelatine over 1 tablespoon water.

2 If necessary, remove the stones (pits) from the fruit. Put all the fruits in a saucepan. Stud the clementine with the cloves and add to the pan with the cinnamon, orange rind and juice, sugar and wine.

3 Bring just to the boil. Reduce the heat, cover and simmer very gently for 10 minutes. Remove from the heat and leave to cool.

4 Remove the clementine and cinnamon, then blend the fruits and liquid in a food processor. Press through a sieve to remove pips, then transfer to a freezer container. Freeze for about 1 hour, until firm around the edges.

5 Turn the mixture into a bowl and whisk until paler in colour and smooth. Return to the freezer, until almost firm.

6 Whisk the sorbet once more and then freeze again until it is firm.

7 Transfer the sorbet to the refrigerator 30 minutes before serving. Scoop the sorbet into glasses and decorate with the shredded orange rind.

COOK'S TIPS

This is a perfect dessert for a celebration dinner as it can be made well in advance. Both the apricot sauce on page 207 and the chocolate sauce on page 205, served chilled, contrast pleasantly with it but for a more elaborate presentation, serve scoops on a pool of fruit sauce (see Sweet Sauces on page 205). For convenience, scoops can be arranged on a tray in a single layer and returned to the freezer until ready to serve.

Christmas Alaska

SERVES 8

1 luxury Swiss (jelly) roll
1.1 litre (1¾ pints/4 cups) dairy vanilla ice cream
1 individual Christmas pudding weighing about 180g (6oz)
2 tablespoons run
4 egg whites
250g (8oz/1 cup) caster (superfine) sugar
icing (confectioner's) sugar, for dusting
holly leaves and glacé (candied) fruits, to decorate

1 Slice the Swiss (jelly) roll and arrange tightly in the base of an 18cm (7in) round loose-bottomed cake tin. Use the sponge trimmings to fill in any gaps and make a solid base.

2 Put the ice cream into a bowl and break up. Leave for 10–15 minutes to soften slightly.

3 Crumble the Christmas pudding, then beat it, with the rum, into the ice cream until fairly evenly incorporated. Spoon over the sponge and lightly pack down. Chill in the freezer overnight or until completely firm.

4 Whisk the egg whites until stiff. Gradually add the sugar, a tablespoonful at a time, whisking well after each addition until stiff and glossy.

5 Lift the ice cream out of the tin and slide onto an ovenproof dish. (A flan dish or base of a flan tin is ideal.) Cover completely with the meringue, spreading evenly over the surface with a palette knife and lifting it attractively into peaks. Return to the freezer until ready to serve.

6 Preheat the oven to 230°C (450°F/Gas 8). Bake the Alaska for 3–4 minutes, watching closely, until the peaks are turning golden. Dust with icing (confectioner's) sugar. Surround with holly leaves, glacé (candied) fruits and serve immediately.

COOK'S TIPS

Many variations can be made of this festive favourite. You could use a sponge flan case for the base and this could be sprinkled with a little rum, brandy or orange-flavoured liqueur. When covering the ice cream with the meringue, make sure it's completely coated. It's this that stops the ice cream from melting, even at such a high oven temperature.

Ratafia Trifle

SERVES 8

1kg (2lb) apricots or sweet plums
315g (10oz) ratafia biscuits
5 tablespoons medium sherry
600ml (1 pint/2½ cups) double (heavy) cream
250g (8oz/1 cup) Greek yogurt
1 teaspoon vanilla essence (extract)
60g (2oz/⅓ cup) dark soft brown sugar

1 Halve and remove the stones (pits) from the apricots or plums. Put in a saucepan with 150ml (¼ pint / ⅔ cup) boiling water. Cover the pan with a tight-fitting lid and cook the fruit for about 3 minutes until slightly softened. Drain and leave to cool.

2 Reserve a few of the biscuits. Place the remainder in a large glass serving bowl or eight tall serving glasses. pour the sherry over the biscuits, then add the cooled fruit.

3 Whip the cream until just beginning to stand in peaks. Stir in the yogurt and vanilla essence (extract). Spread a quarter of the cream over the fruits and sprinkle with half the sugar. Spoon over another quarter of the cream and sprinkle with the remaining sugar.

4 Pile spoonfuls of the remaining cream in the centre of the trifle. Lightly crush the reserved biscuits and scatter over the trifle. Chill for several hours or overnight, to allow the sugar to dissolve, before serving.

COOK'S TIPS

Sprinkle the soft brown sugar right to the edges of the dish or glasses so that it looks attractive as it dissolves into the cream. It is important to chill the trifle thoroughly before serving to let the flavours mingle and the sugar to dissolve, giving the trifle a lovely colour and taste.

If liked, the trifle can be topped with flaked almonds toasted under the grill. Cook until golden brown, turning the almonds frequently. Leave to cool before sprinkling on top of the trifle.

Clementines with Whipped Rosemary Cream

SERVES 8

300ml (½ pint/1¼ cups) double (heavy) cream
5 sprigs of rosemary
1 tablespoon icing (confectioner's) sugar
1.5kg (3lb) clementines
375g (12oz) caster sugar
5 tablespoons Cointreau or Grand Marnier
rosemary sprigs and bay leaves, to decorate

1 Put 150ml (¼ pint/⅔ cup) of the cream in a saucepan with the rosemary sprigs. Bring just to the boil. Remove from the heat and leave for 20 minutes or until cooled. Strain the cream into a bowl and add the remaining cream and icing (confectioner's) sugar. Whip until just beginning to stand in peaks. Transfer to a serving dish and chill.

2 Peel the clementines and prick all over with a fork. Place in a glass serving dish.

3 Put the sugar and 100ml (3½ fl oz /scant ½ cup) water in a heavy-based saucepan and heat gently, until dissolved. Bring to the boil and boil, without stirring, until the syrup turns to a golden caramel.

4 Place the base of the pan in cold water to prevent further cooking. Add 450ml (¾ pint/2 cups) boiling water to the pan and return to the heat until the caramel has dissolved.

5 Leave until cold, then add liqueur and pour over the clementines. Chill for several hours or overnight. Decorate with herbs and serve with the whipped cream.

COOK'S TIP

If making a day in advance, prepare the whipped cream nearer serving time as it will become very thick if left overnight.

Chocolate Cream Truffles

MAKES ABOUT 18

180g (6oz/6 squares) plain (dark) chocolate
60g (2oz/2 squares) white chocolate
100ml (3½ fl oz/scant ½ cup) double (heavy) cream
1 tablespoon brandy or rum
cocoa powder, for dusting

1 Break the plain (dark) chocolate and white chocolate separately into small pieces. Pour the cream into a saucepan and bring almost to the boil. Remove from the heat and stir in two-thirds of the plain chocolate.

2 Stir frequently until the chocolate has melted. Stir in the brandy or rum and transfer to a bowl. Leave to cool, then chill in the refrigerator until the mixture is completely cold.

3 Using an electric whisk, beat until paler in colour and just firm. Take teaspoonfuls of the mixture and shape into balls. Chill for 30 minutes.

4 Put the remaining plain chocolate in a bowl and stand over a pan of simmering water until melted. Melt the white chocolate in the same way. Leave to cool slightly.

5 Line a tray with greaseproof paper (parchment). Using two forks, dip a truffle in the plain chocolate, then transfer to the tray. Lightly fork the surface to give it texture.

6 Coat a third of the truffles in the plain chocolate and a third in the white chocolate. Roll the remaining truffles in the cocoa.

7 Store in the refrigerator for up to 4 days. Serve in paper or foil petit four cases.

Chocolate Hazelnut Layers

SERVES 12

rice paper, for lining tin
60g (2oz) glacé (candied) pineapple
200g (6½ oz / 6½ squares) plain (dark) chocolate
200g (6½ oz/6½ squares) white chocolate
finely grated rind of 1 orange
1 tablespoon Cointreau or orange liqueur
60g (2oz/½ cup) hazelnuts

1 Line an 18cm (7in) round cake tin with rice paper, as you would with greaseproof paper (parchment), letting the rice paper come 12mm (½ in) up the sides of the tin. Chop the glacé (candied) pineapple.

2 Break the plain (dark) chocolate into small pieces and put in a bowl. Stand the bowl over a saucepan of

simmering water and leave until melted.

3 Spread half the plain chocolate over the base of the lined tin. Chill until beginning to harden.

4 Break the white chocolate into small pieces and put in a bowl with the orange rind and liqueur. Melt, stirring, until only just combined as the chocolate will quickly solidify.

5 Spread the white chocolate over the plain chocolate layer, then cover with the remaining plain chocolate.

6 Immediately scatter the glacé pineapple and hazelnuts over the chocolate, then press down into the chocolate until almost submerged. Chill for at least 1 hour. Serve cut into 12 wedges.

Chocolate Coffee Cups

MAKES 12

410g (13oz/13 squares) plain (dark) chocolate
200g (6 ½oz/¾ cup) cream cheese
½ teaspoon vanilla essence (extract)
1 tablespoon coffee, made from espresso ground beans
2 tablespoons Tia Maria or other coffee liqueur
icing (confectioner's) sugar and cocoa powder, to dust

1 Break half the chocolate into small pieces and put in a bowl. Stand over a saucepan of simmering water until melted.

2 Mark six 14 x 10cm (5½ x 4in) rectangles on greaseproof paper (parchment). Use a palette knife or spatula to cover the rectangles with the melted chocolate, spreading the chocolate so that it forms a wavy line along each long edge.

3 Leave on a cool surface until just beginning to harden, then cut through each rectangle lengthways. When almost solid, but still flexible, peel off the strip of chocolate and fold into a case with the straight edge on the bottom. Repeat with the remaining chocolate pieces and chill until firm.

4 Break the remaining chocolate into a bowl and stand over simmering water until melted. Beat the cream cheese in a bowl with the vanilla, coffee and liqueur. Stir in the melted chocolate, then spoon into the chocolate cups. Chill until needed.

5 Dust generously with icing (confectioner's) sugar and cocoa.

Angel's Gateau

SERVES 10–12

8 egg whites
good pinch of salt
1 teaspoon cream of tartar
2 teaspoons vanilla essence (extract)
315g (10oz/1¼ cups) caster (superfine) sugar
180g (6oz/1½ cups) plain (all-purpose) flour
250g (8oz) mascarpone cheese
300ml (½ pint /1¼ cups) double (heavy) cream
2 tablespoons icing (confectioner's) sugar
3 tablespoons Kirsch
1 star fruit
1 pomegranate
1 small honeydew or galia melon
1 pawpaw
small bunch of seedless grapes
small piece of fresh coconut

1 Preheat the oven to 170°C (325°F/Gas 3). Brush a 2 litre (3 pint /1 quart) deep ring tin with oil. Coat the base and sides with flour and shake out the excess.

2 In a large bowl, whisk the egg whites until holding their shape. Add the salt and cream of tartar and whisk again until stiff.

3 Add the vanilla essence (extract) and whisk in 1 tablespoon of the sugar. Continue adding sugar, a tablespoonful at a time, whisking well after each addition until glossy.

4 Sift the flour over the egg whites and carefully fold in. Turn the mixture into the tin and leave the surface. Bake for about 45 minutes until a skewer, inserted into the centre, comes out clean.

5 Invert onto a wire rack and leave to cool. Transfer to a serving plate.

6 Beat together the mascarpone cheese, cream, icing (confectioner's) sugar and Kirsch until the mixture stands in peaks. Spread all over the cake.

7 Thinly slice the star fruit. Remove and separate the pomegranate seeds. Halve and remove the seeds from the melon, then scoop out the flesh with a melon baller. Halve the pawpaw and scoop out the seeds. Peel away the skin and slice the flesh. Remove the grapes from the stalk.

8 Use half the fruit to fill the centre of the ring. Pile the remainder attractively on top of the dessert. Using a potato peeler, pare strips of coconut and scatter over the fruits. Chill until ready to serve.

Yule Log

SERVES 8

280g (9oz/9 squares) plain (dark) chocolate
1 piece of stem ginger plus 2 tablespoons syrup
4 eggs, separated
125g (4oz /½ cup) caster (superfine) sugar
600ml (1 pint/2½ cups) double (heavy) cream
60g (2oz/½ cup) milk chocolate polka dots
1 flaky chocolate bar
2 bags of gold chocolate coins
cocoa powder, for dusting

1 Preheat the oven to 180°C (350°F/Gas 4). Grease and line a 30 x 20cm (12 x 8in) Swiss (jelly) roll tin with greaseproof (wax) paper.

2 Break up 125g (4oz/4 squares) of the chocolate and put in a bowl. Stand the bowl over a saucepan of simmering water. leave until melted, stirring frequently.

3 Finely chop the ginger. Whisk together the egg yolks and sugar until pale and creamy. Fold the melted chocolate into the creamed mixture with the ginger and syrup.

4 Whisk the egg whites until they stand in peaks. Using a metal spoon, fold a quarter into the chocolate mixture. Carefully fold in the remainder.

5 Spread the mixture evenly into the prepared tin and bake for 15–20 minutes, until just firm. Cover with a tea-towel (dish cloth) to prevent drying out and leave to cool for about 20 minutes.

6 Whip 300ml (½ pint / 1¼ cups) of the cream and fold in the polka dots. Turn the roulade out of the tin onto a sheet of greaseproof paper (parchment) and peel away the paper. Spread with the cream mixture. Roll up the roulade carefully but do not roll it too tightly and do not worry if it cracks. Transfer to a rectangular plate or cake board. Cut the log in half widthways, then open out slightly as though broken in half.

7 Break up the remaining chocolate and put in a saucepan with the remaining cream. Heat gently until the chocolate has melted. Chill until cooled.

8 Whip the chocolate mixture until just beginning to stand in peaks, then spread over both the logs. Break up the flaky chocolate bar and scatter over the top. Scatter the coins as shown then dust generously with cocoa powder.

STOLLEN

SERVES 8–10

125g (4oz / ½ cup) butter
375g (12oz/3 cups) strong white flour
good pinch of salt
60g (2oz / ¼ cup) caster (superfine) sugar
2 teaspoons easy-blend dried yeast
150ml (¼ pint/ ⅔ cup) milk
1 egg, beaten
30g (1oz / ¼ cup) glacé (candied) cherries
60g (2oz / ⅓ cup) currants
60g (2oz / ⅓ cup) sultanas (golden raisins)
60g (2oz / ⅓ cup) raisins
30g (1oz / ¼ cup) mixed peel
30g (1oz / ¼ cup) chopped mixed nuts
grated rind of 1 lemon
180g (6oz) marzipan (almond paste)
icing (confectioner's) sugar, for dusting

1 Grease a large baking sheet. Gently melt the butter. Mix the flour, salt, sugar and yeast in a large bowl. Stir in the butter, milk and egg and mix to a dough. Turn out onto a floured surface and knead for about 10 minutes, until smooth and elastic.

2 Put the dough in a bowl. Cover with a clean tea-towel (dish cloth) and leave in a warm place for about 1 hour, until doubled in size.

3 Cut the cherries into quarters. Turn the dough out onto a floured surface. Gradually knead in the cherries, currants, sultanas (golden raisins), raisins, mixed peel, nuts and lemon rind.

4 Lightly roll the dough to a rectangle measuring about 25x20cm (10x8in). Using the rolling pin, mark a line lengthways down the centre of the dough. Roll the marzipan (almond paste) to a sausage shape almost as long as the dough. lay the paste down the marked line.

5 Fold the dough over the paste to enclose. Transfer to the prepared baking sheet. Cover loosely with a clean tea-towel and leave the dough in a warm place for about 45 minutes, until the dough has doubled in size.

6 Preheat the oven to 190°C (375°F/Gas 5). Bake for about 35 minutes, until golden and hollow-sounding when tapped on the underside. Transfer to a wire rack to cool. Serve generously dusted with icing (confectioner's) sugar.

STOLLEN

This German yeast cake freezes well and makes an attractive present, sealed in cellophane and tied with ribbon.

Mince Pies

MAKES 18

250g (8oz/2 cups) plain (all-purpose) flour
pinch of salt
60g (2oz / ¼ cup) butter or margarine
60g (2oz / ¼ cup) lard
60g (2oz) marzipan (almond paste)
375g (12oz/1¼ cups) mincemeat
grated rind of 2 lemons
beaten egg, to glaze
caster (superfine) sugar, to sprinkle

1 Sift the flour and salt into a bowl. Add the butter or margarine and lard, cut into small pieces, and rub in with the fingertips until the mixture resembles breadcrumbs. Add 3 tablespoons cold water and mix to a firm dough, adding a little extra water if necessary. Knead lightly, wrap in greaseproof paper (parchment), then chill in the refrigerator for 30 minutes.

2 Preheat the oven to 200°C (400°F/Gas 6). Roll out the pastry on a lightly floured surface. Using a 7.5cm (3in) cutter and a 6cm (2¼ in) cutter, cut out 18 rounds in each size, re-rolling the trimmings as necessary to make sufficient.

3 Use the larger rounds to line the patty (tartlet) tins. Grate the marzipan (almond paste). Mix together the mincemeat, marzipan and lemon rind and spoon into the cases.

4 Brush the edges with beaten egg, then cover with the smaller rounds, pressing the edges firmly to secure. Cut a cross on the top of each.

5 Brush with beaten egg and sprinkle with caster (superfine) sugar. Bake for about 20 minutes, until turning golden. Transfer to a wire rack to cool, dusting with more caster sugar.

COOK'S TIP

It is worth making mince pies ahead of time as they store well in an airtight tin for several days or they can be frozen. To reheat, arrange them on a baking sheet, ready to pop in the oven for Christmas dinner. Allow about 10 minutes at 170°C (325°F/Gas 3). Pouring cream, brandy butter or custard all make delicious accompaniments. For variety, try different decorations. The pastry lids can be cut with small star, crescent or holly leaf cutters. Alternatively cut thin strips and arrange in a lattice over the filling. Don't forget to dust them generously with icing (confectioner's) sugar or caster sugar before serving.

Party nibbles and drinks

Cheese and Tomato Puffs

MAKES 20

60g (2oz) mozzarella cheese
30g (1oz) sun-dried tomatoes
250g (8oz) puff pastry
1 egg, beaten
2 tablespoons olive oil
1 tablespoon chopped fresh rosemary oregano or basil
coarse sea salt and pepper

1 Preheat the oven to 200°C (400°F/Gas 6). Cut both the cheese and tomatoes into 10 pieces.
2 On a lightly floured surface, roll out the pastry to a 28x23cm (11x9in) rectangle. Trim the pastry edges and cut the pastry into 5cm (2in) squares. Prick all over with fork.
3 Transfer to a lightly greased baking sheet and brush the pastry with the beaten egg.
4 Place the cheese on half the squares and the tomatoes on the remainder. Mix together the oil and herbs and brush carefully over the cheese and tomatoes. Season with salt and pepper.
5 Bake for 12–15 minutes, until crisp and golden. Serve warm.

COOK'S TIP

Take care to roll the pastry very thinly as the puffs rise considerably during cooking.

Champagne Sparkler

SERVES 8–10

1 bottle champagne or sparkling wine, chilled
1 small glass brandy
thin slices of lemon and cucumber
600ml (1 pint/2½ cups) sparkling water, chilled

1 Pour the champagne into a punch bowl and add the brandy, lemon and cucumber slices.
2 Add the sparkling water and serve immediately.

Gruyere and Ham Toasts

MAKES 48

6 slices of smoked ham
12 medium slices of bread
180g (6oz) Gruyère cheese
90g (3oz/⅓ cup) butter
2 tablespoons olive oil
salt and pepper

1 Preheat the oven to 200°C (400°F/Gas 6). Lay the ham over six of the bread slices. Grate the cheese and sprinkle over the ham. Cover with the remaining bread, pressing down lightly. Trim off the crusts.
2 Melt the butter, add the oil, salt and pepper and mix together. Brush half over the sandwiches, then lay the sandwiches, buttered sides down, on a baking sheet. Brush with the remaining butter.
3 Bake for 10–15 minutes, until golden. Cut each toast into four squares, then triangles. Serve hot.

Parma and Pawpaw Sticks

MAKES ABOUT 16

1 pawpaw
60g (2oz) Parma ham (prosciutto)

1 Halve the pawpaw and scoop out the seeds. Cut away the skin, then cut the flesh of each half into eight cubes.
2 Cut the ham into thin strips and wrap a piece around each pawpaw cube. Secure with a cocktail stick (toothpick).

Chicken Kebabs

MAKES ABOUT 35

3 boneless chicken breasts, skimmed
1 small onion
2 garlic cloves
2 tablespoons vegetable oil
2 teaspoons curry paste
2 tablespoons smooth peanut butter
grated rind and juice of 1 lime
2 teaspoons caster (superfine) sugar
salt and pepper
slices of lime, to garnish

1 Preheat the oven to 200°C (400°F/Gas 6). Dice the chicken roughly. Chop the onion finely and crush the garlic.
2 Mix together the oil, onion, garlic, curry paste, peanut butter, lime rind and juice, sugar, salt and pepper.
3 Add the chicken and stir well. Put 2–3 pieces of chicken onto wooden cocktail sticks (toothpicks).
4 Arrange in a single layer in an ovenproof dish and bake for about 15 minutes until golden. Serve warm, garnished with lime slices.

Spicy Fruit Punch

SERVES 10

1 lemon
1 orange
60g (2oz / ⅓ cup) light soft brown sugar
1 litre (1¾ pints/4 cups) cranberry juice
600ml (1 pint /2½ cups) fresh orange juice
2 cinnamon sticks
500ml (16fl oz/2 cups) ginger ale

1 Pare the rind from the lemon and orange, then squeeze the juice. Dissolve the sugar in 300ml (½ pint /1¼ cups) water. Add the cinnamon stick and bring just to the boil, stirring constantly.

2 Leave to cool, then pour into a large jug with the fruit juices and pared rind. Just before serving, top up with the ginger ale.

Cucumber Canapes

MAKES 20

½ a cucumber
60g (2oz) smoked salmon
90g (3oz) thin sliced pastrami or ham
4 tablespoons mayonnaise
2 teaspoons horseradish sauce
salt and pepper
2–3 black olives
small sprigs of dill or parsley, to garnish

1 Cut 20 slices from the cucumber and place on a serving plate.

2 Tear the smoked salmon and cold meats into small pieces. Scrunch up and arrange on the cucumber slices.

3 Mix together the mayonnaise and horseradish and spoon a little onto each cucumber slice. Season lightly with salt and pepper.

4 Garnish each canapé with a small piece of olive and a herb sprig.

Mulled Wine

SERVES 8

1 bottle red wine
4–6 tablespoons brandy
2 clementines
16 whole cloves
1 apple
2 cinnamon sticks, halved
30g (1oz/2 tablespoons) dark soft brown sugar

1 Pour the wine and brandy into a saucepan and add 300ml (½ pint/1¼ cups) water.

2 Halve the clementines and stud with the cloves. Remove the core, then slice the apple widthways. Add the fruit, spice and sugar to the pan.

3 Heat gently for 15 minutes without boiling. Serve hot.

Tomato and Anchovy Dip

SERVES 8

1 onion
1 red pepper
3 tablespoons olive oil
two 440g (14oz) cans chopped tomatoes
2 teaspoons caster (superfine) sugar
1 teaspoon mild chilli seasoning
50g (1¾ oz) can anchovies
1 tablespoon chopped fresh oregano or 1 teaspoon dried
salt and pepper
olive ciabatta or crusty bread, to serve
roughly chopped oregano or flat-leaved parsley, to garnish

1 Chop the onion finely. Cut the red pepper in half, discard the core and seeds and chop the flesh roughly. Heat the oil in a large saucepan. Add the onion and fry gently for 3 minutes.

2 Add the red pepper, tomatoes, sugar and chilli seasoning and bring to the boil. Cook for 10 minutes or until turning pulpy.

3 Drain the anchovies and add to the pan with the herbs. Cook for a further 5 minutes, until thick. Blend lightly in a food processor, then return to the pan and reheat, boiling rapidly if necessary, to evaporate any excess liquid. Season lightly with salt and pepper.

4 Cut the bread into bite-sized pieces and place under a moderate grill (broiler) until crisp on the surface but not toasted.

5 Spoon the dip into a bowl and garnish with the oregano or parsley. Arrange the pieces of bread around the dip to serve.

INDEX

Index

SUPPLIERS

CHRISTMAS IN CROSS STITCH

The following mail order company has supplied some of the basic items needed for making up the projects in this book:

Framecraft Miniatures Ltd
372/376 Summer Lane
Hockley
Birmingham, B19 3QA
England
Tel: 0121 359 4442

Addresses for Framecraft stockists world-wide:

Ireland Needlecraft Pty Ltd
2-4 Keppel Drive
Hallam, Victoria 3803
Australia

Danish Art Needlework
PO Box 442, Lethbridge
Alberta T1J 3Z1
Canada

Sanyei Imports
PO Box 5, Hashima Shi
Gifu 501-62
Japan

The Embroidery Shop
286 Queen Street
Masterton
New Zealand

Anne Brinkley Designs Inc.
246 Walnut Street
Newton, Mass. 02160
USA

S A Threads and Cottons Ltd
43 Somerset Road
Cape Town
South Africa

For information on your nearest stockist of embroidery cotton, contact the following:

UK

DMC Creative World Limited
62 Pullman Road
Wigston
Leicester LE8 2DY
Tel: 01533 811040

USA

The DMC Corporation
Port Kearney Bld.
10 South Kearney
N J 07032-0650
Tel: 201 589 0606

AUSTRALIA

DMC Needlecraft Pty
P O Box 317
Earlswood 2206
NSW 2204
Tel: 02599 3088

Coats and Anchor
UK

Kilncraigs Mill
Alloa
Clackmannanshire
Scotland, FK10 1EG
Tel: 01259 723431

USA

Coats & Clark
P O Box 27067
Dept C01, Greenville
SC 29616
Tel:803 234 0103

AUSTRALIA

Coats Patons Crafts
Thistle Street
Launceston
Tasmania 7250
Tel: 00344 4222

Madeira
UK

Madeira Threads (UK) Ltd
Thirsk Industrial Park
York Road, Thirsk
N. Yorkshire, YO7 3BX
Tel: 01845 524880

USA

Madeira Marketing Ltd
600 East 9th Street
Michigan City, IN 46360
Tel: 219 873 1000

AUSTRALIA

Penguin Threads Pty Ltd
25-27 Izett Street
Prahan, Victoria 3181
Tel: 03529 4400

CHRISTMAS FLOWER PROJECTS

For details of dried flowers, craft ingredients, and pressed flower ingredients and oils by mail order; also two-day craft courses on flowers and other crafts:

Joanna Sheen Ltd

P O Box 52
Newton Abbot, Devon TQ12 4QH

For pot pourri ingredients and oils, and details of shops throughout the country:

Culpeper Ltd

21 Bruton Street, London W1X 7DA

For details of dried flowers by mail order and farm shop:

Caroline Alexander

The Hop Shop
Castle Fam
Shoreham, Sevenoaks
Kent TN14 7UB